£6.95

KING ALFRED'S COLLEGE
WINCHESTER

To be returned on or before the day marked
below:-

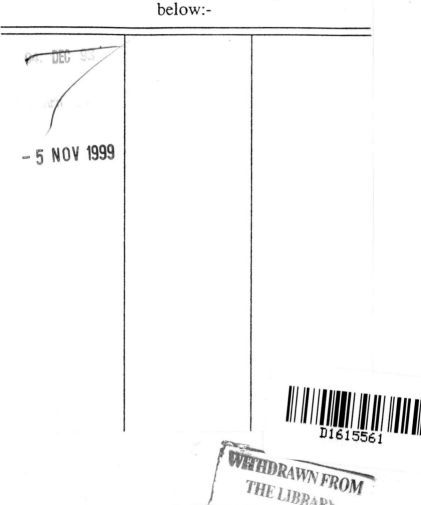

DEC 9

- 5 NOV 1999

D1615561

The Great Civil War in Lancashire

The shaded portion represents royalist territory in August, 1642, just before the outbreak of the Civil War. In August, 1643, only Lathom House, Greenhalgh Castle, and Thurland Castle remained in royalist hands.

...... March of Prince Rupert in 1644. His route was as follows : Stockport, May 25 ; Bolton, May 28 ; Liverpoool, May 29—June 13.

The Great Civil War in Lancashire

(1642—1651)

BY

ERNEST BROXAP, M.A.

MANCHESTER UNIVERSITY PRESS

AUGUSTUS M. KELLEY PUBLISHERS

© 1973 Manchester University Press

Published by the University of Manchester at
The University Press
316-324 Oxford Road, Manchester MI3 9NR

ISBN 0 7190 0539 6

U.S.A.
Augustus M. Kelley
305 Allwood Road, Clifton, New Jersey 07012

ISBN 0 678 06792 9

To

ASPHODEL

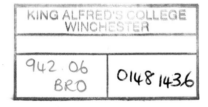
Printed in Great Britain by
Lowe & Brydone (Printers) Ltd, Thetford, Norfolk

INTRODUCTION TO THE SECOND EDITION

R. N. DORE

ERNEST BROXAP, the author of *The Great Civil War in Lanca-shire*, was born in Higher Broughton, Salford, in 1880. From 1897–1900 he was a student at Owens College, Victoria University (now Manchester University), where he took an honours degree in History. Although he went into business his connection with the university and his old tutors, Professors T. F. Tout and James Tait, remained a close one. He worked for and obtained his M.A. under their guidance, choosing for his field of study the Civil War period. In 1902 he contributed a scholarly chapter on "The Siege of Manchester, 1642" to the *Historical Essays* which they edited in commemoration of the jubilee of Owens College. Among the contributors were many distinguished names: besides Tout and Tait themselves there were A. W. Ward, W. A. Shaw, Holland Rose and F. M. Powicke.

In 1905 an article by Broxap on "The Sieges of Hull during the Civil War" appeared in the *English Historical Review*. In 1909 he edited "A Manchester Assessment of 1648" for the second volume of the *Chetham Miscellanies* (Chetham Society, New Series, 63). Then in 1910 the Manchester University Press published *The Great Civil War in Lancashire, 1642–51*. In his preface, after thanking his old tutors, Professors Tout and Tait, for their constant interest and assistance, Broxap added his especial indebtedness to Professor C. H. Firth, saying that the work was really begun at his suggestion. *The Great Civil War in Lancashire* was, in fact, one of a number of histories of the Civil War in particular counties which originated in the interest aroused by Firth's 1900–1 Ford Lectures at Oxford University on the English soldier during the Civil Wars (later published as *Cromwell's Army*). Histories of the Civil War in Worcestershire, Sussex, Dorset and Lancashire came out between 1905 and 1911 and all had received direct encouragement from Firth.

By this time Ernest Broxap had become a partner in the family business—a yarn agency—with his elder brother Henry, also a graduate of Owens College and the author of a book published by Manchester University Press—a biography of Thomas Deacon, the Manchester non-juring clergyman. In 1912 Ernest married and moved from Higher Broughton to Kersal, Salford. Increasing family and business commitments prevented the writing of any further books on the scale of *The Great Civil War in Lancashire*. Yet he always retained a deep interest in cultural matters. Professors Tout and Tait were lifelong friends, and he also became closely associated with C. W. Sutton, the Chief City Librarian from 1879–1920 and the very heart and soul of the intellectual life of Manchester during this period. When Sutton died, Broxap succeeded him as Secretary of the Chetham Society, a position which he held for twenty years. In 1921 he edited "Extracts from the Manchester Churchwardens' Accounts, 1664–71" (*Miscellanies*, 4; Chetham Society, N.S. 80). At the same time he provided a most delightful introduction to a special centenary reprint of II. G. James's Views of Manchester, published under the title of *Manchester a Hundred Years Ago*. In this he not only supplied notes on all the thirty-seven plates reproduced, but pieced together from a number of sources (meticulously given, as in all his work) a most skilful picture of the Manchester of the 1820's. Incidentally this is a useful corrective to the better known descriptions of unrelieved industrial squalor.

Some time after these publications Ernest Broxap moved across the Mersey into Cheshire, living first in Hale and finally in Alderley Edge, where he died in 1963.

As early as 1921 a reviewer of the reprint of James's Views referred to *The Great Civil War in Lancashire* as 'already a classic' and, indeed, this was so. Although written by a Manchester business man it was a product of the new school of professional historians—Gardiner and Firth, Tout and Tait—

followed their canons and maintained their standards. A reviewer of 1910, comparing it with another of the recently published Civil War county histories, said that while that was a vast compilation of interesting but undigested source material — 'exhaustive and exhausting'—Broxap's book was 'selective'. By the judicious use of his material he had enabled the reader to understand "exactly how and why and when the important events occurred—the causes of strength and weakness, of success and failure". Miss Eva Scott, the author of well-known studies of Prince Rupert and the exiled Charles II, praised it as a sound and scholarly piece of work, firmly based on the available sources. These judgements help to explain why today, despite the development of Civil War studies since 1910 and their marked shift of emphasis, the demand for the book is as great as ever and has long outrun the modest numbers of the first edition.

Based on the work of Gardiner and Firth as they were, all the Civil War county histories of this period concentrated on the course of the war itself. Broxap defines the limits of his own book thus:—"It is merely intended to be an account of the Civil War within the borders of the county, religious and social questions and the general course of the war being touched on only so much as is necessary to make the narrative intelligible." It is no mere chronicle, however, of petty and apparently aimless skirmishing. Throughout the emphasis is on 'intelligibility'. The introduction brings out strongly the peculiar geographical features of Lancashire which enabled the war there to be fought almost in isolation for a time. In this and the next chapter on the leaders, the heavy recruitment of soldiers for the King's march on London, which removed many of the most fervent Royalists at the outset; the deficiencies of the Earl of Derby as a military leader in comparison with his lowlier but more vigorous Parliamentarian opponents; the concentration of these opponents in the Puritan area of the south-east, strategically well-placed both for defence and attack—are all developed in explanation of the surprising success of the Parliamentarians in a county where they were not supposed to be numerous and at

a time when the Royalists were in the ascendancy almost every-
where else. Later research has sometimes qualified but not
disproved nor superseded these reasons. The narrative of
military events that follows is admirably clear and firmly
founded on specific references to original sources. There is
a succinct foreword on the main authorities, national and local,
with an assessment of their reliability and value. Sixty years old
though it is, Broxap's book is still a clear and reliable guide to
what actually happened in Lancashire during the Civil Wars
themselves, and the more overt reasons for these happenings.
Knowledge of this is a sound basis for the further study of more
particular aspects or underlying social and economic causes,
subjects which Broxap did not consider were within his terms
of reference.

For the benefit of present-day students three appendices follow:
I. A list of such factual errors as have been discovered in the
   text—a remarkably small list and some of these due to mis-
   takes in the printed versions of the sources Broxap was using.
II. A note on books and articles, published since 1910, concerned in whole or in part with the Civil Wars in Lancashire
   or related fields.
III. For those with a taste for archaeological mysteries, a
   paragraph on the present state of knowledge of the site of
   the Lathom Hall that stood two Civil War sieges—a topic
   to which Broxap devoted four pages.

APPENDIX I: FACTUAL CORRECTIONS

Page 5, line 9. August, *1644*, 'when Newcastle had overrun all Yorkshire'
is an error for *1643*.

Page 18, note 2. Sir Alexander Radcliffe was not committed to the Tower
until November 9, 1642, after having been captured in Essex shortly
before. It was his part in the siege of Manchester and not the skirmish
of July 15 which was given—together with his putting the Commission
of Array into execution—as the reason for his imprisonment. (*Commons
Journals*, 2, pp. 832, 836, 841)

Pages 23-4. In the printed version of his letter which Broxap used, Sir Edward Fytton *is* made to say "The major part of this Hundred of *Manchester*, where I live, will stand right". Not only was there no Hundred of Manchester, however, (it was of Salford) but Sir Edward wrote the letter from his home at Gawsworth which was in the Cheshire Hundred of Macclesfield. So there is little doubt that *Manchester* here is a publisher's or printer's error for *Macclesfield*. Another letter in the same pamphlet purports to come from *Manchester in Lincolnshire!* (*Civil War Tracts of Lancashire*, Chetham Society, Old Series, 2, pp. 15-20)

Page 28, last sentence. The author of *A Discourse of the Warr in Lancashire* said that Tyldesley's estate was sequestered on October 23, 1643, the first to be so treated in Amunderness Hundred. It was still sequestered in 1650, 1651 and 1652 (after his death). As he was in arms against the Parliament for almost the whole period from 1642-51, it is no sign of leniency towards him that he never compounded. Parliament would not have allowed him to do so. (*Discourse*, p. 44; *Calender of the Committee for Compounding*, 4, p. 2568)

Page 32 and note. Although it was undoubtedly true that 'no one was safe in such troublous times', it is unlikely that either of the two Ralph Asshetons mentioned as being imprisoned by the orders of Parliament can have been the distinguished Parliamentary commander and M.P. for the county.

In the first instance Ralph Assheton, 'Receiver of the Duchy', was first commanded by the Commons to pay in '£500 of the monies in his hands' on December 11, 1643. On February 9, 1644, he was ordered to be committed to the Tower for not doing so. Throughout the whole of this period up to January 25, 1644, Colonel Ralph was involved in the campaign against the royal army from Ireland which was invading Cheshire. On January 25 he took part in the battle of Nantwich and was specially commended in Sir Thomas Fairfax's victory dispatch. During the week before the arrest of the Receiver of the Duchy the Commons were receiving accounts of the victory and of the approach of Sir William Brereton with the prisoners taken in it. There is no mention of Colonel Ralph being with him. In any case it is inconceivable that the Commons should so ignore his services as to arrest him without taking them into account or even mentioning them. As the Receiver was said to be a member of the House it is probable that he was the M.P. for Clitheroe, son of Sir Ralph Assheton of Whalley. (*C. J.* 3, pp. 336, 384, 386, 394, 396; *C. W. T.*, pp. 152-4)

In the second instance the Lieutenant-Colonel Ralph Assheton ordered to be brought before the House on a charge of high treason was already 'a prisoner in the Compter for debt'. There are orders of the Council of State for December 12 and 18, 1651, obviously referring to the same man and ordering him to be set at liberty and the charges of his creditors withdrawn. Yet the Colonel Assheton of Civil War fame had, as Broxap himself says, died on February 25, 1651. It is probable that the Lieutenant-Colonel was his son and heir, Ralph, who certainly had had a military command. (*Calender of the State Papers Domestic, 1650*, p. 539; *1651*, pp. 70, 546)

Page 95, note 1. This petition is undated and the date supplied by *Hist. Man. Com.* 10, appendix 4, which Broxap accepts, cannot be right. For in March, 1644, Venables was an unknown junior officer and Parliament in no position to spare troops for Ireland. Nor was Fairfax yet the 'Lord General' as he is addressed in the petition. In 1649, however, the date supplied for the same petition in the *Calender of the Moore MSS* (Record Society of Lancashire & Cheshire, 67, p. 341), he was, and in that year also Venables and his regiment were ordered to Ireland as an advance guard of Cromwell's invading army.

Pages 135, 136 note 2, 137 note 2. Facts concerning the career of Sir John Meldrum. He was called away from the siege of Liverpool to Central, not North Wales, the victory that he won where Tyldesley was captured was at Montgomery, not Oswestry, and he did not lose but failed to capture Scarborough Castle. He died of a wound received in this attempt. (*D. N. B.* J. R. Phillips—*Civil War in Wales and the Marches* 2, p. 64)

Page 137, last line. June 10, *1644*, for the surrender of Greenhaulgh Castle is a mistake for *1645*. As the *Discourse* says (p. 53), the castle did not begin to be besieged until after the defeat of Rupert at Marston Moor (July 2, 1644).

Page 140. Sir Thomas Fairfax is confused with his father, Lord Ferdinando Fairfax. It was Lord Fairfax who was at York in the spring of 1645. Sir Thomas was already at the head of the recently formed New Model Army in the south.

Page 181, line 25. The medium through which Charles II corresponded with the Earl of Derby, then in the Isle of Man, before the Worcester campaign of 1651, was not John Birkenhead, editor of the war-time Oxford news-sheet, *Mercurius Aulicus*, but his brother Isaac, a Royalist captain. Broxap followed Gardiner, but David Underdown has corrected this error in his *Royalist Conspiracy in England, 1649–60*, p. 46 and note 6.

N.B. It should be emphasised that although Broxap entitled his book *The
Great Civil War in Lancashire*, it covers the period not only of the Great
or First Civil War of 1642–6, but also of the Second of 1648 and what is
often known in our own day—though not in his—as the Third of 1649–51.

Since Broxap's day nothing has been published which could claim to be
a history of the Civil Wars in Lancashire. Nevertheless there have been
articles dealing with particular aspects of the struggle or with its course
in certain localities within the county or bordering on it. Books on other
subjects have had sections referring to the Civil Wars in Lancashire; books
concerned with the wars on a national scale have touched on them.

Of the latter Miss C. V. Wedgwood's *The King's War* (London, 1958)
presents Rupert's passage through Lancashire in 1644 in a rather different
light, allowing Rupert himself a much broader strategic view of the
campaign, in which the firm establishment of royalist power in the north-
west was at least as important as the relief of York. Broxap, rather surpris-
ingly for a Lancashire historian, assumes that Rupert's aim was simply to
get to York and by delaying in Lancashire he was 'wasting time'.

A. H. Woolrych, *Battles of the English Civil War* (London, 1961),
contains a chapter on the Preston campaign of 1648 which is longer and
more detailed than Broxap's account, and even contains some extra facts
concerning the Lancashire troops involved in the campaign on both sides.

Peter Young, *Edgehill* (Kineton, 1967), gives details of the Royalist
regiments that took part in the campaign (Part 3, Section 3). This reveals
the full extent of the military support that the King received from the
north-west, and strongly reinforces Broxap's argument (p. 6) that the drain
of its best men from the county in the early stages of the war—not balanced
by a comparable drain on the Parliamentary side—fatally weakened the
Royalist cause in Lancashire and gave the local Parliamentarians the upper
hand.

David Underdown in *Royalist Conspiracy in England, 1649–60* (Newhaven,
1960), has unravelled the tortuous negotiations between Scots Covenanters,
English Presbyterians and English Royalists that lay behind Lord Derby's
reappearance in Lancashire during the Worcester campaign of 1651. Some
of these—particularly the equivocal part played by Colonel John Booth,
late Parliamentary governor of Warrington—were not known to Broxap.
Nevertheless Broxap's excellent diagnosis of the situation in Lancashire—
that the dominant gentry and clergy, being Presbyterian, were hostile to

the new Commonwealth government, but too distrustful of their old enemies, the local Royalists, and too weary of the invading Scots to join the standard of young Charles II—is fully born out by Underdown's briefer account.

In his introduction Broxap sketches the geographical conditions of the Lancashire of Civil War times, and deduces from them an isolation which enabled the local war to be fought almost on its own, and a sharp differentiation between the Roman Catholic west and the Puritan south-east. F. Walker, *The Historical Geography of South-Western Lancashire before the Industrial Revolution* (Chetham Society, N.S. 103, 1939), in a chapter (4) largely devoted to the Civil War, accentuates this religious differentiation, but R. N. Dore—*The Manchester Area in the Great Civil War, 1642-6* (Manchester, 1971) raises some qualifications to the isolation, at least as far as the Mersey boundary was concerned (see below).

R. C. Richardson, *Puritanism in North-West England* (Manchester, 1970), although it deals with the whole diocese of Chester and purports not to go beyond 1642, takes a high proportion of its examples from Lancashire and several from the Civil War and Commonwealth period. It has reinforced Halley's older and more discursive book on Lancashire Puritanism with a more closely argued and analytical study, based on a wide range of sources.

Broxap gives a brief description of the prominent leaders on both sides and, as he says, indicates 'the main lines of division between the various parties'. This does not go much beyond mentioning rank, wealth, religious tendencies and sometimes degree of participation in the war. (He was by no means blind to a phenomenon that has been engaging much attention lately—neutralism.) Much research has been directed in recent years to the economic means, social background, ways of life and thought of the gentry, as a key to their actions during the Civil War. For Lancashire B. G. Blackwood has published "The Lancashire Cavaliers and their Tenants" (*Trans. Historic Society of Lancs. & Chesh.*, 117, 1965) and—a much fuller study—"The Cavalier and Roundhead Gentry of Lancashire" (*Trans. Lancs. & Chesh. Antiquarian Society*, 77, 1973). Unfortunately K. J. Lindley's examination of "The part played by Catholics in the Civil War in Lancashire and Monmouthshire" (Manchester University M.A. thesis, 1965) remains unpublished. Its conclusions, however, are summarised in Blackwood's article on the Lancashire gentry. They bear out Broxap's belief that many of the most vigorous Royalists in Lancashire were Catholics, but show that a majority of the poorer Catholic gentry and the bulk of the Catholic commoners remained neutral.

G. H. Tupling, "The Causes of the Civil War in Lancashire" (*Trans. Lancs. & Chesh. Antiquarian Society*, 65, 1955) is an orthodox survey by broad topics rather than personalities or classes, concentrating more on the causes of discontent under Charles I's personal rule, 1629–40, than those that were operating in the changed conditions just before the outbreak of war.

On particular places inside the county there is a good study of Wigan by A. J. Hawkes, "Wigan's part in the Civil War, 1639–51" (*Trans. Lancs. & Chesh. Antiquarian Society*, 47, 1932), making use of the papers of the Anderton family of Euxton Hall, deposited in the town library. O. M. Tyndale, "The Booths in Warrington during the Civil War" (*Trans. Lancs. & Chesh. Antiqurian Society*, 64, 1954) says something of the importance of Warrington's position, although, as the title implies, it is more concerned with the role of the lords of the manor who supplied the Parliamentary governor during the war.

Broxap gives far more attention to Manchester than Liverpool and probably underestimates the importance of the latter in the war. He only knew the important papers of Colonel John Moore, Parliamentary governor of Liverpool, in the unsatisfactory calendar in *Historical Manuscripts Commission Report* (no. 10, appendix 4, Captain Stewart's MSS). In 1913, after these papers had come into the possession of Liverpool Corporation, a much improved *Calender of the Moore MSS* (Record Society of Lancs. & Chesh., 67) was published. G. Chandler and E. K. Wilson, *Liverpool in the Time of Charles I* (Liverpool, 1965), base much of their narrative on documents in the Moore MSS and also reprint the whole of the Liverpool Town Book for the period. They do, however, fall into an error which Broxap avoided—the belief that when the Parliamentary troops besieged and captured Warrington in May, 1643, they also besieged and captured Liverpool. This originated in a mistaken reading by Ormerod of an ambiguously worded pamphlet that he printed in the *Civil War Tracts of Lancashire* in 1844. He did warn, however, that another pamphlet gave no support to this belief, but Ramsay Muir in his *History of Liverpool* (1907) accepted it and added circumstantial detail by transforming the unnamed church and 'great street' of the pamphlet into St. Nicholas's chapel and Dale Street. A careful reading of the pamphlet and the evidence of other sources, however, leave little doubt that these details refer to Warrington and that it alone was besieged at the time. Broxap takes this view and postulates that Liverpool must have been taken over quietly by the Parliamentarians some time before. This seems a likely explanation, but the tangled skein of Liverpool's fortunes in the Civil War has yet to be unravelled fully.

As already mentioned Broxap places great emphasis on the isolation of
Lancashire—through geographical features—from 'the larger conflict', and
the importance of this in enabling the Parliamentarians to survive in the
Manchester area and, by their vigorous resistance, make their cause triumph
eventually in all Lancashire and Cheshire as well. Of the general truth of
this belief there is no doubt. Yet Broxap almost certainly overestimates the
impenetrability of the Mersey as a physical barrier, and this leads him to
postdate the growth of Parliamentary dominance in Cheshire and play
down instances of co-operation between Lancashire and Cheshire Parliamentarians before 1645. Ties of kinship, upbringing and outlook between
Sir William Brereton, the Parliamentary leader in Cheshire, and Colonels
Holland and Assheton provided the basis for this co-operation. Although
not without its strains and disruptions and not strong enough on its own
to stand against the invasions of the area by the royal troops from Ireland
and Prince Rupert, it was a vital factor in the winning of the local struggle
in 1643. Its military side is dealt with in R. N. Dore, *The Great Civil War
in the Manchester Area, 1642–6* (Manchester, 1971) and *The Civil Wars in
Cheshire* (Chester, 1966). J. S. Morrill's "The Government of Cheshire
during the Civil War and Interregnum" (Oxford University D.Phil.
Thesis: to be published 1973–4) has something to say of the matter from
the administrative angle.

APPENDIX III: THE SITE OF LATHOM HALL

Broxap devotes quite a lengthy appendix (pp. 110–13) to the surprising fact
that the site of the Lathom Hall which stood two Civil War sieges had been
lost completely, although it had been one of the main seats of the Earls
of Derby and, by all accounts, a large mansion. He concludes that, although
there was some evidence of earlier building under the eighteenth century
Lathom Hall, this site was so unlike the description given in Seacome's
House of Stanley of the old hall standing in marshy and hilly ground, that
a site half-a-mile away to the south was far more likely. There were some
earthworks there that could have been those of the besiegers, but the heavily
wooded nature of the ground made more detailed examination difficult.
This unfortunately remains true today. The eighteenth century Lathom
Hall has now been largely demolished and Pilkington Brothers Ltd. have
built extensive laboratories near by. There has been some excavation of

the site which confirms evidence of earlier building on it, but not sufficient to determine whether it could have been anything so extensive as the Civil War hall.

ACKNOWLEDGEMENTS

I wish to thank the following who have been kind enough to give me assistance in the compilation of this Introduction to the Second Edition: Mrs E. M. Broxap (widow of Ernest Broxap); Miss Hilda Lofthouse, Librarian, Chetham's Library, Manchester; Dr W. H. Chaloner of Manchester University; Mr J. J. Bagley of Liverpool University; Mr W. J. Smith of the Lancashire and Cheshire Antiquarian Society; Miss P. A. Pemberton and Dr Copley of Pilkington Brothers Ltd.

CONTENTS

MAPS AND PLANS

PREFACE

THERE has not hitherto been a separate History of the
Civil War in Lancashire, and I venture to think that
the present study, by a native of the County, may
suitably find a place in the publications of the University
of Manchester. It is merely intended to be an account
of the Civil War within the borders of the County,
religious and social questions and the general course
of the war being touched on only so much as is
necessary to make the narrative intelligible. The
principal sources of information are detailed below, and
need not be further referred to here. It only remains to
be said that some care has been taken with topography,
and above all I have tried to give an impartial narrative
of the events. Contemporary writers on both sides
naturally display much prejudice, and it is often difficult
to arrive at an exact knowledge of the facts.

The plan of Manchester is taken from the Owens
College Historical Essays (1902) and my acknowledg-
ments are due to Messrs. Longman & Co. for permission
to reproduce it here. The plan of Liverpool is reprinted
from Transactions of the Historic Society of Lancashire
and Cheshire, Session 6, 1853-4, vol. 6, p. 4. The map
of Lancashire, and the other plans, have been specially
prepared for the present volume, but the plan of the
Preston Campaign in 1648 is based on that given in
Gardiner's " Great Civil War," vol. 3, p. 431.

I take this opportunity of thanking the authorities at
Lathom House, Hornby Castle, Thurland Castle, and
elsewhere, for their courtesy in allowing a personal
inspection of those places to be made. My sincere
thanks are due to Professor T. F. Tout and Professor

James Tait of Manchester, for constant assistance. I share the gratitude felt by so many of their old pupils for their keen and practical interest in the work to which their teaching was the first incentive. Professor Tout's advice has been of great service in preparing this book for the press.

But especially I am indebted to Professor C. H. Firth of Oxford. It was really at his suggestion that the present work was begun nearly four years ago, and he has at all times since been ready to give invaluable help with the utmost kindness. Without his suggestion and help the task would probably not have been accomplished.

ERNEST BROXAP.

Westcliff, Hr. Broughton,
    Manchester,
        March 25th, 1910.

AUTHORITIES

THERE has hitherto been no separate account of the Civil War in Lancashire. The two best accounts in more general works are in Edward Baines' "History of Lancashire" and in Halley's "Lancashire Puritanism and Nonconformity." Baines is a capable historian of sound judgment, but there are now available sources of information which he could not use, and which subsequent editors could not very well include; and the latter book is written from a particular standpoint. The last edition of Baines' work was edited by J. Croston in 5 vols. 1889–93. The Civil War is dealt with in vol. i, chap. 15, pp. 283—321. The other histories of Lancashire by Butterworth, Corry, Britton and others are of no value for the present subject. The few pages devoted to the Civil War in the "Victoria County History of Lancashire" (vol. ii, pp. 232—240) are hurried and inaccurate.

The first main source upon which this work is based is the publications of the local antiquarian societies, the Chetham Society, the Lancashire and Cheshire Record Society, and the Historic Society of Lancashire and Cheshire. The first of the three is the most important; and two books in this series, the "Civil War Tracts" (No. 2), edited by Mr. Ormerod, and the "Discourse of the Warr in Lancashire" (No. 62), edited by Mr. Beamont are invaluable. The editing of the Chetham Society books varies considerably, and it is a great advantage that these two are very ably done. Mr. Ormerod's "Civil War Tracts," published more than 60 years ago, is a most exhaustive collection from contemporary pamphlets and newspapers. In the "Discourse" we have a singularly impartial account of the local war, written by one who himself fought in it; and Mr. Beamont's notes to the narrative add greatly to its value. Other volumes of the Chetham Society which contain material for the Civil War are the "Autobiography of Adam Martindale" (No. 4), the "Moore Rental" (No. 12), the "Farington Papers" (No. 39), the "Shuttleworth Accounts" (Nos. 35, 41, 43 and 46), the "Lancashire Lieutenancy," Part 2 (No. 50), and the "Stanley Papers," Part 3 (Nos. 66, 69 and 70); and some others in a less degree.

All the above numbers refer to the Old Series of the Society's Publications. Where the New Series is mentioned in the following pages the fact is indicated; the later books of the Chetham Society, however, do not contain much material for the purpose.

In the Record Society's Publications (Nos. 24, 26, 29 and 36) are four volumes of extracts from the Composition Papers of the local Royalists. These books contain some valuable details of general information.

The Historic Society Transactions for 1852 give an account of the Siege of Warrington in 1643 by Dr. Kenrick, and the New Series, Volume 5, an article on the Earl of Derby by Mr. F. J. Leslie.

Next come the Public Records, the "Journals of the House of Lords" and the "Journals of the House of Commons," and the " Calendars of Domestic State Papers," which connect the local history with the general course of events. The "Reports of the Historical MSS. Commission" also contain a great deal of very important though scattered information, chiefly in the form of letters. Most valuable are the Denbigh MSS. (Report 4), Sutherland MSS. (Report 5), the "Moore Papers" in Capt. Stewart's MSS. (Report 10, app. 4) and the Portland MSS., vols. 1, 2 and 3. The contemporary Diary of the Siege of Manchester in the Sutherland MSS. (p. 142) is perhaps the best existing account of the Siege. The Kenyon MSS. give much information as to the condition of Lancashire in the 17th century, though not bearing directly on the Civil War.

Clarendon's "History of the Great Rebellion" presents the Royalist standpoint, and amongst other contemporary or nearly contemporary authorities may be mentioned Rushworth's "Historical Collections" (1692 edition in 7 volumes), Whitelock's "Memorials" (1732 edit.), " Autobiography of Captain John Hodgson " (Brighouse, 1882), Seacome's "House of Stanley" (2nd ed. Manchester, 1767), and Hughes' "Boscobel Tracts" (ed. 1830). More modern biographical works are : E. G. B. Warburton's "Prince Rupert" (3 vols. 1849), Léon Marlet's "Charlotte de la Tremoille Comtesse de Derby" (Paris, 1895), and the "Life of the Earl of Derby" prefixed by Canon Raines to his edition of the Stanley Papers (Chetham Society, Nos. 66, 69 and 70). Seacome had the use of the papers of Bishop Rutter, the chaplain of the Stanley family, and gives valuable information not elsewhere obtainable, but he is very inaccurate and biassed. Canon Raines is a violent partisan and quite uncritical. There are notices in the "Dictionary of National Biography" of the Earl of Derby and of the Countess of Derby by Professor A. F. Pollard, and also of a few other local leaders : and of some of the more prominent Lancashire Roman Catholics in Mr. Joseph Gillow's "Dictionary of Catholic Biography."

In the British Museum are some Tracts and Newspapers which escaped Mr. Ormerod's notice. The Tracts are nearly all in the Thomason Collection, which have recently been made much more accessible by the Catalogue in two volumes, issued in 1908. References in the following pages has always been made to the Civil War Tracts where possible, and to the British Museum Catalogue only when the Tract or Newspaper has not been reprinted anywhere. The

xxiv THE CIVIL WAR IN LANCASHIRE

principal newspapers are the Royalist "Mercurius
Aulicus": and "Perfect Diurnall" (which has several
issues), "Certaine Informations, Continuation of Certaine Speciall and Remarkable Passages," and "Letters
from Scotland," &c. on the other side. The last mentioned, which belongs to 1648 and gives a great deal of
local information, is not quoted at all by Mr. Ormerod.
None of the Newspapers are very reliable but the
"Mercurius Aulicus" is hopelessly inaccurate.

Of MSS. in the British Museum, the Rupert MSS.
contain letters referring to the invasion from Ireland,
and Prince Rupert's march north in 1644; the Brereton
MSS. deal with the relations between Lancashire and
Cheshire. They concern us mainly in the Spring and
Summer of 1645, when the two counties co-operated
against the projected royalist march northwards; and
afterwards later in the same year, when Lancashire help
was needed to complete the reduction of Chester. The
Rupert MSS. are Additional MSS. 18980, 18981 : the
Brereton MSS. Additional MSS. 11331, 11332, 11333.

Other MSS. Collections are the Tanner MSS. and the
Carte MSS. in the Bodleian Library. The former
contain some letters of the local parliamentarian committee to the Speaker, and some royalist ones dealing
with the campaign of 1651. With these must be
mentioned the reprints from the Tanner MSS. in Cary's
" Memorials of the Great Civil War " (1842). The
Carte MSS. being mostly Ormonde Papers, relate to
the landing of troops from Ireland in December, 1643,
and the events of the following Spring and Summer;
and many letters of the Earl of Derby to Ormonde of
later date, throwing light on the royalist leader's retirement in the Isle of Man.

Gardiner's History is always valuable to the student
of the period, even in so local a subject as the present.
Naturally the references to Lancashire are, however,
few, and errors of detail sometimes occur.

The following abbreviations have been used :—

C.J.—Commons' Journals.
L.J.—Lords' Journals.
C.S.P.—Calendar of State Papers (Domestic).
C.W.T.—Civil War Tracts of Lancashire.
Discourse.—The Discourse of the Warr in Lancashire.
C.S.—Chetham Society.
R.S.—Record Society.

INTRODUCTION

THE Civil War in Lancashire is an exceedingly interesting and perhaps the most stirring chapter in the history of the county. It was a real struggle; it is sufficiently complete in itself to be studied as a separate subject; while at the same time it illustrates the leading ideas of the Civil War as a whole, and it had a not unimportant bearing upon the course of the war in the North of England.

In some counties either King or Parliament had a sufficient majority of supporters either to prevent fighting, or where there was fighting to make the result certain; but in Lancashire there was a keen struggle for supremacy between the two parties. Lancashire was one of the first counties to take up arms, as it was one of the last to lay them down; and it was for some time doubtful which side would win.

Geographical conditions were most important and must be described at some length. Lancashire was in the 17th century an isolated, remote, and backward part of England. The eastern counties were then the richest and most populous, and the political centre of England was for long after this in the south. Lancashire lay aside from the main lines of communication. It had no great river and no considerable port, Liverpool being still a very small town. The soil is not fertile, and before the opening up of the coalfields and the development of the cotton trade made Lancashire one of the richest parts of England, it was a poor and thinly populated county. Much of it was and still is barren moorland; much of it was then marsh land which has since been drained. A glance at the map will show that the words 'moor' and 'moss' in place names occur dozens of times. Moreover the natural boundaries are very sharply defined. Lancashire consists roughly of a coast plain divided into two by the estuary of the Ribble, and a higher eastern portion rising toward the border of the county. Its shape can be roughly contained in an acute-angled triangle, the two longer sides being the west and east. The west is coast line, the east is an almost continuous range of hills, forming part of the Pennine Chain. From the Lune valley in the north to the extreme south-east of the county there is only one good natural entrance into Lancashire. This is by the Ribble valley, a smaller break in the hills to the south of the Forest of Pendle joining the Ribble valley lower down. Between the Lune and the Ribble are Burn Moor and Bowland Forest; and south of the Ribble Trawden Forest, the Forest of Rossendale, and Blackstone Edge stretch almost to the south of the county. It was by the Ribble valley that Prince Rupert marched out of Lancashire on his way to York in 1644; and it was by this road that Cromwell entered the county in pursuit of the Scots in 1648. All the moors are fairly high; the eastern border of Lancashire is seldom lower than 1000 feet above sea level, and rising in places to 1700 and 1800 feet. Along the southern and most accessible side of Lancashire the boundary is formed by the river Mersey, which is a considerable stream for much of the border; and the low-lying land to the north of the river was in the 17th century mostly undrained marsh, forming a strong barrier. Thus Lancashire was effectually isolated by its natural boundaries from the neighbouring counties.

These geographical conditions had two great effects on the war in Lancashire. In the first place they enabled the issue to be decided within the county without help or hindrance from outside. There was of course some connection with Yorkshire and Cheshire, but mostly in the later years of the war; at first the war was fought

out by local troops within the county itself. This is
no drawback to the study of our subject, for the Civil
War was very largely a local war and can best be studied
locally. It was not, like the Wars of the Roses, a
dynastic struggle, in which the nation generally had
no direct interest; but its causes, political, religious and
social, went down to the primary divisions of opinion
among Englishmen which have existed ever since, and
to some extent do so to-day. The course of the Civil
War in Lancashire shows the working out on a smaller
stage of the main principles of the period. The religious
question was of course very prominent. The local
royalists were either in sympathy with the King's
ecclesiastical policy, or they were Roman Catholics.
Lancashire had been conservative in religion, and there
was a very large Roman Catholic population; particularly the west coast and the Fylde adhered, as to some
extent they still do, to the ancient faith. And though
at first Catholics were not openly included in the royalist
armies, and indeed Lord Strange's first warrants
definitely excluded them,[1] the exclusion was only
temporary. A petition of the Lancashire recusants to
the King to bear arms 'for their own defence' was
granted, and paved the way for their admission to the
royalist ranks. Some of the most prominent of the
Lancashire royalist leaders were Roman Catholics.
The Puritan element was strongest in the east and
south-east of the county, especially in Manchester and
in Bolton, 'the Geneva of the North'; and it was these
places which formed the stronghold of the Parliament's
cause in Lancashire. The Hundreds of Salford and
Blackburn were the only two out of the six Hundreds
of the county which were on the popular side in 1642.
But a distinctive development took place in the later
years of our period. The Lancashire Parliament men
were Presbyterians; indeed so strong was Presbyte-

1. " A Copy of Lord Strange's Warrant," 669, f. 3 (74)

rianism as to produce in this county the most completely organized system in England of Presbyterian church government. This development occurred after the end of the first Civil War. The Parliament therefore had the steady support of the Lancashire leaders in the early part of the struggle; but with the growth of Independency, they became more and more out of sympathy with the ruling powers. By 1648 the relations between the two had become so strained that there was some doubt about the support of Lancashire being forthcoming against the Scotch Invasion. Eventually the differences were overcome because the invaders were Scots, and the Lancashire troops rendered valuable service at the battle of Preston. But there was no common ground for the Presbyterians and Cromwell; and in 1651, when Charles II. marched through Lancashire, the county was really in his favour. The Earl of Derby, Charles' general in Lancashire, had an interview with the leading Presbyterians, and it was only the impossibility of reconciling their opinions, and the exhaustion of the county after nine years of war which prevented Lancashire from being completely raised in Charles' favour.

The side of the war from which it appears as a class struggle is also illustrated in Lancashire. The head of the local royalists was James Stanley, seventh Earl of Derby, representing the great house of Stanley which had been for generations all-powerful in the north-west of England; the leaders on the other side were the lesser gentry who stood to gain by the weakening of his power, and behind them was the awakening spirit of the towns. The first event of the war in September, 1642, was Derby's unsuccessful siege of Manchester; the hardest fought engagement was the royalist capture of Bolton in 1644; the last scene, seven years later, was Derby's own execution in Bolton market place. These things are significant of the place which the towns were beginning to take. And with the Earl of Derby in 1651 died the last of feudalism in Lancashire.

The geographical conditions had another effect in that as the two parties were divided the Parliament held in this respect the advantage. Their territory was the south and south-east of the county which was the most accessible part of it. Thus the royalists were cut off from the neighbouring counties, and once at least, in August, 1644, when Newcastle had overrun all Yorkshire and sent from Halifax a summons to Manchester, the moorland barrier saved the Lancashire Parliamentarians from having an invasion to face. Blackstone Edge was fortified and the difficulty of the ground was enough to secure the safety of the county.

Yet although the war in Lancashire was mostly fought out locally, the result had a considerable effect on the war in the north of England generally. This has been too much neglected in the general text books. The north-west of England was in 1642 mainly Royalist; so was the neighbouring district of North Wales; and in 1642 Lancashire was mainly royalist too. The King's party thought themselves and their opponents thought them the stronger side. Yet in less than twelve months after Edgehill the Royalist party in Lancashire was completely defeated; and though Prince Rupert's hurricane descent on the county on his way to York in 1644 changed things for a little while, it was only a temporary change, and had no permanent result on the war in Lancashire. This meant much, for it was in the summer of 1643, when the Lancashire Parliamentarians were carrying all before them in their county, that the King's cause generally was at its height; and not only in the south of England but even in Yorkshire and Cheshire. In the spring of 1643 Sir Wm. Brereton was holding his own in Cheshire with difficulty; after Newcastle's victory over the Fairfaxes at Adwalton Moor in July all Yorkshire except Hull was royalist

territory. If the royalists had kept Lancashire in 1642
as they expected, or had regained it afterwards as they
were always hoping to do, the King would have been
supreme in the north of England, and the war might
have been considerably prolonged.

In mere numbers the royalists in Lancashire were
probably at all times equal to their opponents; it may
be doubted whether the supporters of the Parliament
ever counted a numerical majority in the county. Their
success was due partly to the fact that their attention
was concentrated on Lancashire, while the royalist
leaders were concerned also with other parts of the
country. The soldiers first raised by the Earl of Derby
were withdrawn to swell the regiments of the royalist
army at Edgehill; and several royalist gentlemen raised
troops of horse for the King from among their tenants
in Lancashire. No Parliamentarian troops were ever
marched out of the county until the issue at home was
decided. But when this allowance has been made it
must be acknowledged that the Parliament's success
was due to the greater ability of its supporters. Derby
was no leader though personally brave; no one could
supersede him on account of his rank, and the conduct
of the war in Lancashire for the King demanded far
more ability than he possessed. On the other hand it
happened that the Parliamentarian leaders, Assheton,
Shuttleworth, Moore, Rigby and others were if not
brilliant generals at least capable men. And not only
had the Parliament the advantage in leaders but in the
rank and file. Its soldiers were better led but they were
better soldiers also. Clarendon's words on this subject
may be quoted :—

> " the difference in the temper of the common people
> of both sides was so great that they who inclined to
> the Parliament left nothing unperformed that they
> might advance the cause, and were incredibly vigorous
> and industrious to cross and hinder whatsoever might

provoke the King's; whereas they who wished well to him thought they had performed their duty in doing so, and that they had done enough for him that they had done nothing against him." [1]

This judgment of the relative zeal of the two parties is true at any rate of Lancashire.

Small as Lancashire is it is not very easy to connect in one plan the necessarily somewhat scattered incidents of the war. On the whole, however, its course at first shows a gradual advance by the Parliamentarian party northwards and westwards from their base at Manchester. They first met successfully an attack in their own quarters; the remainder of 1642 saw them fighting mostly on the defensive in Salford and Blackburn Hundreds; but early in 1643 they began to extend their lines until all the county was gradually conquered. The next two years were occupied in reducing the last royalist strongholds, in meeting Rupert's invasion, and after he had gone in doing over again the work which his coming had undone. During the remainder of the period the outstanding military events are the coming of the Scots in 1648 and the rising when Charles II. invaded England in 1651. With the defeat and death of the last royalists at Wigan Lane, and the execution of the Earl of Derby the Civil War in Lancashire may be said to end.

1. Clarendon (Macray), Vol. 2, p. 472 (bk. 6, par. 273).

CHAPTER I.

Preliminaries.—Petitions.—Seizure of Magazines.— The Array and the Militia.—First Skirmish at Manchester.

THE actual fighting of the civil war was preceded by some months during which both parties attempted to seize stores of arms and to win over the local troops; this again followed a long series of proclamations by the King and by Parliament. Many petitions and memorials were presented to both from different parts of the country. A number of these petitions came from Lancashire. The first was presented to the Houses of Parliament in February 1641-2, and represents the wishes of their supporters in the county. It praises the work already done in the reform of civil government and the church, the disposal of the Militia, and in other ways. As far as Lancashire is concerned it is asked that recusants be disarmed and the number of 'preaching ministers' increased, also that provision should be made for the crowds of destitute refugees from Ireland who were daily arriving in the county; and that a fleet of small ships be sent for the defence of the coast. As evidence of the natural but exaggerated fear produced by the Irish rebellion the petitioners described themselves as "seated in the mouth of danger," and evidently expected an invasion from the other side of the channel. This petition was presented to the House of Commons on February 10th, 1642, and the House promised to take it into consideration.[1]

1. This petition is given in "C. W. T.," pp. 2–5. Cf. "C. J.," Vol. 2, 476. Lancashire being a Catholic county the Puritans were exceedingly afraid of their probable action. Cf. "C. S. P.," 1641–3, p. 166.

Two petitions were also sent to the King at York in April and May respectively. The first merely urged his return to Parliament, but the other which is much longer and more elaborate, was drawn up by Richard Heyrick, warden of the Collegiate Church at Manchester, and contained nearly 8,000 names. It professes great loyalty to the King's person, and gives him credit for the reforms which had already been carried through; but asks him to find out some way for an accommodation with the Parliament. The signatories of this petition afterwards became the Presbyterian party in the county and five years later they presented the petition to the Parliament for the establishment of Presbyterianism in Lancashire.

A few months after this the Recusants in Lancashire petitioned Charles for permission to take up arms for their own safety, which was very readily given. Recusants were, however, as yet forbidden to serve in the Royal armies.[1]

The next step was the raising of the local trained bands, the winning over of men of influence, and seizing magazines of arms which had been collected in various places in view of the rebellion in Ireland. The famous Militia Ordinance, which was the first exercise of Parliament's claim to legislate without the King's consent, was made on March 5, 1641—2; the King's proclamation forbidding any of the trained bands of the kingdom to obey the Ordinance was dated at York, May 27th, 1642. Parliament replied on the following day with their Order beginning "Whereas it appears that the King seduced by wicked Councell intends to make War against the Parliament." The King's

---

1. " C. W. T.," pp. 38–40. The petition and answer are also given in the "Discourse," pp. 12–14. While taking stronger measures against the recusants, Parliament ordered the documents to be printed in order to arouse public opinion against the King. On Aug. 29 the King issued instructions to the Commissioners of Array to disarm all " Popish Recusants, all Brownists, Anabapists and other sectaries." " Rushworth," Vol. 4, p. 415.

Commissions of Array were sent out early in June, and afterwards the raising of troops was pushed forward by either side.[1] Parliament had early in the year appointed its own list of Lords Lieutenant of all the counties in England, the King also naming his own representatives. In the list presented to the House of Commons on February 10, 1641-2 Lord Wharton is put in for Lancashire in place of Lord Strange who had previously been Lord Lieutenant; but curiously enough Lord Strange was nominated by the Houses for Cheshire. On March 18, however, Sir William Brereton informed the Commons that his lordship desired to be excused, and the desire being repeated a week later his name was removed and that of Lord Say substituted. Lord Strange was made Lord Lieutenant of both Lancashire and Cheshire by the King.[2] Parliament also appointed a long list of Deputy-Lieutenants for Lancashire which was afterwards added to during the ensuing month.[3]

During the summer Commissions of Array were voted to be illegal, and the House of Lords appointed a Committee to devise means to prevent their going out; 9000 copies of a Declaration to this effect were printed and circulated, and the Judges on circuit were each given a copy and ordered to publish it.[4] (July.)

In the preceding month the Lancashire members of Parliament had been sent down to form with the Deputy Lieutenants a county Committee for putting the Militia Ordinance into operation. Their instructions were to put the Ordinance in force, to collect trained bands, to publish the Declarations of both Houses, to disarm

1. The Militia Ordinance and the King's Proclamation are printed in Gardiner's "Constitutional Documents," pp. 166 and 169. For the Parliament's Order of May 28, v. "C. W. T.," p. 7.

2. "C. J." 2, pp. 424, 486, 496. Lord Strange was the royalist of greatest influence in Lancashire and Cheshire and so could not be passed over. But he was so unpopular at court that the appointment was an unexpected one. Cf. "Hist. MSS. Com.," Rep. 9, app. 2, p. 391.

3. "L. J.," Vol. 5, p. 178; Vol. 6, p. 125. "C. J.," Vol. 2, pp. 495, 499, 591, 598.

4. "C. J.," Vol. 2, pp. 629, 650, 681.

recusants and see that they confined themselves to their
own houses. It was expressly stated that no evil was
intended to the King, whose greatest danger lay in
separating himself from his Parliament.[1] Active preparations now began on both sides in Lancashire as in
other parts of the country. It is rather surprising and
testifies to the extreme reluctance to begin a war of
which no man could see the end, that the Militia and
the Array did not come to blows before they did. The
royalists were the first to move. Lord Strange returning
from a visit to the Court at York called a meeting of his
supporters on Fulwood Moor near Preston in accordance
with a letter from the King to Sir John Girlington,
High Sheriff; the ostensible purpose being to hear read
Charles' two Declarations and his answer to the Lancashire petition. This gathering though by no means so
large as the corresponding royalist demonstration on
Heworth Moor, near York, nevertheless numbered
about 5000 people; but if the Parliamentarians are to be
believed it was not at all unanimous in favour of the
King. Rigby and the elder Shuttleworth hearing of
the summons on their way to Lancashire hastened on
towards Preston, hindering as many people as possible
from obeying it as they went. At Standish they
deprived the Constable of his warrant, which had that
day been published by the Vicar in church. (Sunday,
June 19.) Reaching Preston the same night they
attempted though without success to prevent the meeting
being held; and the following day they attended the
meeting themselves. Lord Strange was accompanied
by his eldest son Charles, a boy of 14, Lord Molyneux,

1. "L. J.," Vol. 5, p. 129. It was on June 9 that the Lancashire
members were directed by the Commons to go down ("C. J.," Vol. 2,
p. 615), and they must have started almost immediately. Several letters
were received before the end of the month both from them and from
Sir W. Brereton. On Saturday, July 16, a report from the Committee
and Deputy Lieutenants was received by the House of Commons, and
referred by them to the Committee for the Defence of the Kingdom.
("C.J.," Vol. 2, p. 676.)

Sir George Middleton, Sir Alexander Radcliffe, Mr. Tyldesley of Myerscough, Mr. Farington of Worden, and other prominent Lancashire royalists. The King's Declarations were read by the Sheriff, the Under Sheriff and others in different parts of the crowd, and most of the people dispersed. Rigby, however, attempted to read the Votes of Parliament in answer to the King and demanded Girlington to deliver up his Commission of Array; whereupon 400 of the more ardent royalists rode up and down the moor shouting, 'For the King, For the King.' The remainder stayed and shouted ' For King and Parliament,' and Rigby declared that the royalists could only count on the support of a small minority of those present and that they had in reality lost more than they had gained by the demonstration. On hearing of the occurrence Parliament summoned Sir John Girlington, Sir George Middleton, and Sir Edward Fitton to attend as delinquents.[1] Meanwhile under cover of the excitement on the Moor a servant of Mr. Farington's, William Sumpner, seized part of the magazine in the town of Preston, conveying it away secretly on packhorses as ordinary merchandise. The magazine, which consisted of 13 barrels of powder and some match, had been mostly collected by Farington and stored in a private house. Early next morning the remainder was removed by order of the Sheriff. Rigby hearing of what had taken place again protested, but to no purpose; and he was not in a position to use force.[2]

1. "C. W. T.," p. 14. "Discourse," p. 6. Rigby wrote a long letter giving an account of the meeting to the Speaker from Manchester on June 24. He calls the majority of the 400 adherents of Lord Strange "popish recusants." The "Discourse" implies that a majority of the meeting were in favour of the King. Cf. "L. J.," Vol. 5, p. 166.

2. For Rigby's Letter to the Speaker, v. "C. W. T.," p. 329. He suggests that for so small an amount of powder it was not worth while to use force; but it was a sufficient reason that he did not know where the powder had been taken. On July 26th it was ordered by both Houses that the removal of magazines might be resisted by force. ("L. J.," Vol. 5, p. 242. "C. J.," Vol. 2, pp. 692, 693.)

This was part of a royalist plan for securing all the ammunition in the county. Considerable stores had been established by Lord Strange when Lord Lieutenant, the principal centres being Preston, Warrington, Liverpool and Manchester. Warrington was royalist in sympathy and that also was seized by the King. Strange in person secured most if not all of the powder at Liverpool. Rigby, however, warned Mr. Assheton of Middleton in time to save the magazine at Manchester.[1] When the royalist design became known in Manchester a petition was addressed to the Committee asking them if necessary to remove the magazine to a more secure place. The answer refers to great levies of money made by Lord Strange, much of which had been spent in providing ammunition in various places. But there were in Manchester only 10 barrels of powder and a few bundles of match; they were kept in the then disused College of the Church which had been granted to the Earl of Derby by the Crown. This building was afterwards purchased by the executors of Humphrey Chetham from Charles, eighth Earl of Derby, and is still the Chetham College. The royalist Commissioners of Array, Sir Alexander Radcliffe and Mr. Prestwich, with Mr. Nicholas Mosley and Thomas Danson, the Under Sheriff, endeavoured to seize these stores as they had seized the others; but Assheton and Sir Thomas Stanley, another Deputy Lieutenant, prevented them. Judging, however, that the powder was not safe on

1. The Committee's Letter to Lenthall on June 25 ("C. W. T.," p. 16) states that Lord Strange took 30 barrels of powder and some match from Liverpool. The "Valley of Achor" ("C. W. T.," p. 111) implies that this was all the magazine in Liverpool. The report that Strange was intercepted at Liverpool by Mr. Moore ("C. W. T.," p. 332) is probably false.
   The Manchester petition and answer are given at length in the "Valley of Achor" ("C. W. T.," p. 111). No other places are mentioned except Manchester, Warrington, Preston and Liverpool, and apparently the royalists secured all these except the first-named. Cf. A Copy of a Letter from Chester, etc., 669, f. 6 (78), where it is stated that Strange armed his troops at Chester with arms sent by the Parliament for service in Ireland.

Lord Strange's property, it was removed to other parts of the town.[1] Lord Strange was very angry at the rebuff and threatened to attack the town. He collected troops at Bury and more than 1000 armed volunteers came in for the defence of Manchester. These outnumbered the royalists, and negotiations were thereupon entered into for the disposal of the magazine. Two or three Deputy Lieutenants visited Lord Strange at Bury; but his offer to replace the magazine in the College in the joint keeping of the Parliament men and of Robert Holt, one of his own Deputy Lieutenants, was refused. (June 23.) Next day the forces were dismissed; but Lord Strange, having received fresh instructions from York, called a second muster at Bury and caused an order to be published at Manchester Cross for the removal of the magazine, part to Rochdale and part to Bury, only a small part to be left in Manchester.

It was now evident that actual hostilities could not be long delayed. The Parliamentarians sent to London for help from Lord Wharton. Lord Strange was required to redeliver that part of the county magazine which he had seized.[2] On Saturday, June 25, Sir William Brereton was in Manchester, and reported to the Speaker that he found the townsmen "up in arms in defence of their magazine," and most of the shops shut. A Journal, of the first week in July, by a Preston man who accompanied Rigby to Manchester, relates

1. "C. W. T.," pp. 16 and 112. Cf. "Hist. MSS. Com.," Vol. 5, p. 32; and also a letter from Richard Radcliffe to Sir John Gell, July 1, 1642 : "Lord Strange threatens to procure aid from the King; but we think His Majesty has not much to spare." ("Hist. MSS. Com.," Vol. 9, app. 2, p. 391.)

2. "L. J.," Vol. 5, p. 166. Sir William Brereton (1604–1661) was the son of William Brereton of Handforth, Cheshire, and of Margaret, daughter and co-heiress of Richard Holland of Denton. He was the Parliamentarian Commander-in-Chief in Cheshire, and was concerned in all the military operations in that county. But he was also a Deputy Lieutenant for Lancashire, having close relations with the leaders there. There is a notice of Brereton, by Mr. T. F. Henderson, in the "Dictionary of National Biography."

that 7000 or 8000 militia armed with muskets and pikes were being daily trained there.   On the other hand reports were brought of royalist musters numbering 4000 at Preston, and 600 on Knutsford Heath in Cheshire.[1]   A letter about royalist movements from Sir Edward Fitton to Sir Thomas Aston at York was intercepted and sent to London.   News came of the King's siege of Hull.   But no one was anxious to strike the first blow in Lancashire, and relations were not yet so strained between the leaders but that Rigby, going to see Sir Gilbert Hoghton about a letter of his which had been seized, could be asked to stay to dinner.   While he was there a Mr. Dawton who was a recusant came in, and Rigby with characteristic rudeness told his host that "he should like him better if he were not so familiar with Papists."   In royalist Preston, however, it needed a report that Lord Wharton was on his march with 20,000 men to make it possible for "honest men to go through the streets without scoffing at them and calling them Roundheads." (Friday, July 8.)   And a man who directed the Sergeant coming to deliver a message from Parliament to Lord Strange's house had his head broken by the royalists. [2]

A week later the first actual bloodshed of the war in Lancashire took place at Manchester (Friday, July 15), the occasion being a visit of Lord Strange and some of his supporters to the town.   There is an account of a previous skirmish on July 4, when it is stated that Lord Strange attempted to force his way into the town and was repulsed with loss; but this is usually thought to be

---

1. "L. J.," Vol. 5, p. 174. Cf. a further letter to the Speaker in "H. L. Cal." ("Hist. MSS. Com.," rep. 5, p. 31), written on June 24, in which Brereton states that Lord Strange is prepared to enforce his Commission of Array when Parliament does the Militia Ordinance. He desires further instructions, for the Commission cannot be stopped without violence, which "once begun may not be so easily composed."

2. This "Journal" is given in "C. W. T.," p. 24. The writer seems well informed and fairly impartial.

false.[1] Lord Strange's visit on July 15 was in response
to an invitation. Apparently negotiations were still in
progress about the Manchester magazine, and some of
his lordship's supporters, of whom there were a good
many in the town, wished to entertain him at a banquet
in the house of Mr. Alexander Green, in order that the
negotiations might be completed. Green was a vintner
and lived on the Conduit, now the bottom of Market
Street.[2]

The condition was made that Strange should come
peaceably with his own attendance; but in the excited
state of affairs it was almost impossible that the occasion
should end peaceably, especially as Lord Strange had
earlier on the same day called a muster of troops at
Bury which was attended by about 2000 men from the
immediate neighbourhood of Manchester. There are
several accounts of what happened, and as may be
expected the two sides give very different views. The
royalists describe the expression of joy by the inhabitants, "continued acclamations, bonfires, the streets
strewed with flowers, &c.," as Lord Strange entered
Manchester in his coach with his ordinary attendants
only; the other side represent him as coming in a

1. The chief authority for this skirmish is a tract called "The
Beginning of Civil Warres in England, etc." ("C. W. T.," p. 24). It is
a circumstantial account giving the times at which the battle began and
ended and the number killed on both sides. But nevertheless it is
almost certainly an entire fabrication. None of the main authorities
mention it; and if any skirmish occurred at all on July 4 it would
certainly have been mentioned in Lord Strange's impeachment. Cf. also
"C. W. T.," pp. 27 and 331. The "Victoria County History of
Lancashire," referring to this date, says: "Doubt has been cast on the
truth of this report," but this statement is not strong enough (Vol. 2,
p. 235).

2. Green had given £1. 10s. to the building of Salford Chapel in 1634.
Judging from the amounts at which he was assessed in the levies made
upon the town during the war, he was a well-to-do man; the Conduit
was then one of the streets inhabited by the richer citizens ("Manchester
Municipal Records"). Green does not seem to have been an ardent
royalist, for he was not sequestered, but he afforded shelter to one
George Leigh of Barton-upon-Irwell, who at first supported the royalist
cause, but on Prince Rupert's invasion fled to Manchester ("Royalist
Composition Papers," Vol. 4, p. 82).

warlike manner attended by many horsemen, "with
cocked pistols and shouts that the town was their own."
The local militia under Captain Birch and Captain
Holcroft was, however, in Manchester, and the surprising thing is not that an affray occurred, but that it was
not a great deal more serious than it turned out to be.
Hardly had the Royalists sat down to dinner when word
was brought that Birch and Holcroft accompanied by
Sir Thomas Stanley of Bickerstaffe[1] were marching their
men about the streets. The Sheriff immediately ran
downstairs, mounted Lord Strange's horse, and near the
Cross met Holcroft, whose men he endeavoured unsuc-
cessfully to disperse. Alarmed at Girlington's non-
return Strange himself followed him, and missing his
horse pushed his way on foot through the crowd to the
end of the street. The attitude of the townspeople was
very threatening and Lord Strange was several times
fired at from houses. As he and the Sheriff were
returning they met Birch who ordered his men to fire,
but the rain put out their matches. To avoid a general
skirmish the royalists decided to leave the town. In the
melée, however, a royalist gentleman was knocked off
his horse and the assailant was shot; this was Richard
Perceval, a linen weaver of Kirkmanshulme; he was
buried at the Parish Church on July 18. ·Lord Strange
proceeded for the night to Sir Alexander Radcliffe's
house at Ordsall Hall;[2] and he never entered Manchester again. Next morning, twenty-five gentlemen
of the town, including Green and Nicholas Mosley, the

1. Sir Thomas Stanley was the son of Edward Stanley of Bickerstaffe,
who was made a Baronet in 1627–8. He was a consistent, if rather
lukewarm, supporter of the Parliamentary cause. He was the direct
ancestor of the present Earl of Derby. ("Lancashire Lieutenancy,"
Pt. 2, p. 246.)

2. "C. W. T.," p. 33, note. Sir Alexander Radcliffe was committed
to the Tower for his part in this disturbance, and remained a prisoner
until the following year. Ordsall Hall, then about 1½ miles from the
town, stands now in the midst of cottages and workshops. It is the
property of Lord Egerton, and was until recently used as an Anglican
Training College.

Boroughreeve, waited on him at Ordsall to apologize for what had taken place, and declared Stanley, Holcroft and Birch to be disturbers of the peace; but that they did not speak for a majority of the townsmen subsequent events were to show.[1]

It has been very commonly stated that this July 15th skirmish was the first bloodshed of the whole Civil War; the statement is made by Mr. Gardiner and is repeated in so recent a work as the "Cambridge Modern History," but is almost certainly incorrect. It is not of course the fact that Lancashire was before any other county in hostile preparations. In the months of June and July 1642, the two factions in arms were facing each other all over England and it was really an accident rather than otherwise in which county the first blow was struck. On June 4, the King wrote to Lord Willoughby of Parham forbidding him to raise the trained bands of Lincolnshire, and in the same week the Earl of Warwick put the Militia Ordinance into force in Essex. In Leicestershire a fortnight later bloodshed was narrowly averted. On June 21, Mr. Hastings, son of the Earl of Huntingdon, who was a royalist, arrived at Loughborough and marched on Leicester; but finding a superior force under the Earl of Stamford in possession, he retreated and most of his men were disarmed. There was an affray in Dorsetshire in August at which some lives were lost. It would seem, however, that actually the first blood of the war was shed at Hull. The King

---

1. There are a Parliamentarian paper describing the affray, two royalist tracts and an account in the "Valley of Achor" ("C. W. T.," pp. 29, 30, 31 and 113). The reference in the "Discourse," p. 6, may be dismissed as worthless; that writer is not often well informed on matters relating to Manchester. It is evident that the banquet was a pre-arranged affair in spite of statements to the contrary ("C. W. T.," p. 30), and also that the rising of the townsmen was not wholly the result of the Parliamentarian leaders' agitation. Probably each party in the town made its own arrangements entirely neglecting their effect on the other; and probably each side gave afterwards what it honestly thought to be the statement of the facts. There is an account of this affray in Burghall's "Providence Improved" (R. S., No. 19, p. 29); but it adds no new details.

in person was present at the siege of that town which
began on July 4. His troops were not close to the walls
but in the following week there had been three or four
skirmishes, one of which lasted for several hours and
some lives must have been lost.[1] It is fitting that the
war should begin at Hull, for that was the city which
was first seized for the Parliament and which first
offered defiance to Charles.

It might have been expected that the affray in Manchester would be followed by further hostilities; but this
was not the case, and two months elapsed before fighting
really began in Lancashire. The intervening time was
spent in active preparations by both sides; of the two
the royalists at first appeared to have the advantage.
Manchester had declared for the Parliament, but there
was not much of the county which that party could rely
upon, and even Manchester was not unanimous. Perhaps the majority of the crowd in the streets on July 15
were not anti-royalists.[2] The immediate outcome of the
affray was that proceedings were begun against Mr.
Tyldesley, who was reported to have killed Perceval,
and by the other side against Stanley, Birch and
Holcroft. Parliament stopped both actions. It was
Birch who reported the affair to the House of Commons,
and the committee named to deal with Commissions of
Array was asked to consider it.[3]

In the following month there was a prospect of

1. "Rushworth," Vol. 4, p. 670, 676, 678. Cf. an article by the
present writer on the "Sieges of Hull during the Great Civil War," in
the "English Historical Review" (1905), Vol. 20, p. 464.
2. The account given in the "Valley of Achor" ("C. W. T.," p. 113)
suggests this. The statement that the other side were in a vast majority
is, however, made by both parties.
3. The judges in Lancashire were ordered to stay proceedings against
Tyldesley, "who, as this House is informed, slew the man at Manchester,"
and other proceedings begun for the same reason. There is a similar
order concerning proceedings against Stanley, Birch and Holcroft
("C. J.," Vol. 2, p. 714). Assheton, Rigby and Moore were members of
this Committee ("C. J.," Vol. 2, pp. 689, 690). It seems probable that the
man actually responsible for the death of Perceval was Richard Fleetwood
of Rossall ("C. W. T.," p. 72).

Lancashire being made the centre of the Royalist operations. Several places were considered for the raising of the royal standard, and the Earl of Derby suggested Warrington as suitable. He promised to raise at once 3000 foot and 500 horse, and within three days to make up their number to 10,000 men. After a few days' consideration Strange was sent back to Lancashire to make preparations, but in his absence the place was altered to Nottingham. It is suggested that court jealousy of Strange was responsible for the alteration.[1] Whatever the reason, however, Strange's loyalty was unwavering. He returned to Lancashire, and on August 17 dated from Lathom a warrant to all knights, freeholders and others able to bear arms (popish recusants excepted) to assemble at Preston on August 23. A week later Lady Strange wrote to her cousin, Prince Rupert, on his arrival in England, asking him to send a few troops of horse into Lancashire for a few weeks to assist in raising foot. Clarendon says that Strange was looked upon 'as of absolute power over that people,' and as yet there seems to have been no doubt at Lathom that this was the case.[2] Strange joined the King at Shrewsbury with three troops of horse and three regiments of foot. Lord Molyneux raised two regiments, one of horse and one of foot, and other Lancashire royalists contributed to the main royal army in a lesser degree. This draining of Lancashire of royalist troops, a process which was continued later, was to have a disastrous effect on their cause within the county.

A week after the raising of the royal standard at Nottingham (August 22, 1642), the Commons set about the impeachment of Lord Strange. The energetic

1. The authority for this statement is Seacome's "House of Stanley," p. 70-74. Though Seacome is very inaccurate, there seems to be no reason for doubting his statement here.

2. "A Copy of Lord Strange's Warrant," 669, f. 6 (74); Marlet's "Charlotte de la Tremoille," pp. 76-7; "Clarendon" (Macray), Vol. 2, p. 342 (bk. 6, par. 67). Marlet is of the opinion that Prince Rupert would have acceded to the request, but was prevented by the King.

Rigby .was one of the five members appointed to prepare
the accusation, but it was nevertheless a fortnight before
it was sent up to the Lords, who agreed next day
(September 15).   The articles of Indictment are the
raising of forces at Manchester on July 15 and in other
places, the death of Perceval, and the being in actual
rebellion against the King, Parliament and Kingdom.
It was, however, evident that it would be much easier to
publish such an impeachment than to have it carried
into effect "considering that if messengers be sent they
will be imprisoned, and if proclamation writs be sent
down they will not be sealed."   Several conferences
were held between the two Houses as to the best means
of executing the impeachment.   On September 16,
publication of the charge was ordered to be made in all
churches and chapels and in all markets and towns;
and all Sheriffs and other officers were urged to do their
best to secure Lord Strange's arrest and to send him up
to Parliament.[1]   The impeachment no doubt had some
effect on public opinion in Lancashire, but it made no
difference to the royalist preparations which continued
to be actively pushed forward.

1. The Impeachment was moved in the House of Commons on August 29,
and Sir Robert Harley took it to the Lords on Sept. 14 (" C. J.," Vol. 2,
p. 742; " L. J.," Vol. 5, pp. 353, 354, 355, 357).   The order for publishing
the Impeachment and carrying it out was dated Friday, Sept. 16
(" L. J.," Vol. 5, p. 358).   The Impeachment and Order are printed in
" C. W. T.," pp. 35–37.

CHAPTER II.

The Leaders on Both Sides.

In September, 1642, when the two parties in Lancashire faced each other before coming to blows, the royalist prospects appeared considerably the better. Their leaders were the men of chief rank in the county; they had the undivided support of the numerous Catholic families; they held nearly all the defensible positions and fortified houses, and they had secured nearly all the stores of arms and ammunition which the county contained. In four out of the six Hundreds of Lancashire their influence was entirely predominant. With the possession of the greater part of the county, and the support of two out of the three religious parties it appeared that the King had a far better prospect of success than the Parliament. In the light of the events of the next two years this expectation is seen to have been unjustified, but in September, 1642, the result could not be foreseen. There was reason for expressions such as that of the author of the " Discourse " " That part of the Civill Broyles that fell within this County shewes a Divine hand to have overruled them, considering that a handfull in respect of the multitude always caried it." [1] For even the east and south-east parts of the county where Puritanism had its stronghold were not all of one mind, and the strength of their resistance had not yet appeared. Sir Edward Fitton could write in June, 1642, "I may assure you that the

1. "Discourse," p. 5. Cf., however, " MSS. of Lord Montague of Beaulieu," p. 153. J. Dillingham to Lord Montague, May, 1642 : " I am assured from a good hand that in Lancashire and Cheshire the Puritans are able to encounter the papists, and the Protestants are rather for the Puritan party than the popish. This you may build upon for my authority is very good."

major part of this Hundred of Manchester where I live
will stand right," meaning of course it would support
the King. And that there were many royalists even
in Manchester itself the events of July 15 and 16 had
plainly shown. Moreover even the possibility of raising
the royal standard within the borders of Lancashire
would seem to show that it was a county whose loyalty
could be relied upon.

It is not possible in the present work to give a detailed
account of all the families in Lancashire during the
Civil War; all that can be done is to indicate the main
lines of division between the various parties and to give
brief descriptions of the more prominent leaders on
both sides.

The unquestioned leader of the royalists was the head
of the great house of Stanley, James Stanley, Lord
Strange, afterwards 7th Earl of Derby. Though not
actually succeeding to the title until September, 1642,
his father William the 6th Earl had resigned all his
estates in his son's favour five years before, and Strange
had been since then the leader of the county. Born on
January 31, 1606-7, he was educated in Bolton and at
Oxford, and entered public life very early, becoming
member of Parliament for Liverpool in 1625. Two
years later he was summoned to the House of Lords as
Baron Strange under the impression that this title was
held by his father; that however not being the case the
summons amounted to the creation of a new peerage.
In June, 1626, Strange married, and lived for a time at
court; but he soon retired to his estates in the north of
England, living chiefly at Lathom House, and finding
ample scope for his activities in local affairs in Lancashire, Cheshire and the Isle of Man. Strange was not
a man fitted by temperament or inclination to shine at a
court like that of Charles I., and though his loyalty was
conspicuous and undoubted, he had evidently made
himself very unpopular with the royal advisers who

hindered rather than helped him during the Civil War.
"Court friendship," he writes, "is a cable that in storms
is ever cut," and probably the words had a personal
significance. But however objectionable he may have
been to the Court, Strange was marked by his position
for leadership when the King needed help from Lancashire.

In February, 1638-9, he was summoned by Charles at
the outbreak of the first Scotch war, and in 1640 he
joined the King at York. When the Civil War began
he was Lord Lieutenant of Lancashire and Cheshire,
and was continued in those positions by the King,
though of course removed by Parliament.

In 1642 Strange was 35 years of age. He was in
many ways not unworthy of the great traditions of the
famous House which he represented. There is no need
to subscribe to all the panegyrics which royalist writers
have showered upon the 'martyr earl'; and no doubt
his personal worth, unhappy history, and tragic death
are some excuse for them. Personally he was honourable, high minded and brave; even his enemies speak
of him as a "worthy gentleman, courteous and friendly"
and suggest that his actions were rather due to evil
counsels than to his own disposition. Indeed it is
remarkable that of contemporary judgments, Clarendon's is the most unfavourable. He was personally
religious, as his Book of Private Devotions shows, and
he was a patron of literature and art. But there seems
to have been in his character some underlying flaw of
weakness and irresolution which paralysed all his
actions. He broke with the Court, yet he made himself
no party in Lancashire; and finding himself in 1642 in
command of great resources, he had not the strength to
concentrate his efforts, and lost control in the county
while sending to the main royalist armies troops over
which he had no command. His leadership was marked
by no foresight or capacity; he left Lancashire just at

a time when his presence was most needed there; and
on his return obeyed, though with reluctance, the
Queen's orders to go to the Isle of Man, when it was
far more necessary that he should remain in England.
During his absence the famous first siege of Lathom
House was sustained by the Countess of Derby.
Refusing all overtures after the end of the first war, he
retired to the Isle of Man, which became a refuge for
the more irreconcilable royalists. Pursued to the last
by ill-fortune and bad judgment Derby emerged from
his retirement to join Charles II.'s expedition in 1651;
he escaped wounded from his own defeat at Wigan to
join in the general rout at Worcester; and finally,
having surrendered on promise of quarter to a Captain
who could not keep the promise, he was the only Lancashire royalist to suffer death on the scaffold.   But if
unswerving loyalty and sincerity in a lost cause consti-
tute a claim to martyrdom, the leader of the Lancashire
royalists is abundantly entitled to the honour.[1]

Lord Derby was ably seconded if not directed by his
wife; indeed she was the stronger character of the two.
She was the daughter of Claude de la Tremoille, Duc de
Thouars, and grand-daughter of William the Silent,
Prince of Orange. On coming to England her mother
had endeavoured, though without success, to have her
attached to the household of the Queen. After the
outbreak of the war it would seem as if Lady Derby
had endeavoured to secure herself against possible
reverses of the royalist cause; but she showed no waver-
ing afterwards, and her defence of Lathom House in

1. The chief authorities for Lord Derby's career are the article in the
"Dict. Nat. Biog."; The Life by Canon Raines in the "Stanley Papers,"
C. S., No. 66, and Seacome's "House of Stanley." Seacome had
access to the papers of Bishop Rutter, the supposed author of the
Journal of the first siege of Lathom House, and his work contains
valuable information about the Stanley family not otherwise obtainable;
but he is a bitter partisan and very inaccurate. The first edition of his
work was published at Liverpool in 1741; the references in the following
pages are to the second edition, printed by Joseph Harrop in Manchester
in 1767.

1644 was the one conspicuous success of the royalist cause in Lancashire. After her husband's death she was with difficulty persuaded to surrender the Isle of Man when all other resistance had come to an end.[1]

Next in rank was Richard, Second Viscount Molyneux, the son of Sir Richard Molyneux of Sefton, who had been created in 1628 Viscount Molyneux of Maryborough in the Irish peerage. He was only 19 at the outbreak of the Civil War, and though he took some part in the fighting he was not personally of much advantage to his party in Lancashire. There are several references to him by contemporaries as Lord Derby's son-in-law, the fact being that a 'child marriage' was contracted in 1639 between Molyneux and Henrietta Maria, eldest daughter of Lord Derby, who was then only 9 years old. There was some legal doubt as to whether the marriage was not actually valid; but it was never consummated, though apparently the matter was still in abeyance in 1650 when Molyneux received permission to send messengers to the Isle of Man to receive the lady's answer. He died in July, 1654, and was succeeded in the title by his brother Caryll, who also had taken some little part in the war in Lancashire.

Molyneux surrendered after the capture of Ludlow

---

1. *Vide* "Dict. Nat. Biog." "Hist. MSS. Com.," Rep. 11, pts. 1–3, p. 85. Despatch of the Tuscan Resident at Whitehall : "The Duchess is very desirous of attaching her (Lady Strange) to the household of the Queen ; but with little prospect of success, either because no more French are desired, or because she has no influence with those who dispose of these offices." Cf. also "Moore Rental," pp. 136, 137.
"Hist. MSS. Com.," Rep. 10, "Bouverie MSS.," p. 91, November 10–20, 1642. W. Strickland to John Pym from the Hague : The States General have received a letter from Lady Derby which has been communicated to Strickland by Lord Vosbergen. Lady Derby desires the States General to mediate with Parliament that her person, children and house may be secured from dangers to which she may be exposed by Lord Derby following the King's party. "I told Lord Vosbergen that some of her letters were said to show but little good affection to Parliament, and I knew not how far Parliament had power to exempt any from these common dangers."
Same Day and Place : "Do what you please about Lady Derby's business ; a civil answer will serve, though it be not to expectation. I desire to speak for malignants, but I could do no less" (*ibid*, p. 93).

and took the Covenant and the Negative Oath in August 1646.   His fine at a sixth was £9,037.[1]

By far the ablest of the Lancashire Royalists, and next to Derby the most prominent, was Thomas Tyldesley.   He was a Roman Catholic, of a younger branch of the Tyldesleys of Tyldesley, and resided at Myerscough Hall near Garstang.   He married Bridget Standish, whose mother was sister of Richard, first Viscount Molyneux, and was therefore a cousin by marriage of the second Viscount.   He is better known as Sir Thomas Tyldesley, being knighted for his services when with the Queen at Burton Bridge in July, 1643.   Tyldesley was concerned in all the early Royalist movements in Lancashire.   He was in command at Liverpool when it was first surrendered to the Parliament in 1643; and attended Rupert in the following year at the sack of Bolton, the recapture of Liverpool, and the relief of Lathom House.   When the Royalist cause in Lancashire was finally lost, Tyldesley was active in other parts of the country, and was three times taken prisoner. He was Governor of Lichfield when that town was captured in 1646; he then served in Ireland, and took part in Hamilton's invasion in 1648.   Afterwards Tyldesley found refuge in the Isle of Man, joined Derby's invasion in 1651, and was killed at the Battle of Wigan Lane.   He was a good specimen of the best type of chivalrous Cavalier.   He never compounded for his estates, and considering the very prominent part which he took in the War, the ruling powers treated him very lightly, for no forfeiture is known to have followed his death. [2]

1. For a sound account of Molyneux *vide* " Hist. Soc.," Vol. 7 and 8, pp. 245-278.   This contains an account of the " child marriage." Particulars of his sequestration are given in "Royalist Composition Papers," R. S., No. 26, p. 157.

2. " Dict. Nat. Biog."   " C. W. T.," pp. 306, 353.   " Discourse," p. 92. Myerscough Lodge lies just aside from the main road from Preston to Garstang, and about half-way between the two.   Until comparatively recently some parts of the old house remained, but in 1887 the Lodge was entirely re-built.   Clarendon's estimate of Tyldesley is a very high one (" Hist. Rebell.," ed. Macray, Vol. 5, p. 186; bk. 13, par. 70).

After Tyldesley the three most prominent Lancashire royalists were Sir Gilbert Hoghton of Hoghton, Sir John Girlington of Thurland, and Mr. William Farington of Worden Hall, near Chorley. Hoghton was the son of the Sir Richard Hoghton who, when Sheriff in 1617, had entertained King James the First at Hoghton Tower. He was an elderly man at the outbreak of the war, and took a more prominent part in the earlier operations. In Blackburn Hundred, however, Hoghton was the first royalist to take action, and he was present at the loss of Preston in February, 1642-3. Later he served at Chester, but became involved in a dispute with Colonel Byron the royalist Governor. He died in 1647.[1]

Sir John Girlington of Thurland was Sheriff of Lancashire in 1642. He was one of the first to be sent for by the House of Commons as a delinquent, on account of his energy in plundering his opponents. He was twice besieged in his strong castle at Thurland, and after surrendering it for the second time in October, 1643, Girlington took refuge in Yorkshire, where he was killed in action in the following year.[2]

William Farington of Worden had been Sheriff of Lancashire in 1636. He was a member of the Commission of Array and one of the royalist collectors for Leyland Hundred. His principal military service was at the first Siege of Lathom House, where he was Lady Derby's most trusted adviser. He suffered imprisonment and sequestration and did not compound until 1649. His fine was £511.[3] Farington acted in the attempted pacification in the Autumn of 1642.

---

1. "Discourse," p. 91. "Rupert MSS." ("Add. MSS.," 18981), fol. 266.
2. "C. W. T.," p. 344. "Discourse," p. 90.
3. "Farington Papers" (C. S., No. 39). "Discourse," p. 94. Worden Hall, some three miles from Chorley, is still standing, though it was largely dismantled when the new Hall was built. The old stables remain. About half a mile away across the fields is Buckshawe Hall, the residence of Major Robinson, the supposed author of the "Discourse." Both are now used as farmhouses. Several stone gate-posts bearing Robinson's initials are now built into the walls at Buckshawe.

It is significant of the strength of the popular movement against the King that even in Lancashire a
majority of the members of the Long Parliament were
opposed to him.   There were at this time two members
for the County and two each for Lancaster, Preston,
Clitheroe, Wigan, Newton and Liverpool, fourteen in
all; and the popular party had eight to the King's six,
while in weight and ability their advantage was far
greater.   The full list of the Lancashire members is as
follows :—

LANCASHIRE.
  Ralph Assheton, Esq.
  Roger Kirkby, Esq.
LANCASTER.
  John Harrison, Knight.
  Thomas Fanshaw, Esq.
PRESTON.
  Richard Shuttleworth, Esq.
  Thomas Standish, Esq.
CLITHEROE.
  Ralph Assheton, Esq.
  Richard Shuttleworth, Gent.

WIGAN.
  Orlando Bridgeman, Esq.
  Alexander Rigby, Esq.

NEWTON.
  William Ashhurst, Esq.
  Roger Palmer, Knight.

LIVERPOOL.
  John Moore, Esq.
  Richard Wyn, Knight
    and Baronet.

Of the above, Kirkby, Fanshaw, Harrison, Bridgeman,
Palmer and Wyn were nominally royalists, but three
of them took no part in the war at all, and only Kirkby
had anything to do with it in Lancashire.   Roger
Kirkby of Kirkby Lonsdale was a member of the
royalist County Committee, and one of their collectors
for Lonsdale Hundred; he was concerned in the capture
of Lancaster in 1643, and in the attempt to raise the
siege of Thurland Castle later on the same year, but his
name does not afterwards appear.[1]
  Sir John Harrison was a native of Beaumont, near
Lancaster, but he lived in London, where he had

1. " C. W. T.," pp. 67, 84, 149, 347.

acquired considerable wealth as an official in the Customs. At the outbreak of the war he was arrested, but he escaped and joined the King at Oxford. Harrison outlived the Restoration by ten years, and died at the age of eighty. His daughter was Anne Lady Fanshawe, the wife of Sir Richard Fanshawe.[1]

Bridgeman was the son of the Bishop of Chester of that name, and a lawyer. On the day on which Lord Strange's impeachment was moved Bridgeman was disabled from sitting any longer, it having been reported to the House that he had raised fourteen men to assist Lord Strange and had been active in persuading others to do so. Bridgeman came into some prominence after the Restoration, being created a Baronet in 1660, and in 1667 Lord Keeper. He was the ancestor of the Earls of Bradford.[2]

Ralph Assheton of Middleton, one of the members for the County, was head of that branch of the ancient family. In the seventeenth century the three principal branches were that at Middleton, Whalley, and Downham near Clitheroe, the last being now the only one which remains. He was the son of Richard Assheton, and his wife Mary, daughter of Thomas Venables, Baron of Kinderton in Cheshire, and he married Elizabeth, only daughter of John Kay of Woodsome in Yorkshire. Born on March 31, 1606, Assheton was quite a young man at the beginning of the Civil War, but he at once came to the front, and was first Colonel and afterwards Major-General in command of all the forces in Lancashire. He was a man of great energy and ability and of moderate views. He fought in nearly every engagement of the first war, and on January 2, 1644-5, was specially thanked by the House of Commons for his services to the public. This vote was repeated

1. "Memoirs of Anne Lady Fanshawe" (ed. H. C. Fanshawe, 1907), pp. 21–25.
2. "C. W. T.," 340. "C. J.," Vol. 2, p. 742.

after the Battle of Preston in 1648.   But no one was safe
in such troublous times.   In 1644 Assheton was committed to the Tower for a fortnight on refusing to obey
an order of Parliament about the payment of some
money; and in May, 1650, a warrant was issued by the
Council of State for him to be brought before the
Council on a charge of high treason.   Whether the
warrant was executed or not does not appear.   Assheton
died early in 1651, and was buried in Middleton Parish
Church on February 25, 1650-1.[1]

He must be distinguished from two other Ralph
Asshetons, both of them on the Parliamentary side.
These were Ralph Assheton, eldest son of Sir Ralph
Assheton of Whalley, who was M.P. for Clitheroe in
the Long Parliament, and Ralph Assheton of Downham
who was a Deputy-Lieutenant and a sequestrator of
delinquents' estates.   The latter of these, however, died
in 1643.

Richard Shuttleworth of Gawthorpe near Padiham,
ancestor of the present Lord Shuttleworth, was born in
1587, and had been Sheriff of Lancashire in 1618.   His

---

1. "C. W. T.," 337.   "Discourse," p. 100.   Both these notices, however, give the date of Assheton's death incorrectly.   The entries in the
Parish registers of Middleton put the question beyond doubt ("Lanc.
Parish Register Soc.," Vol. 12, pp. 45, 98).   For the votes of the House
of Commons v. "C. J.," Vol. 4, p. 7; Vol. 5, p. 680.   The former
referred to Assheton's "great, constant and very faithful service."   He
was committed to the Tower on Feb. 9, 1643/4, for not paying £1,500 of
the King's revenue in his hands, as one of the Receivers of the King's
Revenue.   The Order for his arrest in 1650 was issued by the Council of
State on May 1, "To deliver Lieut.-Col. Ralph Assheton, prisoner in the
Compter for debt, into the custody of the Serjeant-at-Arms, to be
brought before Council on a charge of High Treason, he having been
informed against as a very dangerous person" ("C. S. P.," 1650, p. 539).
It is difficult to see how this warrant can refer to anyone else.   In
"Iter Lancastrense' (C. S., 6), p. 29, a description of Assheton's
tomb in Middleton Church is given, and the situation of it is exactly
indicated.   This book was published in 1845; but on the restoration of
Middleton Church by Bishop Durnford in 1869, the stone was removed
with others bearing brasses into the sacrarium.   The floor of the
Assheton Chapel is now occupied by pews.   The Albany Mill stands on
the site of old Middleton Hall.   There is a pedigree of the Middleton
Asshetons in Baines' "Lancashire" (ed. Croston), Vol. 2, p. 396.

experience and standing in the county, as well as his
ability made him of great value to his party. He was
a moderate man of Presbyterian views, and became a
lay elder of the third Lancashire Classis. He was the
only one, however, of the original Lancashire leaders
who had an interview with Lilburne in the campaign of
1651. Four of his sons took part in the war, three of
them becoming colonels, while one of them was killed
at Lancaster in 1643 while still a captain.[1]

Alexander Rigby of Middleton near Preston, was
certainly the most active of the Lancashire Parliamentarians. He seems to have attempted to control local
affairs and to attend Parliament at the same time, and
was constantly travelling about between London and
Lancashire. He was one of the first to take action on
the Parliament's side in Lancashire; his chief military
commands were at Thurland Castle in 1643 and at the
first siege of Lathom in the following year. He commanded a cavalry regiment against Hamilton in 1648.
In the following year Cromwell appointed him a Baron
of the Exchequer, and he died in 1650 from fever caught
whilst trying a case. Rigby was named as one of the
King's judges but he refused to sit. In spite of his
ability he was never popular with his own party, and
Lady Derby's description of him as "that insolent
rebel" fairly represents the royalist opinion of him.
He was nevertheless closely connected with the opposite
party by relationship. A curious illustration of Rigby's
activity was his 'Governship' of Lygonia, a district in
the province of Maine in North America. He bought
the charter and described himself as Governor until his

1. "C. W. T.," p. 352. "Discourse," p. 101, note. Pedigree in
Whitaker's "Whalley," p. 339. Robert Shuttleworth (1784–1855) had
an only daughter Janet, who married, in 1842, Sir James Kay-Shuttleworth;
the present Lord Shuttleworth is their son (Burke's "Peerage").
Colonel Ughtred Shuttleworth was committed to the Tower in March,
1651 ("C. S. P.," 1651, p. 104).

D

death, though he never visited America and discharged his duties by deputy.[1]

John Moore was head of the family of Moore of Bank Hall, near Liverpool. He was the leader of the Puritans in that district and was returned for Liverpool in the Short Parliament. He took little part in the early military operations in Lancashire but commanded at the first siege of Lathom; and he was Governor of Liverpool when that place was stormed by Prince Rupert in August, 1644. Moore was blamed for his surrender, but apparently without due reason. He was a Deputy-Lieutenant, Sequestrator, and one of the judges at the King's trial, his name appearing in the death warrant. He afterwards served in Ireland and died in 1650. His son Edward, was created a Baronet by Charles II. Moore was a restless, bitter, and unscrupulous man, and his household was described as a 'hell upon earth' by Adam Martindale, who for a time acted as his clerk.[2]

William Ashhurst took no part in the operations in Lancashire but looked after the interests of the county at Westminster. He attained some prominence in the House of Commons, and was one of the commissioners sent to Scotland in 1647-8. His brother Major Ashhurst who had at first fought on the Parliament's side joined Charles the Second in the expedition of 1651, and

1. "C. W. T.," p. 351. "Discourse," p. 127. "Palatine Note Book," Vol. 3, pp. 137–140. Rigby's elder brother, George Rigby of Peel, was the ancestor of the present Lord Kenyon.

2. "C. W. T.," p. 349. "Discourse," pp. 101–2. "Martindale's Life," pp. 36–7. "There was such a pack of arrant thieves and they so artificial at their trade, that it was scarce possible to save anything out of their hands except what I could carry about with me or lodge in some other house. Those that were not thieves (if there are any such) were generally, if not universally, profaned bitter scoffers at piety." For the surrender of Liverpool *vide* "Hist. MSS. Com.," Rep. 10, app. 4, pp. 102–3 (Depositions of Capt. Andrew Ashton concerning the loss of Liverpool). It is here stated that when Moore heard of the royalists' entry into the town he drew his sword and asked for volunteers, but his men refused to follow him, and he then reluctantly proceeded to the waterside, many shots being fired at him as he embarked. The fullest account of Moore is in the "Moore Rental," pp. v–xxxix.

William Ashhurst was for a time imprisoned as a suspected person.[1]

It has already been indicated that the division of Lancashire between the two factions followed the same lines as the division of the country generally, that is, the Parliament had the south-east and the King the north-west. The divisions of the families also on the whole followed this arrangement. But no hard and fast lines can be drawn. The Parliament for instance had one firm supporter, Colonel Moore, in the extreme west, and one, Colonel Dodding, in Lancaster; Rigby himself lived near Preston : while on the other hand the Nowells of Read lived in what was chiefly a Parliamentarian district, and we find the Traffords, Mosleys, and the Radcliffes who were Royalists in or near Manchester itself.

Moreover hardly a single family of note was to be found entirely united. Even the Stanleys had their representative in the Parliament's ranks, Sir Thomas Stanley. Sir Gilbert Hoghton's eldest son was a Parliamentarian, whilst Capt. Standish, son of the M.P. for Preston, was killed in the royalist ranks at Manchester. The two bitterest opponents of the King in Lancashire were Rigby and Moore; and Rigby's wife was the sister of an active royalist, while Moore's son was created a Baronet after the Restoration.

1. " C. W. T.," p. 337. " Tanner MSS.," Vol. 59, fol. 503. Another brother, Henry, became a prominent London merchant and philanthropist.

CHAPTER III.

The Siege of Manchester.

FROM the days when it was a Roman fortress Manchester
had probably been the most considerable place in
Lancashire. Leland had referred to it in the previous
century as the "fairest best builded quickest and most
populous town of all Lancashire" : and as in those days
the ring of towns now surrounding it, the creation of
the cotton trade, were non-existent, Manchester was in
proportion larger than now. It was the principal market
for the fustians which were manufactured at Bolton,
Leigh and the places adjacent. The following quotation
is from Lewis Robert's "Merchant's Map of Commerce"
written in 1641.

" The town of Manchester buys the linen yarn of
the Irish in great quantity and weaving it returns the
same again to Ireland to sell; neither doth their
industry rest here for they buy cotton wool in London
that comes first from Cyprus and Smyrna and work
the same into fustians vermilions dimities etc., which
they return to London where they are sold, and from
thence not seldom sent into such foreign parts where
the first materials may be more easily had for their
manufacture."

Though Manchester was in the 17th century no more
than a small unwalled town its position at the junction
of the Irk and Irwell gave it some natural strength on
the north and west sides; but there were no walls or
defences of any kind. The town consisted of a half
circle of houses round the Collegiate Church, with

Deansgate and Market Stead Lane branching off to the
south-west and south-east respectively.   The population
was probably from 5000 to 6000, and of Salford about
one-fourth of that.[1]   The bridges over the Irwell and
Irk described by Leland were still all that existed during
the Civil War; but the Chapel on Salford Bridge which
he mentions had fallen into ruin, and was during the war
often used as a prison.   All that now remains above
ground of the Manchester of that day besides a few old
public houses and one street corner is the Collegiate
Church, now the Cathedral, and the old College, which
is now Chetham Hospital.

If the Civil War had not broken out when it did
Manchester might have attained a distinction for which
it had to wait for another 250 years.   In March, 1640-1,
a proposal was made to establish a University in the
town.   A petition was presented to Parliament urging
the great distance of Oxford and Cambridge and the
great expense which was incurred at those places, " so
that divers gentlemen are induced to send their sons to
foreign universities or to allow them only country
breeding."   It was pointed out that the north of
England generally would benefit "which by reason of
the distance from Court and University suffers a double
eclipse of honour and learning," and Manchester was
stated to be the fittest place, being central in position
and an old town "formerly both a city and a sanctuary."
Lord Strange was much interested in the scheme and
had promised to contribute liberally towards it; and the
old College, at that time disused and much neglected,
was indicated as a very suitable place for the University
to be established.

1. The population is probably estimated from the list of Manchester
signatures to the Protestation of 1641–2, which are given at length in
the " Palatine Note Book," Vol. 1. This is supposed to be a complete
list of the householders in Manchester at the time. The whole total,
however, is 1,305, and as 120 or more are names of officers mostly
outside the town, and there are many reduplications besides, the estimate
of 5,000 seems nearer the mark.

Unfortunately the success of this very interesting scheme was made impossible by the agitated condition of public affairs. An attempt was made to secure Lord Fairfax's support, but he pointed out that even if the opposition of Oxford and Cambridge and other difficulties did not prove insuperable, Parliament had no leisure to discuss matters of such local interest. In view of the trials of Stafford and of Laud and the state of church affairs, a Manchester University bill had no chance of a hearing.[1]

It was fortunate for the Parliamentarian cause in Lancashire that the largest town in the county was on its side. The 'very London of those parts' had as much weight then as now in local affairs, though not its present importance in the national life. The Civil War gave Manchester a national position such as it had never had before. There was no doubt that the majority of the townsmen were against the King; the town was not unanimous as the affray on July 15 had shown, but the fact that the Manchester magazine alone was not secured by the royalists is significant enough; we cannot credit the statements made to the contrary. Curiously enough, however, Salford was royalist in sympathy.[2]

During September, 1642, it was definitely known in Manchester that Lord Strange was collecting troops for

1. "Fairfax Correspondence" (2 vols., 1848), Vol. 2, pp. 271-4. "Hist. MSS. Com.," Rep. 9, app. 2, pp. 431-2. Fairfax writes to his brother, Henry Fairfax, at Ashton-under-Lyne: a bill in Parliament would cost 100 marks, and would have very small chance of success.
2. The Reeve of Salford at this time was Henry Wrigley, a successful cloth merchant and banker. He gave £20 towards the £200 which was subscribed for the building of Salford Chapel, the remainder being paid by Humphrey Booth. Wrigley was Constable for Salford Hundred, and in that capacity issued the summons under the Commission of Array for the muster at Bury on July 14, 1642. He was a lukewarm royalist, however, and prevented two of his servants from joining the royalist army. Afterwards he closed his house and fled to London, where he appeared definitely on the Parliament's side. Attempts were afterwards made to convict him as a malignant, but without success. Wrigley, who was a very prosperous merchant, afterwards lived at Chamber Hall, near Oldham. He was one of Humphrey Chetham's executors and High Sheriff of Lancashire in 1651. ("Palatine Note Book," Vol. 3, pp. 103, 104.)

an attack upon the town. Towards the end of the
month the Parliamentarian newspapers contained disquieting rumours about the royalist plans. Lord Strange
was said to have 1000 foot, and it was thought possible
that Rupert, and even the King might join him.[1] The
situation was critical; for the majority of the county
was on his lordship's side, and there was no garrison
in Manchester, and no fortifications of any kind. The
townsmen were able, however, to secure the services of
a capable engineer to direct the defence. This was
John Rosworm, a German by birth, who had seen
service in the Low Countries, and had been in Ireland
until the insurrection there broke out. He had come to
Manchester early in the summer of 1642; and when the
war began entered into an agreement signed by 22 of
the principal citizens of Manchester to defend the town
for 6 months for the sum of £30.[2] This engagement
was renewed 6 months later, and eventually Rosworm
remained in the service of the town for more than six
years at a salary of £60 a year. Also in January,

1. "Perfect Diurnall" (Cooke), Sept., 19–26. "Perfect Diurnall"
(Cooke and Wood), Sept., 19–26. "The Cavaliers have disarmed most
of Lancashire; Lord Wharton has been ordered north."

2. Rosworm's connection with Manchester is given in greatest detail in
his "Good Service Hitherto Ill-Rewarded ("C. W. T.," pp. 215–244),
which was an appeal to Parliament against the arrears of his salary from
the town; and it cannot therefore be called an impartial account of his
services. His estimate of himself is always a great deal higher than
that given by other writers. Moreover his complaints of arrears would
seem to have been considerably exaggerated. From the "Good Service"
one would gather that the town never paid Rosworm anything at all;
there are, however, given in "C. W. T.," pp. 246, 247, particulars showing
that Rosworm was paid £135 between Dec., 1644, and July, 1647, which
is not very far short of his amount due for the period. He also received
£28 in 1648 ("Chetham Miscellanies," Vol. 2, New Series, No. 63;
"Manchester Civic Records). It must be remembered that our information of payments made is necessarily very fragmentary. The details in
"C. W. T." are said to be "from an old Book of Accounts of the town
of Manchester in the custody of the Boroughreeve," but it is an example
of the way in which the Manchester Municipal Records have been
neglected that this book does not now exist, and no information as to
its contents can be obtained.

In 1651 Rosworm was recommended by the Council of State to be
employed as engineer at Yarmouth, where some works were to be erected
in prospect of an attempted landing by the enemy ("C. S. P.," 1649–50,
pp. 225–235).

1642-3, he became Lieutenant-Colonel in Assheton's regiment of foot. Rosworm was a capable officer and served the town well; but his own estimate of his services is much higher than anybody else's, and his statements about the arrears owing to him from the town must have been greatly exaggerated. His service during the siege, however, was most valuable. It was only in September that he was engaged by the town, and he at once began to make such defences as were possible, by building mud walls at the street ends, and fixing posts and chains to keep out the enemy's horse. These preparations were only just completed in time; and even so it was accident rather than otherwise which gave the town another reinforcement. Sir Edward Fitton and Mr. Leigh of Adlington beginning to disarm their tenants, the supporters of the Parliament from all the neighbourhood round Manchester flocked into the town and completely silenced any objections which the royalists there were making to the works. All the present suburbs of Manchester were not, however, favourable to the Parliament. On September 24 one John Scholes being sent to ring the bells at Prestwich Church 'backwards,' was prevented by the Rector, Isaac Allen. Allen was afterwards deprived of his living, but it was urged in his favour that he was a man of blameless life, and he had not directed his parishioners to take either side in the war. In 1645 he was allowed £40 per annum for maintenance.

Lord Strange mustered his troops at Warrington, and it was 10 o'clock at night on Saturday, Sept. 24, when news reached the town that he was on his march. The distance is only 18 miles, but delayed by the breaking of a wheel of one of the gun carriages and probably also by bad roads, his troops did not arrive before the town until the following day. Their numbers are variously stated from 2000 to 4000 men, and they were probably about half way between these estimates.

With Lord Strange were Lord Molyneux, Sir Gilbert Hoghton, Sir Alexander Radcliffe, Sir John Girlington, Sir Gilbert Gerard, Mr. Tyldesley, Mr. Farington and many others of the royalist gentry of the south and west of Lancashire. The force included four troops of horse and one of dragoons; the foot were trained bands and some Welshmen. They were divided into two somewhere on the march, one division keeping north of the Irwell and occupying Salford, the other crossing the river and approaching Manchester by way of Alport Lane. Lord Strange was with the latter party and took up his quarters at Alport Lodge belonging to Sir Edward Mosley.[1]

When the royalists approached the alarm was given by ringing the bells 'backwards'; it was 9 o'clock on Sunday morning, and the townsmen were called out of church. Two envoys were sent out to Lord Strange, who kept one of them with him for some hours, sending the other back with Captain Windebank to demand an entrance into the town; he promised to respect life and property if this were conceded. This demand was of course refused, and next day hostilities began.[2]

1. Alport Lodge stood half a mile from the town, on the site of the present Great Northern Goods Station. It seems to have been burnt down by accident during the siege. Sir Edward Mosley contributed £20,000 to the royal cause. He afterwards joined Sir Thomas Aston in Cheshire, and was taken prisoner near Middlewich. One-tenth levied on his estate amounted to £4,874. His pardon was passed by Parliament in October, 1647. (Axon, "Lancashire Gleanings," p. 3. "H. L. Calendar, Hist. MSS. Com.," Vol. 6.)

2. The principal authorities for the Siege of Manchester are a number of Tracts in the Thomason Collection :—" Newes from Manchester"; "A True and Faithfull Relation of the Besieging of the Town of Manchester, etc."; "A True and Exact Relation of the Several Passages at the Siege of Manchester, etc."; "A True and Perfect Relation of the Proceedings at Manchester, etc.," E. 121 (13). The first two of these are given in "C. W. T.," pp. 44 and 49; the third is summarised in the appendix to that volume, p. 332. The fourth Tract differs greatly from the other accounts. There are also several other Tracts of little value. To these must be added Rosworm's narrative ("C. W. T.," pp. 219–223) and that in Lancashire's "Valley of Achor" ("C. W. T.," pp. 111–123). And perhaps the most interesting account of all is the Diary contained in the Sutherland MSS., "Hist. MSS. Comm.," Report 5, p. 142. The present writer contributed an essay on the Siege of Manchester to the "Owens College Historical Essays" (1902), p. 377.

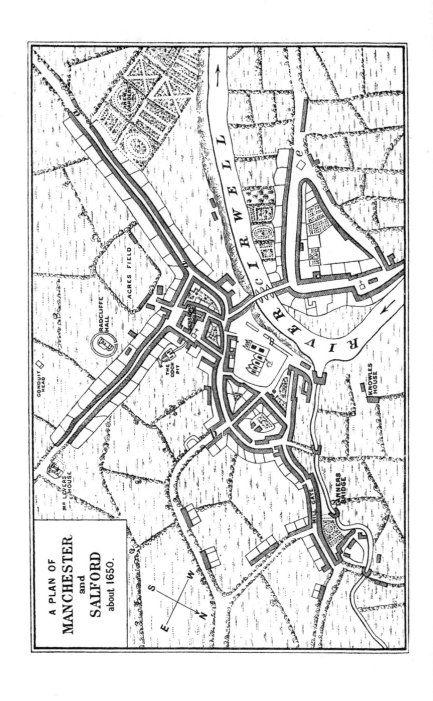

A PLAN OF
MANCHESTER
and
SALFORD
about 1650.

The Parliamentary troops in the town, which numbered about 1000, consisted partly of the militia under
the command of Captain Radcliffe and partly of those
who had come in from the surrounding country to its
assistance. The best of the latter were 150 tenants of
Mr. Assheton of Middleton under Captain Bradshaw.
The various positions had already been assigned.
Bradshaw was posted at the end of Deansgate; Salford
Bridge, which he rather unreasonably calls "the only
place of manifest danger, greatest action and least
defence," Rosworm took for himself; Captain Radcliffe
held Market Stead Lane and Captain Booth Millgate.
Lieutenant Barwick was posted in Hunt's Bank; and
on Shudehill 'a company of resolute soldiers without
any commander.' The guns or gun, for perhaps there
was only one, defended Bradshaw's position, which was
really the most difficult.[1]

1. The Captain Bradshaw here mentioned was probably Robert
Bradshaw, younger brother of John Bradshaw, of Bradshaw Hall, near
Bolton, Sheriff of Lancashire in 1645 (often wrongly confused with
President Bradshaw). He did good service in command of the Assheton
tenantry at Manchester : "Captain Bradshaw hath quit himself most
valiantly to his everlasting renown; he prays with his soldiers every day
himself," E. 240 (23). His name does not, however, appear much
afterwards, but if he was the Captain Bradshaw who was taken prisoner
later in the year, and carried to Lathom House, he died soon after his
release from there. The "Discourse" calls him "a very moderate man
and of good parts" (p. 20).

Richard Radcliffe lived at Radcliffe Hall, a moated house then
standing south of Market Stead Lane. It was afterwards called Pool
Fold, and the name is still preserved. The Hall was pulled down in
1811. This is usually supposed to have been the Richard Radcliffe who
was elected Member of Parliament for Manchester in Cromwell's Parliament of 1656; but as he is called 'old Mr. Radcliffe' in the following
year, this may be doubted. The return of the Burgess to Parliament
in 1656 simply calls the Member "Richard Radcliffe, Esquire, of
Manchester." Radcliffe served at the second defence of Bolton against
the royalists in 1643. ("C. W. T.," p. 351. "Manchester Municipal
Records." "Palatine Note Book," Vol. 3, pp. 265–6.)

Captain, afterwards Colonel, John Booth, was the fifth son of Sir
George Booth, Lord of the Manor of Warrington; for a full account of
his career *vide* a note in the "Discourse," p. 120–122. He must be
distinguished from Colonel (afterwards Sir George) Booth, grandson of the
Sir George Booth referred to, who at first fought on the Parliament's
side, but headed a rising for Charles the Second in 1659, and became
first Lord Delamere after the Restoration.

On Monday morning Lord Strange sent another
message formally demanding all the arms in the town
to be delivered up, and quarter for a troop of his horse;
but the townsmen replied that this was forbidden by the
Protestation, and by Ordinance of Parliament.   About
mid-day the royalist batteries opened fire, shooting
bullets of 4 lbs., 6 lbs., and 8 lbs. weight; but little
damage was done except to the houses.   They then
attacked Deansgate at close quarters and setting fire to
some buildings at the end of the town, almost effected
an entrance.   Rosworm was obliged to send 20 of his
50 musketeers as reinforcement, and the royalists were
at length driven back with some loss.   Later in the
afternoon an assault was also made on Salford Bridge,
but this was more easily repulsed as the royalists had
there to charge uphill, and their position was commanded by the higher ground of the churchyard.
There is also said to have been a royalist attack of horse
against the east of the town, but this also was beaten
off.   Firing continued until dark, and at midnight a
party of royalists went down to the water's edge in
Salford, and attempted to set fire to the town by means
of lighted faggots.   The royalists are said to have lost
120 men against 3 of the defenders.[1]

1. These numbers sound very disproportionate, but the statement is
made in the "Sutherland MSS.," which seems much the most reliable
in the matter of numbers. "These were estimated," the account continues,
"from the graves found in the fields about the town, and five more
were found in the sands of the river; and it is supposed that more were
cast into the river, among whom was Mr. Mountain, a Colonel of horse,
and Captain Skirton and a lieutenant, with others of note" ("Hist.
MSS. Com.," Vol. 5, p. 142).   The tract called "A True and Faithful
Relation, etc.," which is supposed to have been written by Heyrick,
says roundly : "In this day's fight, blessed be to God, we lost not one
man."
Richard Heyrick, the Warden of the Collegiate Church, was son of
Sir William Heyrick, Alderman of London, who afterwards lived at
Beaumanor, in Leicestershire.   He was born in London in 1600,
became Rector of North Repps, in Norfolk, and Warden of Manchester
in 1635, his father obtaining the Wardenship for him in satisfaction of
some monetary transactions with the Crown.   Heyrick was a man of
great energy, and was the leader of the Presbyterian party in Manchester.
He was a cousin of Herrick the poet. (Art. by C. W. Sutton, "Dictionary
of National Biography.")

Next day no direct attacks were delivered at Deansgate or the Bridge. The former seems to have been left quite free, but a cannonade was begun by the royalists in Salford which so terrified Rosworm's raw soldiers that 16 of them took to their heels; and he says that some of those who stayed did so from fear of his drawn sword.[1] As he had sent away 20 of his men on the previous day only 14 now remained at this important position; but volunteers brought up his men to their original number again. On this day the other street ends were attacked by the royalists, especially Market Stead Lane; but they were beaten back at all points. Gaining confidence, the townsmen began to sally out on their own account and cut off several small parties which were straggling in the fields. Seven troopers with their horses were taken and one quarter-master shot with the loss of two of the garrison.

At 5 o'clock in the afternoon Lord Strange called a parley and again proposed surrender; after some negotiation a truce was agreed upon until 7 o'clock on the following morning, but it seems to have been observed by neither side.[2] Lord Strange's proposals were considered, but it was not likely that after having repelled his attacks for two days the townsmen would be more ready to treat than before; and all the royalist terms were refused.[3] Strange made many proposals, less and less being asked for on each refusal. First he demanded to march through the town, then £1000 in money, then

1. No other account mentions this incident.
2. The royalists continued plundering, if they suspended their actual attacks upon the town; and evidently the garrison took opportunity to bring in reinforcements. They came from Bolton, and two of them were killed by the royalists during a skirmish outside the town; " Coming peaceably with 150 more to assist the town," Heyrick says quaintly (" C. W. T.," p. 55).
3. The terms offered are variously stated, the fullest account being given in a tract entitled, " The Lord Strange, his Demands, etc." (" C. W. T.," p. 47). Rosworm mentions only a demand for 100 muskets. Heyrick says that the question was finally referred to the soldiers, " who all resolutely answered they would not give him a yard of match, but would maintain their cause and arms to the last drop of blood."

200 muskets; finally he offered to depart if 50 muskets were surrendered. " The town said they would not give him so much as a rusty dagger"[1]; and next day hostilities were resumed.

The defenders were, however, not quite so unanimous as the defiant replies would suggest. There was a party in the town led by Colonel Holland the Governor, which desired to come to terms with the royalists. They pointed out that the stock of ammunition was running very low, and that the country people who had come in as volunteers were becoming restive owing to the plundering by the royalists in the neighbourhood.[2] Rosworm describes a scene when Holland on Wednesday afternoon came down to him at the Bridge urging these considerations; Rosworm referred the matter to his soldiers, who declared they would stand firm, and Holland went away in anger. Shortly after this Mr. Bourne, the aged fellow of the Collegiate Church coming by, Rosworm urged him to go along Deansgate to Bradshaw's men and persuade them if necessary to resist. They, however, needed no persuasion but declared "by a general shout that they would part with their arms and their lives together." [3]   It was perhaps

1. " Sutherland MSS."

2. " As also their foot plundered, which gave the occasion and example for all the plundering that after happened in the county " (" Discourse," p. 7).

Richard Holland (afterwards Colonel in the service of the Parliament) lived at Heaton, in Prestwich. He was a magistrate and sequestrator, and served at Preston, Wigan and the first siege of Lathom House. Rosworm was his bitter enemy, and accused him of great cowardice.

3. The shortage of ammunition was evidently a very grave danger, for all the accounts mention it. Rosworm confesses that he had only 6 lbs. of powder and 18 fathom of match left, but he had told no one. Cf. a letter from Sir John Hotham to the Speaker on Nov. 25, 1642, in which he refers to his having sent from Hull five barrels of powder to Manchester "when they were in that extremity with Lord Strange " (" Portland MSS.," Vol. 1, p. 174). This powder arrived on Oct. 14 (" C. W. T.," p. 122). The " Valley of Achor " refers to the fact that the very wet weather made the country people more willing to stay in Manchester, it being harvest time (" C. W. T.," p. 118).

Rev. William Bourne was senior fellow of the Collegiate Church. He died in the following year. He "had long been a blessing to the town, and had seen a resurrection of it from the Plague, nigh forty years before " (evidently the visitation of 1605), and "was lifted up from the gates of death and raised in spirit to promote this work."

a concession to the faint-hearted that on the following day Mr. Alexander Butterworth of Belfield was sent towards London for aid.[1]

There was, however, no need to bring help from London or anywhere else, for the royalist attack was nearly spent. When hostilities were resumed the Parliamentarians were the assailants. At 10 o'clock on Thursday, September 29, 200 men sallied out from Deansgate to relieve a house which had been occupied by the royalists; they were attacked by 100 musketeers and a troop of horse, but after an hour's fighting the royalists were defeated, most of the horse being driven into the river and an officer[2] and two men drowned. The losses are given as 13 on each side and the town made two prisoners. In Salford some guns previously placed in a position which was commanded by the churchyard were removed. On this day also the royalists lost one of their leaders in Salford, Captain Standish, who was shot by a marksman posted at the top of the church tower.[3] There was no further fighting after this. The following day desultory firing continued from Deansgate and Salford, and at the former position the royalists began to dig a trench as if they intended to establish a blockade; but it was only a

1. Cf. also a letter dated Sept. 26, signed by Holland, Booth, Egerton and Hide, to Colonels Shuttleworth and Starkie "at Haslingden or elsewhere," asking them to send powder and match for the relief of Manchester ("Lancs. Lieutenancy," pt. 2, p. 273).
2. This was Captain Snell, who "had two rings on his hands worth £20" ("Sutherland MSS.").
3. Captain Thomas Standish was not of the royalist family of that name at Standish; that branch was represented at the siege of Manchester by its head, Ralph Standish, the uncle of Lord Molyneux and father-in-law of Colonel Tyldesley; but was the eldest son of Thomas Standish of Duxbury, near Chorley, Shuttleworth's colleague as M.P. for Preston. Heyrick says he was killed whilst "reproaching his soldiers because they would not fall on," but the "Discourse" less picturesquely, but probably with more accuracy, that "quartered in a house upon the north side of Salford, well up towards the Chapel, was, by a bullet shot from the top of Manchester Steeple, slain" (p. 7). The "Sutherland Diary" gives a touch of human interest in the statement, "He was to have married Mr. Archbould's kinswoman, who married Sir John Harper of Cork." There is no doubt that the loss of Standish was a serious blow to the attack.

pretence for they dared no longer to come to close quarters. [1] On Saturday the Earl of Derby, as he now was from his father's death on the previous day, sent for an exchange of prisoners, of which the town is said to have taken 85. The royalists made up their number by seizing non-combatants from the surrounding district. When the exchange had been effected the royalists decamped in such haste that Rosworm was able to send out a party openly to capture their arms.

It is not very easy to estimate satisfactorily the losses on both sides during the six days of the siege. We have very full details, but unfortunately all the accounts are written by Parliamentarians, and no one-sided descriptions of Civil War battles can be relied upon. Heyrick for instance roundly says of the Monday operations when fighting was the most severe of all, "in this day's fight blessed be God we lost not one man." One writer states that the townsmen lost no one at all except one boy who was looking on from a stile; and they all estimate the royalist casualties at some hundreds. It is of course to be expected that few of the defenders were killed but surprising that many lives were lost at all. Seventeenth century musketry was very erratic, and the besieger's cannon was probably wholly useless; and the combatants came to close quarters very little except on the first day of the siege. The "Sutherland Diary," which seems altogether the most accurate and moderate account estimates the royalist losses at 220 killed and 85 prisoners; detailed losses of the defenders amount only to 19. But on the first day the losses are said to be 125 and 3 respectively, which sounds very unlikely. It is, however, not possible to arrive at any greater

1. "On Friday Lord Strange's forces were so scattered that they durst not come within pistol shot of the town" ("Sutherland Diary"). When Derby requested an exchange of prisoners and a cessation of plundering, the town retorted that they had not plundered at all, but his lordship had done so much damage "that £10,000 would not make a recompense" ("C. W. T.," p. 55).

accurateness for all the accounts agree in the main that about 80 prisoners were taken by the town, and that the royalists lost from 100 to 250 men. Nineteen is the largest total given for the defenders' losses.[1] A very glowing picture of the state of the town during the siege is given by Heyrick and other writers. Heyrick says "our Souldiers from first to last had prayers and singing of Psalmes daily at the street ends, most of our Souldiers being religious honest men of a civill and inoffensive conversation, which came out of conscience of their oath and protestation. The Townsmen were kind and respective to the Souldiers; all things were common : the Gentlemen made bullets night and day ; the Souldiers were resolute and coragious and feared nothing so much as a Parley; the deputy Lieutenants, Captaine Chantwell and other gentlemen took paines night and day to see that the Souldiers did their duty.[2]

If this description is not somewhat overdrawn, it is because the town did not stand by itself in the matter of defence. The neighbouring Deputy-Lieutenants and Bradshaw's men probably did much not only in numbers but in moral effect to strengthen the resistance. For there was certainly a party in the town less inclined to stand out. Manchester contained many royalists; and as we have seen, they were at least the majority in Salford. Probably Lord Strange counted on a far less stubborn resistance than he encountered; and judging by the support given him in July he was justified in

1. These figures are from the authorities cited above. The only independent estimate is in a letter from Stephen Charlton to Sir R. Leveson : " News confirmed by several letters from Manchester that they of the town have slain about 300 of Lord Strange's forces " (" Hist. MSS. Com.," Vol. 5, p. 161).
2. The " Valley of Achor " goes further than this : " A spirit of Piety and Devotion in Prayers and singing of Psalms rested generally upon Persons and families, yea Taverns and Innes where it might not put in the head formerly " (" C. W. T.," p. 120). Cf. however " Salford Portmote Records," C. S. (new series), 48, Vol. 2, p. 77 ; on Oct. 16, 1644, Edward Rosterne was presented " for making an affray on the Bridge with the soldiers that kept the Bridge there."

doing so. This may have had something to do with the badly organised state of his force, though there is no need to credit all the stories which the other side told about its composition. It was evidently without discipline or efficiency;[1] and the attack was ill-planned and conducted with no vigour. The royalists attacked Manchester which was not a strong position on the whole, at two of its strongest points. At Deansgate they had no advantage of ground, and in Salford they were at a disadvantage, having to advance across a narrow sloping bridge which was commanded by the higher opposite bank of the river; whereas at Shude Hill or at Market Stead Lane the royalists would have had the advantage of ground, and their guns would have proved much more effective at these positions than pointing up Salford Bridge. The principal attacks should have been delivered at these two points.

The weather was no doubt an item in favour of the town. It was a very wet week, and not only did the rain make communication impossible between the two divisions of the royalists, for the Irwell rises rapidly in flood; but as the besiegers were mostly out in the open the discomfort of their position served to demoralise them still further.

"By reason of cold and wet hunger and thirst and labour want of sleep and a bitter welcome that we gave them, their hearts were discouraged mightily."[2]

Moreover no attempt was made by the royalists to blockade the town, which kept open communications during all the week of the siege. It was, however, a mistake to divide the royalist forces at all.

Nevertheless Manchester might congratulate itself on

1, It was stated that the royalist forces had been summoned to Warrington to meet the King, and the direction of their march was at first concealed from them. "The Lord Strange's Souldiers some of them wept, others protested great unwillingness to fight against Manchester, affirming they were deceived and deluded else they had not come hither" ("C. W. T.," p. 56).

2. "A True and Exact Relation of the Several Passages at the Siege of Manchester," etc., E. 121 (45).

a very considerable and well deserved success. The thanksgivings of October 2nd, and of October 6th, when there was a special service in the church for the soldiers, were amply justified; for it was the first trial of strength, and the royalists were thought to be the stronger. The effect of their failure was therefore very great. And it is surely not only local pride which sees in the siege of Manchester an event which had an importance quite out of proportion to that which is at first apparent. As a Parliamentarian writer says, "had not that town stood very firmly for the King and Parliament in all probability the whole county had been brought into subjection to the oppression and violence of the Cavaliers." [1] This is quite true. Manchester became the Parliamentarian headquarters, though even after their first success that party was for three months very largely on the defensive. Manchester was the key of the position, and had it fallen in October, 1642, and remained in royalist hands the King would have been supreme in the whole county. And to have been supreme in Lancashire would have enormously strengthened Charles' cause in all the north of England.

1. "Exceeding Joyful News out of Lancashire, etc." ("C. W. T.," p. 103). Cf. "Clarendon" (Macray), Vol. 6, p. 67 : "For Manchester the Lord Strange, who had by His Majesty's favour and encouragement recovered his spirits (after the impeachment), undertook, without troubling His Majesty further northward in a very short time to reduce that place (which was not so fortunately performed because not so resolutely pursued) and to send a good body of foot to the King to Shrewsbury."

CHAPTER IV.

First Operations of the Manchester Garrison.
Capture of Preston.

WHEN the House of Commons met on Monday, Oct. 3, letters were read giving information of Lord Strange's retreat. It was, however, feared that he would very soon return to make another attempt. There was a false alarm in Manchester on the same day that the royalists were coming back, and the rumours were repeated on October 5 and October 10; and at intervals all through the rest of the month the town lived in fear of a second royalist attack. It was again reported in the newspapers that the King was to join the Earl of Derby against Manchester and then to march into Yorkshire against the Hothams.[1] Fortunately all these rumours were false. Manchester was never to see any more fighting and only once again the march of a hostile army. And there was never any real prospect at this time of Charles invading Lancashire. The Earl of Derby sent some of his troops to join the royal army, but he does not seem to have himself joined the King.

Parliament had realised the importance of retaining Manchester, and already during the siege a commission had been issued for raising 1000 dragoons under Sir John Seaton for service in Lancashire. Unfortunately it was easier to issue commissions than to carry them out; in spite of newspaper reports to the contrary the dragoons had not reached Manchester by the end of November. Indeed it is doubtful whether they were

---

1. On Monday, October 3, the state of Lancashire was referred to the Committee of Safety. Thanks were voted on the 6th. The "Valley of Achor" gives details of the false alarms ("C. J.," Vol. 2, p. 792. "C. W. T.," p. 122. "Perfect Diurnall," Oct. 15).

ever sent at all, though Seaton was in command in
Lancashire early in the new year.[1] Supplies of powder
were, however, sent to Manchester; a large amount
reached the town on October 22, besides that which had
been sent from Hull; though several convoys were
intercepted by the royalists, one on its way from
Worcester, one by Sir Edward Mosley at Stafford, and
one later on October 24. Mr. Assheton had also a
warrant from the Speaker for conveying four small
brass pieces to Manchester and one for the defence of
his own house at Middleton.[2] The whole county was
organised for military purposes by the Parliament,
companies being raised and Colonels appointed for each
Hundred; Assheton and Holland in Salford Hundred,
Shuttleworth and Nicholas Starkie in Blackburn, Rigby
for Amounderness and Leyland, Moore and Peter
Egerton in West Derby, and Mr. Dodding for Lonsdale
Hundred. The local captains were those who had
already served at the siege of Manchester, Birch,
Bradshaw, Radcliffe and Venables. Salford Hundred
was the most active for the Parliament, and Manchester
led the way. The troops there were steadily drilled,
the magazine replenished, and fortifications consider-

1. Some troops of horse are mentioned at first, but not afterwards.
It was intended to borrow £16,000 in London for this purpose at the
usual rate of 8 per cent. "All persons who are willing to go soldiers in
the service under Col. Sir John Seaton as dragoniers, are to resort to
Capt. Henry Legh at the Sign of the Sun near Cripplegate, and Capt.
William Stackhouse at his house in St. Thomas Apostles, and there are
to be listed for that service" ("L. J.," Vol. 5, p. 377). In "England's
Memorable Accidents," Oct. 17–24, mention is made of the 1,000 dragoons
being on their march. Some of these dragoons are part of those men
that came out of Holland in the ship that was forced by a leak to put
into Yarmouth ("C. W. T.," p. 60). A letter written on Dec. 2, however,
makes it clear that the men had not arrived then, and it is doubtful if
they ever did so. Cf. "Tanner MSS." 59, fol. 683, where Rigby speaks
of the "remains of the money raised for the Lancashire dragoniers taken
into the Lord General Essex's army."
2. "C. J.," Vol. 2, p. 833. "C. W. T.," p. 123. Cf. also "Portland
MSS.," Vol. 1, p. 160. A. Stavely, Leicester, to the Speaker. The
Parliamentarian garrison there is between Ashby and Belvoir, two
royalist strongholds, and on the road from Nottingham and Derby to
Manchester; so that their small strength of horse is constantly employed
in convoy of ammunition and other commodities (Nov. 24, 1643).

ably strengthened. Not content with this the garrison
began to make small expeditions on its own account to
plunder the houses of royalists in the neighbourhood.[1]
Alport Lodge where Lord Strange and Tyldesley had
stayed during the siege was destroyed;[2] a party was sent
to disarm the town of Bury, where the first royalist
musters had been made; and Captain Birch led a force
into Blackburn Hundred to capture Townley Hall. As
soon, however, as the war had actually broken out men
began to realise what consequences its long continuance
may have. It was, writes Clarendon, "the opinion of
most that a battle would determine all"; and when
Edgehill had been fought and small skirmishes occur-
ring in all parts of the country had left matters much
as they were, local attempts at pacification began to
be made in many places. These merely attempted to
make a temporary arrangement for cessation, and were
quite distinct from the negotiations between King and
Parliament which continued all through the autumn of
1642. Questions of principle were not raised, and as
the local opponents had usually been on good terms
before the war began, it was not difficult for them to
come to some agreement. In Devon and Cornwall a
treaty was entered into by the two parties; in Yorkshire
and in Cheshire, and no doubt in other counties also,
pacifications were arranged. Parliament, however,
steadily refused to countenance them, and the position
was no doubt a sound one.

In Lancashire negotiations were opened through the
medium of Roger Nowell of Read, a royalist captain,
but a relative of Colonel Shuttleworth, and it was

1. The Parliamentarian soldiers were guilty of much vandalism in
these operations, "taking out of Churches the Books of Common Praier,
Surplisses, Fonts, and breaking down of Organs where they found any."
At Bury they seized the surplice "and put it on the back of a Souldier,
and caused him to ride in the cart the Armes were carried in, to be
matter of sport and laughter to the Behoulders" ("Discourse," p. 11).
2. Some of the timber from Alport Lodge was used to strengthen the
defences of Manchester.

decided to attempt a meeting of a certain number from each party at Blackburn on Thursday, October 13. Shuttleworth wrote to Holland and Egerton in Manchester asking for their co-operation, and they replied on October 10 agreeing to the meeting, but suggesting Bolton as a better place since they were not willing to leave their own Hundred.   Shuttleworth replied next day to Nowell naming Bolton as the place, and offering either the following Monday or Tuesday, October 17 or 18 for the date. Nowell fixed October 18 with William Farington, and it was arranged that six leaders from each side should meet. The Parliamentarians were Shuttleworth, Starkie, Egerton, Holland, John Bradshaw and John Braddyl; the royalists Farington, Alexander Rigby of Burgh, John Fleetwood, Savile Radcliffe, and it was hoped Sir Thomas Barton and Robert Holt of Castleton. But the intended meeting never took place. Parliament somehow had news of the arrangement, and promptly put their veto upon it. On October 15 Holland wrote from Manchester that Parliament had forbidden any local attempts at pacification; Shuttleworth forwarded the letter to the royalists, and the incident closed.[1]

There seems to have been one further attempt to bring about a pacification in Lancashire, or perhaps it would be more correct to say that Manchester was included in negotiations which were proceeding in Cheshire at the initiative of Lord Kilmorey and Lord Brereton.   It was

1. Seven of the letters referred to above are printed in the "Farington Papers" (C. S., 39), pp. 80–86, and three of these also in the "Lancashire Lieutenancy," pt. 2 (C. S., 50), pp. 282–286. Nowell himself was unable to take any part in the negotiation after October 12, as he started on the following Friday to join the King. Richard Nowell, the younger brother of Roger Nowell of Read, was killed at the capture of Bristol by Prince Rupert, being then captain in Lord Molyneux's regiment. Dugdale's "Visitation of Lancs.," 1664 (C. S., 84), p. 122. The Bradshaw here referred to was probably of Bradshaw Hall, near Bolton, elder brother of Capt. Bradshaw. Braddyl lived at Portfield, near Whalley. Fleetwood and Farington were the royalist collectors for Leyland Hundred, and Holt one of those for Salford Hundred.

proposed that the troops in and near Manchester should
be disbanded and the town 'secured' by the Earl of
Derby. But the Parliamentarians had nothing to gain
by the terms suggested, and the former failure had
made them more cautious. They replied that they had
done nothing consciously to provoke Lord Derby's
hostility; but that if satisfactory proposals for pacification were submitted they would send them up to Parliament immediately by a special messenger.[1] Meanwhile
the royalists in the county were also arming, and in
spite of peace proposals all preparations were being
made for a protracted struggle. After retreating a little
way from Manchester Lord Derby seems to have sent
some regiments to the King and made his own headquarters at Warrington. But he was reported to be in
a very despondent frame of mind, "for the last Thursday
(November 24) at Warrington at dinner he said he was
born under an unfortunate planet and that he thought
some evil constellation reigned at the time of his birth,
with many such other words of passion and discontent."
There was even a report about this time that his life
was in danger, which is the more credible as it comes
from a royalist source. He summoned a meeting of his
supporters on October 10 at Warrington,[2] and it was
resolved to call out the trained bands and freehold bands.
of Lancashire and to raise horse, and also to bring about
an association with the counties of Shropshire, Flint,

1. These proposals are printed in " C. W. T.," 61; also in "Lancs.
Lieutenancy," pt. 2, 300, together with a letter from the Committee at
Manchester to Col. Shuttleworth. The proposals were evidently made
about the middle of October, as the letter above referred to is dated
Oct. 22, and states that an answer was to be returned to the Earl of
Derby on the following Monday morning, *i.e.*, Oct. 24.

2. Cf. "Ashmolean MSS." 830, fol. 289, for an 'oath imposed by the
Earl of Derby upon Lancashire.' No date is given. He who takes it
promises "to the uttermost of my power and with hasard of my life
maintain and defend the true Protestant religion established in the
Church of England, His Majesty's sacred person, his heirs and lawful
successors, His Majesty's just powers and prerogatives and the just
powers and priveleges of parliament against the forces now under the
command of the Earl of Essex and against all other forces whatsoever,"
etc.

Denbigh, Cumberland and Westmorland. The resolutions were signed by Derby and 23 others; it is rather surprising to find that the Parliamentarian leaders were also summoned to this meeting.[1] Shuttleworth and Starkie certainly had invitations, and probably some others also. The chief royalist garrisons were established at Warrington, Wigan and Preston. Wigan was the nearest town to Lathom House, and was described by its opponents as the "most malignant town in all the county"; Warrington, however, on account of its geographical importance as commanding the only bridge into Cheshire, was the most strongly fortified, and contained the most numerous garrison. At the end of October the Parliamentarian leaders had information that there were royalist troops to the number of 1400 in six garrisons, of which 400 were at Warrington, 300 at Preston and 200 at Wigan.[2] In December another royalist meeting was held at Preston and the organisation was further completed. Collectors were appointed for every Hundred to raise the sum of £8,700 to be employed for the payment of 2000 foot and 400 horse and for the provision of a magazine. The collectors were Girlington and Roger Kirkby for Lonsdale Hundred; Adam Mort, Mayor of Preston, and Alexander Rigby of Burgh for Amounderness; Farington and John Fleetwood for Leyland; Henry Ogle, John Bretherton and Robert Mercer for West Derby; Robert Holt and Francis Sherington for Salford; and Sir John Talbot and Radcliffe Assheton for Blackburn. The rates of pay were fixed; and Girlington, Mort, Kirkby and James Anderton or any three of them were to form

1. "Sutherland MSS." Hist. MSS. Com.," Vol. 5, p. 347. "Lancs. Lieut.," pt. 2, pp. 296–298. Shuttleworth's letter of refusal is given. Assheton and Rigby were at this time in London, and Shuttleworth sent them weekly reports of affairs in Lancashire.
2. The other three places were Ormskirk, Eccleston and Prescot. Through the medium of George Rigby of Peel the Parliament appointed informants in Wigan and Warrington ("Lancs. Lieut.," pt. 2, pp. 289–291).

a standing council at Preston to give reports periodically to Lord Derby, and having power to summon other advisers as they pleased.[1]

Actual hostilities began again about the end of November, and for two months in spite of the winter, there was constant fighting in various parts of the county. The climax of the campaign, which on the whole went greatly in favour of the Parliamentarians, was their capture of Preston in February, 1642-3. A number of skirmishes occurred almost simultaneously at the end of November, the first being in Blackburn Hundred.[2] There had been a general meeting of royalists at Preston on November 7, and a week or two later Sir Gilbert Hoghton fired his beacon as a signal to the Fylde. Hoghton Tower occupies a conspicuous position, and the light of the beacon would be seen all over the low lying country nearer the sea. With the troops thus raised he disarmed Whalley and occupied Blackburn. Colonels Shuttleworth and Starkie, hearing of this, hastily raised 8000 men and attacked the royalists by night. Moonlight prevented a complete surprise, but the victory was complete. After two hours fighting they gained an entrance into Blackburn, and the royalists fled in such haste that they left their own arms and all that they had seized in Whalley. Hoghton himself escaped with difficulty.

A few days after this engagement, on Sunday,

1. "C. W. T.," p. 66. "Discourse," p. 16. The Rigbys of Burgh were royalists. This is Alexander Rigby the elder, who died in 1650 ; it was his son who was Sir Thomas Tyldesley's cornet at the Battle of Wigan, and erected the monument to his Colonel ("C. W. T.," 351. "Discourse," pp. 106, 126). Radcliffe Assheton lived at Chadderton ; this was the only branch of the Assheton family which took the King's side in the Civil War.

2. This seems to have been the first in point of time, though the dates are somewhat confused. Shuttleworth is said to have halted his men on Hinfield Moor (according to one account it was the scene of the battle, but that is evidently an error), but this name does not now appear on the map of Lancashire. The nearest approach to it is Inchfield Moor, which is on the extreme eastern border of the county, and cannot be the place intended here.

November 27, a skirmish occurred in which Lord
Derby's troops were concerned, though it does not
appear that he himself was present. The countryside
was going to church when a post rode in with the news
that the Earl's troops were marching towards Chowbent;
about 3000 men were hastily collected against him and
a running fight ensued all the way to Leigh, some two
miles distant. The royalists were gradually driven
back, some being killed and many wounded. On
Lowton Common, two miles beyond Leigh, they turned
and faced the Parliamentarian horse which had left the
foot far behind; but after a short stand they again broke
and fled, many prisoners being taken in the pursuit.[1]

It is worthy of remark that most of the actual fighting
during the Civil War in Lancashire was running
fighting. This first instance is only one of many more
in the next few years. The decisive battle in the county
covered many miles of ground, and even the battle of
Preston itself was, after Langdale's first stand, a long
and straggling engagement half way across the county.
Attacks on houses or towns excepted, there were few if
any pitched battles until that at Wigan Lane in 1651,
which was the last battle of the war.

The next encounter went in favour of the royalists,
and, as all the Parliamentarians admit, it was a great
disaster. During the next few weeks both parties sent
out from their garrisons plundering expeditions against
houses in the neighbourhood which belonged to the
other side. In retaliation for some plunder by the

1. The name Chowbent has recently disappeared from the map, being
represented by Atherton, the two railway stations which used to
bear the name being now called respectively Atherton (Central) and
Howe Bridge. The ground descends gradually towards Leigh. Lowton
Common is still partly an open space. The language of this description,
"A true and full relation of the troubles in Lancashire, etc." ("C. W. T.,"
p. 63), is very picturesque, "For now the men of Blackburn, Paduam,
Burnely, Clitheroe and Colne, with those sturdy churles in the two
forests of Pendle and Rossendale have raised their spirits, and have
resolved to fight it out rather than their Beefe and fatt Bacon shall
be taken from them."

Wigan garrison, a local company of Parliamentarians together with two from Manchester, attacked the house of a Roman Catholic gentleman near Wigan. They were surprised by a superior force of royalists, but abandoning their booty they managed to escape. A day or two afterwards, however, they were again surprised near Westhoughton by a force of 1000 men, and being surrounded they were all compelled to surrender at discretion. This was on December 15, 1642; 160 men together with Captains Bradshaw and Venables were captured. Venables was probably some months in captivity at Lathom House; Bradshaw was released earlier, but soon afterwards died.[1]

This was, however, the only royalist success for some time to come. The two remaining engagements of the year went in favour of the Parliamentarians. Both took place on Christmas Eve. On that day the Manchester garrison accompanied by Rosworm marched out by way of Chowbent, which they cleared of the enemy, to Leigh. This was a measure of retaliation for plundering by the Wigan garrison in the neighbourhood. The royalists made some resistance, but being largely outnumbered by the attacking force they were surrounded and overpowered. The Parliamentarians marched on the market place from different sides, and they recovered many of the arms which had

1. "C. W. T.," pp. 63 and 125. "Discourse," p. 20. The details of this engagement are very confused, but the above seems the most probable course of events. There is no doubt about the large number of prisoners. There is a story told by one Parliamentarian writer of the conduct of the royalist troop which may be set against that of the Manchester soldiers at Bury. "The carriage of the cavaliers about Wigan was most insolent, yea blasphemous, for after they had pulled down the pulpit in Hendon Chapel, and played at cards in the pews and upon the desk, they surprised the Holy Bible, took it away, and afterwards tore it in pieces, and then stucke up the leaves of it upon the posts in severall places in Wigan, saying, 'This is the Roundheads' Bible.'"
Venables was of the ancient Cheshire family of that name at Antrobus. He was afterward Commander-in-Chief of the Parliamentarian troops in Ulster, and later, with the rank of General, led the expedition to the West Indies which took possession of Jamaica. He acquiesced in the Restoration, and died in 1687, aged 75 ("Discourse" note, p. 99).

been captured a fortnight before. The victory was
regarded with great satisfaction as a revenge for
Venables' surrender.   Within three days the Parliamentarian troops were back in Manchester.   The other
engagement was also fought on previously contested
ground at Blackburn, in this case the assailants being
the royalists.   Sir Gilbert Hoghton had a special case
against this garrison as it was only three miles from
his own house.   Accordingly on Christmas Eve he
marched out of Blackburn, it was said with 5000 men,
to attack the town.   The garrison numbered only 400.
But there was no fighting at close quarters; the royalists
had with them one small piece of cannon which they
discharged repeatedly without effect, but they hardly
approached within musket shot at all, and under cover
of night they retreated.   No lives were lost and the only
result was the plundering of the countryside.[1]

In January, 1642-3, there was very little done by
either side.   Some Manchester troops set out to capture
the house of Mr. Leigh at Adlington in Cheshire, but
they returned without doing anything.   The only other
incident was an unsuccessful plot by Sir John Talbot,
which is reported incorrectly in details though there
seems to be no doubt of the main facts.   Talbot was
one of the royalist collectors for Blackburn Hundred and
lived at Salesbury Hall near Ribchester.   Early in
January he invited some of the Parliamentarian leaders
to pay a visit to his house; but suspecting some treachery
they sent a troop of horse instead, and found that it was

---

1. "Discourse," pp. 21–2. The humour of this narrative can hardly
be unconscious : "The greatest execution that it did, as was heard of, a
bullet enterd into a house upon the South syde of the Church Yard and
burst the bottom out of a fryen pan.   There was no nearer assault to
the towne than a quarter of a mile.   They wear afraid of comming near
one another.   The soldiers within the Towne went out of it and
discharged there muskets towards them at randome for anything was
knowne there was not a man sleyne or hurt.   Upon Christmas day at
night Sir Gilbert withdrew his forces being weary of the Siege, and his
Souldiers and Clubmen were glad of it, that they might eate their
Christmas pyes at home."

a plot to capture the supposed guests. Returning with reinforcements they attacked the ambush with superior numbers and sacked the house.

The next trial of strength, the capture of Preston by the Parliamentarians, was an important event. Confident in its strength and thinking no doubt that an attack was improbable, the royalists had relaxed their vigilance, and Preston was only weakly garrisoned. News of this being brought to Colonel Shuttleworth, he planned a joint attack with the Manchester garrison, which was now under the command of Sir John Seaton. Seaton left Manchester on Monday evening, February 6, accompanied by Colonel Holland, Serg.-Major Birch, Serg.-Major Sparrow, Captain Booth and other officers, with three foot companies from Manchester and three from Bolton. They came to Blackburn on Tuesday night, and were joined there by four or five companies more. These altogether numbering about 1000 men together with about 600 'club-men' set out from Blackburn late on Wednesday evening, February 8, for Preston, which is ten miles away. It was a clear night and the whole force having crossed Ribble Bridge, which was almost if not entirely undefended, drew up in the fields a little distance from the town walls. The attack was made at about half past seven o'clock, a little while before sunrise, at two places. A few men attacked from the south and the main body from the east of the town; the former being guided by somebody familiar to the ground soon gained an entrance, but elsewhere the royalists offered a most determined resistance. For two hours the garrison fought stoutly. There were outer and inner walls, and the garrison kept both with pikes and swords. Captain John Booth showed conspicuous bravery, and was the first to scale the outer defences, bidding his soldiers either follow him or give him up; in another place a small body of the Parliamentarians driven back from the outer walls gained entrance by means of a house. The Manchester troops under Holland showed great bravery. After other resistance had been overcome the royalists occupied the church tower, and were dislodged with difficulty. Then the defence collapsed, and the besiegers became masters of the town. The losses do not seem to have been very great on either side; but the royalists' killed included Adam Mort, the Mayor, and his son, both energetic supporters of the cause, Radcliffe Hoghton, brother of Sir Gilbert Hoghton, and others of note. Very few of the Parliamentarian officers were killed. There were many prisoners taken, including Lady Hoghton, Lady Girlington, Mr. Towneley, Mr. Anderton of Clayton, a son of Sir John Talbot, and a nephew of Sir Gilbert Hoghton. Sir Gilbert only saved himself by a hasty flight to Wigan.[1]

The capture of Preston was an enormous blow to the King's party in Lancashire. An account, written by John Tilsley, Vicar of Dean, describes the engagement as " much to the advancement of the public work in this county and not so altogether impertinent to the Kingdom"; and there is justification for his statement. In attacking Preston the Manchester garrison were venturing for the first time right into the enemy's country, No longer on the defensive as at the end of 1642, they were now reversing the original position of the two parties in the county. And if the royalist standard had fallen at Preston it could hardly be raised with safety anywhere in Lancashire. Preston was also important geographically, as being on the main road through

1. "The true relation of the taking of the Town of Preston by Colonell Seaton's forces from Manchester, etc." ("C. W. T.," p. 71). "A perfect Relation of the Taking of the Towne of Preston in Lancashire, etc." ("C. W. T.," p. 73). Also shorter accounts in "C. W. T.," pp. 127, 224; and "Discourse," p. 23. The first of these tracts was written by John Tilsley, Vicar of Dean, near Bolton. "So soon as matters were settled we sung the praises to God in the streets (Sir, it was wonderfull to see it), the sun brake forth and shined brightly and hot in the time of the exercise, as if it had been Midsummer."

Lancashire. "It blocks up the way to all the north-east part of Lancashire, where were the chief malignants and the cream of the Earl's forces." [1] Moreover Preston symbolised the royalist cause, and since it was (as it still is) a stronghold of Roman Catholicism, it was specially obnoxious to the Puritan party. The Lancashire Parliamentarians, therefore, had captured their enemy's stronghold and broken the lines of communication between Newcastle, Chester and Shrewsbury.

1. "C. W. T.," p. 72.

F

CHAPTER V.

The Crisis. January to June, 1643.

THE next six months was the really critical time in the
Lancashire Civil War. In it the issue was finally
decided, and by the end of the summer the royalist
resistance was practically overcome. In this period it
was for a time quite possible that the royalists would
gain the upper hand; their best planned operations
were in these months, and they showed more enterprise
and energy than either before or afterwards. For a
time at least they more than stemmed the tide of defeat
which was rising against them. The fighting was now
chiefly in royalist territory, mostly in Amounderness
and Leyland Hundred; but the engagements in the
Fylde in March were rather due to accident than otherwise, and the real struggle resolved itself into mutual
attacks on Preston, Lancaster and Wigan on the one
hand and on Blackburn and Bolton on the other. The
Earl of Derby was said to have intended a second
assault on Manchester, but there was never any probability of his being able to carry it out.

The isolation of Lancashire is illustrated in the early
part of 1643, as it is seen how events were developing
here without regard to the course of the general war or
even of that in the neighbouring counties of Yorkshire
and Cheshire. The spring and summer of 1643 saw the
highest point of success which the King's cause attained
during the war. In the beginning of the year the
royalists advanced in the west with the victory of
Bradock; and in the north by the beginning of the
invasion of Yorkshire by the Earl of Newcastle. In
May, Hopton's victory over the Earl of Stamford at
Stratton secured Cornwall for the royalists; and they

won further victories over Sir William Waller at
Lansdown and at Roundway Down in July. Rupert
took Bristol by storm. And in Yorkshire by the end
of the summer Newcastle was nearly supreme. After
his defeat of the Fairfaxes at Adwalton Moor in July,
all the county except Hull was in his hands. It was,
on the other hand, just in these two months that the
royalist cause was being overthrown in Lancashire. In
February they had lost Preston, and though they made
a short revival in the following month, by the end of
April their complete reduction was only a question of
time, and by the end of the summer only a few places
remained in their power.

The Parliamentarian leaders spent some days in
Preston in disposing of the numerous prisoners which
they had taken, and in erecting new fortifications.
This was done under the direction of Rosworm. Colonel
Shuttleworth also sent out summonses for surrender to
all the neighbourhood, and many came in and made
their subjection. It was, however, only a matter of
necessity, for the district remained royalist in sympathy.
An expedition was then sent out to take possession of
Hoghton Tower.[1] It consisted of three foot companies
mostly Blackburn men, one of them being commanded
by Captain Starkie, son of Colonel Starkie of Huntroyd.
They found Hoghton Tower garrisoned by no more
than 30 or 40 musketeers, far too few to hold so large a
place.   The house was summoned and the garrison
asked for a quarter of an hour delay. When that time
expired they asked for another quarter of an hour in
which to decide, and finally surrendered the Tower upon
promise of quarter. This was a victory, however, which
was more costly to the Parliamentarian party than many

1. Hoghton Tower was practically a ruin half a century ago, but has
since then been very carefully restored, and is now to outward appearance
much as in the old days. It occupies a commanding position on a hill
six miles from Preston and four miles from Blackburn, standing
about 550 feet above sea level.

defeats; for after Captain Starkie and his company had entered the Tower an accidental explosion of gunpowder wrecked part of the building, and killed the captain and 60 of his men. An accusation of treachery was of course made against the garrison, and six of the royalist soldiers who had not been able to escape were detained; but there seems no reasonable doubt that the explosion was due to accident only.[1]

Two days after this occurrence (Thursday, Feb. 16) a determined attack was made on Bolton by the royalist garrison from Wigan. Though the actual assault was a surprise some danger must have been expected, for Bolton was garrisoned by 500 men under the command of Colonel Assheton, drawn from various places. It included the companies of Captain Buckley of Oldham, Captain Schofield of Rochdale, Captain Holt of Bury, and Captain Ashhurst from Radcliffe Bridge. The royalists, consisting of 11 companies of foot and two of dragoons, together with two troops of horse, left Wigan, which is nine miles by road, early in the morning, surprised the enemy's scouts, and were within sight of Bolton before their movements were suspected. If they had attacked the town immediately the surprise would have been complete; but they made a detour instead, and approached from the south. As it was, however,

1. "A punctuall relation of the passages in Lancashire this weeke, etc." ("C. W. T.," p. 79). Lancashire's "Valley of Achor" ("C. W. T.," p. 127). "Discourse," p. 24. "Certaine Informations," No. 6, Feb. 20–27. The first and last of these accounts make allegations of treachery but not the other two; and the "Valley of Achor" would not have omitted the charge if it had not been quite baseless. The "Discourse" ascribes the disaster to "want of heedfulnesse," and the "Valley of Achor" is still more definite : "It dispossessed them by the help of Powder to which their disorders laid a Train fired by their neglected matches, or by that great Souldiers' Idoll, Tobacco." "O that this thundering alarm might ever sound in the eares of our Swearing, Cursing, Drunken, Tobacco-abusing Commanders and Souldiers unto unfaigned Repentance. For do they think that those upon whom the Tower fell and slew them, were sinners above the rest of the Army ?"
In his "Pilgrimages to Old Homes" (1906), p. 84, Mr. Fletcher Moss says that it was the gate house into the second court which was blown up; but it would rather seem to have been the Tower itself, which then crowned the building on its eastern side.

they had a great initial advantage, for they surrounded Bolton on all sides before help could be summoned. They then advanced towards Bradshawgate, and over-powered the soldiers in the three outworks which were at a little distance from the walls. Captain Ashhurst with 24 men was intercepted by 60 royalists as he retreated towards the town; but with some loss he cut his way through, and gained the shelter of the chain and mud walls at the end of the street. The royalists followed and set fire to a house outside the chain, while they occupied some others and from them fired on the Parliamentarian troops, who were forced to fall back along the street. Then, having secured an entrance into a royalist house, they took the defenders in the rear. One Parliamentarian officer, Serg.-Major Leigh, had his horse shot under him, and was himself wounded in the arm while mounting another. Finally, however, two of the garrison forced an entrance into the royalists' houses, and Captain Ashhurst with 16 men breaking in from the other side, the town was gradually cleared of the royalist troops. While the fight lasted their horse without the town had prevented reinforcements from coming in, but now hearing the shouts of approaching troops they hastily retreated towards Wigan. Captain Radcliffe arrived with 200 fresh soldiers from Man-chester, but too late to take any part in the battle.[1]

1. "Speciall Passages and Certain Informations from severall Places" ("C. W. T.," p. 77). "A punctuall relation, etc." ("C. W. T.," p. 79). The latter of these accounts is an extremely vivid narrative, and must have been communicated, if not written, by an eye-witness. The former tract gives the defenders' losses as five, the latter as eight or ten; and it is stated that 100 of the royalists were either killed or mortally wounded. These numbers must be received with considerable reservation. The "Discourse" states incorrectly that Alexander Rigby of Burgh was killed in this engagement. The "Valley of Achor" mentions a "new invented mischievous Instrument which received this description at Bolton: An head about a quarter of a yard long, a staffe of two yards long or more, put into that head, twelve iron pikes round about, and one in the end to stab with. This fierce weapon (to double their scorn) they called a Roundhead." The Editor of "C. W. T." (p. 129) states that the "Mercurius Civicus," June 2–16, 1643, gives a picture of one of these "Roundheads."

This first royalist attack on Bolton was one of the hardest fought encounters of the whole war. Colonel Assheton himself is said to have showed much bravery, and the hand-to-hand fighting was severe. The losses on either side are difficult to estimate; they seem as usual to have been understated by the Parliamentarian writers. The day after the unsuccessful royalist attack on Bolton, Serg.-Major Birch was sent from Preston with a company of foot to occupy Lancaster. The royalists had never had a garrison in that town, probably thinking it quite secure from attack; there were only a few soldiers in the Castle. Birch entered the town without opposition, and summoned Sir John Girlington and Mr. Kirkby, who were in the Castle, to surrender; being quite unable to defend the place they did so, and were allowed to march away; Birch thereupon took possession of the town for the Parliament. A garrison was left in the Castle under the command of Captain William Shuttleworth.

The Parliamentarians did not long retain possession of Lancaster at this time, but their expedition represents a great advance on former operations. Lancaster is 17 miles north of Preston, which had hitherto been the limit of their territory.

After this there was some weeks quiet in Lancashire, and the actual recommencement of hostilities was due to a rather curious accident. A large vessel appeared off Rossall Point at the north-west corner of the Fylde, and lay off shore at anchor discharging her guns, for three or four days. She was at first thought to be a royalist vessel; but as no attempt was made to land, a pilot was at length sent out and the ship found to be the Saint Anne of Dunkirk, a Spanish frigate, belonging to the Dunkirk squadron, which had been driven out of her course by contrary winds. She carried recruits on their way to be trained in the Low Countries. Finding that her presence in those waters was quite accidental, the ship was beached in the mouth of the Wyre on the Rossall side (that is in the present Fleetwood Harbour), and she was taken possession of in the name of the Parliament. The Earl of Derby, however, who was at Lathom, heard of the occurrence, and setting off hastily with one troop of horse, he crossed the Ribble and stayed that night (Saturday, March 4) with Mr. Clifton at Lytham Hall. The same day four foot companies of the Parliament's troops arrived in the Fylde from Preston under the command of Major Sparrow, and quartered round Poulton and Singleton. But the conduct of the Parliamentarians was incomprehensible. Next morning (Sunday, March 5) Sparrow drew out his men at a place called The Hoes (now Layton Common), but hearing that the Earl was on his march northwards from Lytham, he retreated, ferried his men over the Wyre, and marched them along the eastern bank of the Estuary to a point opposite to the present town of Fleetwood.[1] Meanwhile Derby rode straight to the ship without resistance; he took prisoners Colonel Dodding and Mr. Townson of Lancaster who were on guard, set the ship on fire, and taking with him the Spanish officers and their ladies rode hurriedly back to Lathom the same night, stopping only to search Rossall Hall for arms on the way.[2] As the Saint Anne burned the guns discharged, and fell either into the bottom of the ship or into the water. But the Parliamentarians recovered most of them and sent them by sea to Lancaster to strengthen the fortifications there.

Major Sparrow explained that he had crossed the

1. Apparently Sparrow crossed somewhere about the present Shard Bridge. Unless it happened to be high tide, however, there would be no need for a ferry. The River Wyre at this point is a broad expanse of water when the tide is full, but at low water it shrinks to a width of eight or ten yards, and can easily be forded for a long stretch.

2. Rossall Hall is now the headmaster's house at Rossall School. The Fleetwoods of Rossall were royalists, and the statement that Derby plundered the house for arms can only be correct on the assumption that the Parliamentarian party had previously taken possession of it.

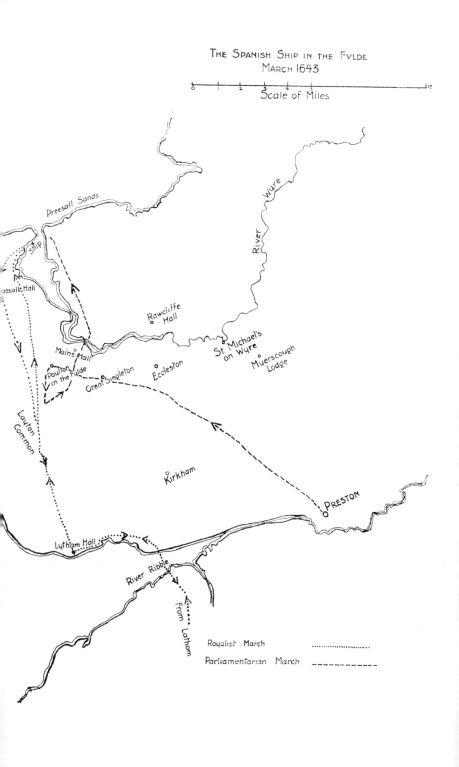

THE SPANISH SHIP IN THE FYLDE
MARCH 1643

Scale of Miles

0   1   2   3   4   5   10

Preesall Sands

River Wyre

Ship

ossall Hall

Rawcliffe Hall

St. Michael's on Wyre

Muerscough Lodge

Mains Hall

Poulton in the Fylde

Great Singleton

Eccleston

Lawton Common

Kirkham

PRESTON

Lytham Hall

River Ribble

From Latham

Royalist March   ....

Parliamentarian March   — — — — — —

river in order to guard the ship more effectually, but it is impossible to see how this could have been so. He was apparently guilty of carelessness if not of cowardice; as the "Discourse" put it "being as feared of the Earl as the Earl was of him." If he had only done as he was advised and retreated towards Rossall, he would have saved the ship and checked the royalist advance, for Derby could not have attacked in face of such superior numbers. The Spanish Ambassador disclaimed all intention of interfering in the English Civil War, and requested that the crew might be sent safely to London and so to Flanders. The House of Lords passed two resolutions to this effect, and as far as the officers were concerned they were probably carried out; but the unfortunate sailors were thrown on the hostile countryside. Some of them died of hunger, and some of them more fortunate who obtained shelter were unable to recover from the privations which they had endured while at sea.[1] This incident is a somewhat unpleasant illustration of the customs of war in the seventeenth century. No one seemed to consider that the foreign ship cast ashore by accident had any claim to fair treatment. Each side took possession of it in turn; and after the royalists had burnt the vessel the Parliamentarians returned and seized as many of the guns as they could. Both parties were quite indifferent to the fate of the unhappy crew.

1. The "Discourse" (pp. 25-27) gives much the fullest account of these operations; this writer is usually especially well informed with regard to the Fylde. His estimate of the ability of Serj.-Major Sparrow is very different from that given by Tilsley in his narrative of the capture of Preston, but is probably more reliable. It is only fair to state, however, in Sparrow's defence that Seaton says that the Earl also had foot with him and 300 horse, and that there were 400 Spaniards; and that Sparrow crossed the river in order to guard the ammunition which had been taken from the ship. From Lytham to Rossall Point is about 13 miles, Layton Common lying half-way between the two places; Poulton is a little nearer Rossall, and closer to the river. For the fate of the Spaniards, Cf. "L. J.," Vol. 5, p. 652; "Hist. MSS. Com." Report 8, p. 63. Five names of officers are given, the chief being Don Francisco de Aco and Don Alonzo Navarro. The date of the burning of the ship by the royalists is given by the Earl of Derby in his Diary ("Stanley Papers," Pt. 3, Vol. 3, C. S. 70, p. 3, ed. Raines).

During the months of March and April there was almost incessant fighting in Lancashire with varying fortune. At the end of February the Parliament held both Preston and Lancaster, and Blackburn and Bolton besides, the royalists still keeping possession of Wigan, Warrington and Liverpool; and repeated attempts were now made by each party on the positions of the other side. The royalists showed in these two months better generalship and greater energy than at any other time during the war; it almost seemed at one period as if they might gain the upper hand; but they were gradually overcome and the early summer found the fate of the county practically decided.

The royalists were the first to take action. About the middle of March a plan was formed to recover the Spanish guns from Lancaster.[1] The Earl of Derby marched out of Wigan on Monday, March 13, with 600 foot and 400 horse, and on the Tuesday night stayed again with Mr. Clifton at Lytham Hall, his men being quartered round Kirkham. He stayed a day or two in order to summon the Fylde, which was entirely royalist in sympathy, and so added to his numbers 3000 clubmen over whom officers were appointed. He was then joined by Sir John Girlington and Mr. Tyldesley with 600 more soldiers from York, of whom half were musketeers, and the whole force set forward to Lancaster. Early in the morning of March 18 the town was summoned, but they returned answer that all their arms were in the disposal of the Parliamentarian troops in the Castle; and the royalists prepared for an attack.

The Parliamentarians were disorganised and showed much irresolution. There had been trouble among their troops at Preston, in which for a time Sir John Seaton's

1. Seaton says that the guns were 22 in number, including 8 brass pieces, 2 demi-cannon, one minion, and 3 sacres. At first there was some competition between Manchester, Bolton, Preston and Lancaster as to which town should receive the guns, but the matter was decided in favour of Lancaster, which was in more royalist territory, and perhaps also because of rumours of the projected attack.

life was in danger, and he had had to escape for a while to Lancaster. When it was known that the royalists were on their way to Lancaster Colonel Assheton marched in pursuit, but probably because he was out-numbered refused to go any further than Garstang, in spite of Seaton's remonstrances. In Lancaster there were some 600 Parliamentarian troops under Holcroft and Sparrow, but they were not able to hold an open town against such superior numbers as the royalists possessed and retreated into the castle. Captain William Shuttleworth was killed before they were able to gain the shelter of the walls. The Castle was not provisioned for a siege, and had no adequate water supply, but the royalists made no attempt to take it, and dispersed their troops through the streets, plundering and setting fire to the houses. The town was thoroughly sacked.[1] The following day, hearing that Assheton and Seaton were on their march from Preston they retreated. In the meantime the garrison had broken out of the Castle while the royalists were plundering and had secured provisions for some days. The Earl of Derby seems to have been a great deal better informed about the enemy's movements than were the Parliamentarians; for he was able to outwit them again and escape their advance.[2]

1. On July 7, 1645, Parliament ordered that "when this unnatural war shall be ended" Lancaster should receive the sum of £8,000 out of the estates of delinquents who were actually present at the siege ("C. J.," Vol. 4, p. 168). Payment of this relief was long delayed; and on December 23, 1647, the House ordered that the inhabitants of Lancaster should farm papists' and delinquents' estates to the value of £2,000 for one year, in part of their former vote. The Castle was later to cause considerable trouble to the authorities. In March, 1646-7 Parliament ordered that it be dismantled, but for some reason the order was not put into effect until years afterwards, in spite of its having been repeated several times ("C. J.," Vol. 5, 101; "C. S. P.," 1649-50, pp. 385, 536, etc., etc.).

2. The royalist opinion of their prospects in Lancashire at this time was very favourable. Cf. "Mercurius Aulicus," March 15, 1643 : "By letters of March 7, it is certified that affairs in Lancashire are not so bad as reported. Wigan and Warrington still hold good for the King, and in Liverpool, the principal town toward Ireland, there are some foot companies of Sir T. Salisbury's regiment and a troop of Flintshire horse. Lancaster is recovered by Col. Tyldesley." And again on March 31 : "Last Monday Mr. Kirkby came to the Queen asking for arms and reporting that Lord Molyneux had taken Bolton."

Both Seaton and Assheton were now on their march from Preston with eleven companies of foot and "some few ill-mounted horse that durst not look the enemy in the face"; Assheton having collected what men he could from Salford Hundred, and reached Preston on the 18th. On Monday, March 20th, Derby removed his troops to Ellel about five miles south of Lancaster on the main road; and hearing that Assheton was at Cockerham waited just long enough to escape being caught, and marched with all speed to Preston, which he expected would be left but poorly defended. He was right in his conjecture, and the action of the Parliamentarian commanders showed great carelessness or undue haste. It is only three miles from Ellel to Cockerham, and the latter place is hardly on the direct route between Preston and Lancaster. The Parliamentarians therefore reached Lancaster only to find the enemy gone, and they had to content themselves with reinforcing the garrison and replenishing the stores in the Castle. Meanwhile Derby had marched straight on Preston, using great care to prevent his approach being known; and he had almost reached the town before news of his advance was brought. In Preston there had only been left four companies of foot and five hundred clubmen under Colonel Holland, and Colonel Duckenfield's troop of horse; but late at night as it was the Friars Gate was strongly guarded, and all preparations made for resistance. The townsmen, however, were strongly royalist in sympathy, and as the Earl approached the garrison gradually melted away, and led by Colonel Shuttleworth most of them made their escape as best they could. The royalist ostlers had locked the stable doors and secured the keys; so that many of the Parliamentarians being unable to get at their horses were taken prisoners. The royalists again garrisoned Preston, and plundered unmercifully any in the town who had been suspected of disaffection to their cause (March 20).

Assheton hearing that the royalists had regained Preston, found his own position at Lancaster untenable, and leaving a garrison in the Castle marched into Blackburn Hundred, and by way of Chipping and Whalley into east Lancashire. A week later Seaton writes from Manchester in great despondency. He was without troops and his personal unpopularity was still so great that he hardly dared to show himself in the streets. The "Mercurius Aulicus" reported with rather less than its usual inaccuracy that "all Lancashire except Manchester is in royalist hands." [1]

This was indeed the most spirited and successful operation conducted by the royalists. They derived no doubt some advantage from the disorganisation of the enemy's troops and their demoralisation owing to insufficient pay and clothing, as also from the carelessness which success had produced in the Parliamentarian officers; for their tactics show to much greater advantage than those of Assheton and Seaton, and for a time at least they regained much of the ground which they had lost. It is possible that there were other successes besides those which have just been described; one Parliamentarian writer even mentions a capture of Blackburn; and in any case a bold following up of the victories might possibly have led to a royalist reconquest

1. There are two accounts of the capture of Preston in the "Mercurius Aulicus," 1643, pp. 150 and 159 respectively. The former is given in "C. W. T.," p. 84. The fullest Parliamentarian account is in the "Discourse," p. 29. Cf. also "Valley of Achor" ("C. W. T.," p. 132) and Seaton's Letter "Chetham Miscellanies," Vol. 3 (No. 57). Seaton says that though he was suffering from a fall from his horse he would have at once pursued the royalists at Preston, but his men refused to follow him. On the next morning, when news came of Derby's occupation of Preston, none of them would remain in Lancaster; and Colonel Stanley's three companies flatly disobeyed his orders. Evidently the men had got quite out of hand, and Seaton was very unpopular. He gives as the reason that he had restrained the soldiers from plundering at Preston. The dates of the capture of Lancaster are given by the Earl of Derby in his Diary ("Stanley Papers," C. S. 70, ed Raines, Pt. 3, Vol. 3, p. 3).

of the county.[1]   The royalist star was now in the ascendant in the north of England.   Queen Henrietta Maria who had landed at Bridlington in February, had overrun the greater part of Yorkshire; some of her troops had advanced as far as Skipton, and were thus an additional menace on the north-east of Blackburn Hundred.

As might be expected, the Earl of Derby now began to plan an advance into the enemy's country.   It is stated, probably with truth, that he intended to form a second siege of Manchester; and he certainly did make a second attack on Bolton on March 28, 1643.   Bolton was, however, prepared, and was well garrisoned, while the Parliamentarians had also established a garrison for its additional protection, in the town of Bury.   The royalists came in sight of Bolton about 3 o'clock in the afternoon, but after their summons for surrender had been refused, they made no attack until dark.   They then delivered a sharp assault on the outworks and there was fighting at close quarters for some time.   The assailants were at length beaten off with the loss of ten men.   After some reinforcements to the town had come in from Bury the royalists delivered another attack upon the south side of the town, and owing to the darkness were able to get quite close to the mud walls before they were observed; but this attempt met with no better success and they finally retired with the loss of 23 men.[2]

This was, however, almost the end of aggressive tactics

1. "Valley of Achor" ("C. W. T.," p. 132).   Probably one reason for the unmanageableness of the troops was want of supplies and of pay. Cf. a letter from Col. Holland to John Booth, Manchester, March 19, 1643, concerning the condition of the regiments with which they have been ordered to join Lord Denbigh for the relief of Wem.   What with "sicknesse, diseases, and other disasters of warre" the two regiments together do not exceed 600 men, and these are so discouraged and mutinous through want of pay and clothing that it is feared that they will refuse to march ("Denbigh MSS.," Vol. 4, p. 265).

2. "C. W. T.," p. 133.   The "Mercurius Aulicus" contains a description of a defeat of two Parliamentarian troops of horse by Lord Derby's regiment; but this seems to have been invented.

on the part of the royalists. By this time the Parliamentarian leaders seem to have restored the morale of their troops, and they soon regained the upper hand in the county. The recovery was shown when four days after Lord Derby's unsuccessful attack on Bolton, they besieged Wigan itself. This was on Easter Eve, 1643. Their force consisted of 2000 foot, mostly musketeers, and 200 or 300 horse, with 8 guns, under the command of Colonel Holland; as Assheton's regiment was included Rosworm also accompanied the expedition, and as usual he represents his own share in the operations as very great. Wigan was commanded by Major-General Blaire, a Scotchman who had been recommended to the Earl of Derby by the King. Attacking fiercely at the southeast end of the town Assheton's musketeers forced an entrance after an hour's fighting, and the Wigan garrison which numbered 1,400 men broke and fled in disorder; many prisoners were taken. Some of the garrison, however, retreated to the Church Tower, and shooting from there did considerable execution on the attacking force; and a threat to blow up the church with gunpowder was necessary before they were reduced to surrender.[1] The town was then thoroughly plundered by the Parliamentary soldiery. They did not, however, occupy Wigan, but marched away the same night, their departure being probably hastened by a report that the Earl of Derby was on his way to its assistance. The Earl came as far as Standish Moor; but hearing there that Wigan had been taken, plundered and abandoned by the enemy he returned to Lathom. One Parliament-

1. "Discourse," p. 36. "C. W. T.," pp. 134, 226. The last of these is from Rosworm's "Good Service," and is the fullest. It has sometimes been treated as if referring to the first attack on Warrington ("Discourse" note, p. 113), but though the language is rather ambiguous, Rosworm is evidently describing the taking of Wigan, where he himself was present. He makes a strong charge of cowardice against Holland, whom, he states, refused to leave any garrison in Wigan, though Rosworm himself offered to remain there; and finally Holland marched away in such haste as to endanger the safety of the forces. But the Parliamentarians cannot as yet have hoped to garrison Wigan.

arian writer estimates the amount of plunder taken in
Wigan at £20,000.[1]   Its loss naturally caused some
consternation at Lathom House which is only six miles
distant.   Lady Derby wrote to Prince Rupert, "In the
name of God, Sire, take pity on us, and if you will
come you may reconquer Wigan easily and with much
glory to your Highness.   I know not what to say; but
have pity on my husband, my children, and myself who
are altogether lost if God and your Highness have not
pity on us."[2]   There was some reason for her agitation.
As Preston and Lancaster had been lost in the north,
so now Wigan had been lost in the west; and a great
effort would be necessary if the royalist cause in Lancashire were not to suffer defeat.

The next encounter, however, went in their favour.
Elated at their success at Wigan, " that impregnable
piece the enemy's pride and presumption our fear and
despair," the Parliamentarian troops assaulted Warrington on April 5th.   In this they joined Sir William
Brereton, the commander-in-chief in Cheshire, who
towards the end of March was quartered with his horse
at Nantwich; and he had sent for 500 foot to join him in
the attempt.   Warrington was strongly held, the Earl
of Derby being there in person.   On Monday, April 3,
Captain Ardern and some other captains approached the
town from the Cheshire side, but the royalist garrison
seeing the smallness of the force, sallied out and routed
them on Stockton Heath, having by a ruse given Ardern
to understand that they were of his own party.   Brereton's main forces shortly afterwards coming up were at
a second attack also defeated by the royalists.   Brereton,
however, remained on the ground, and having been
joined by Holland's troops from Manchester the two
together made an attack on Warrington on April 5th.
The advance was from two sides, from the east near

1. Vicars' "Parliamentary Chronicle," Pt. 1, p. 297 ("C. W. T.," p. 94).
2. Marlet, "Charlotte de la Tremoille," p. 86.

the Parish Church, a battery being placed on Moot Hill, and from the west where Brereton's men occupied the house of one Edward Bridgman at Sankey, about a mile from the town. The royalists, however, fought with great determination, and in spite of their numbers the Parliamentarians were unable to effect an entrance on any point. " Wigan (thought impregnable) proved easy; Warrington (thought easy) proved now impregnable." [1]

It has been stated that the operations round Warrington at the beginning of April, 1643, were the critical events of this Spring; but really the decisive contest occurred at the end of the month and was fought in north-east Lancashire between Padiham and Whalley. The Parliamentarian forces in Blackburn Hundred were still very disorganised and evidently discouraged by their reverse at Warrington on April 5th. After that action the Earl of Derby removed to Preston, where he made preparations for following up his success, calling a general muster there about the middle of April. Accompanied by Lord Molyneux, Sir Gilbert Hoghton, Colonel Tyldesley, and other well known royalists he marched out of Preston at the head of eleven troops of horse, 700 foot, and many clubmen mostly from the Fylde, numbering in all about 5000 men. Keeping on the north bank of the Ribble they reached Ribchester at noon on Wednesday, April 19, crossed the river by ferry at Salesbury, and marched on Whalley. The Parliamentarians were completely taken by surprise. Two troops of horse at Dukenhalgh Hall

1. " C. W.T.," pp. 94, 135. "Discourse," p. 31. There is a long note in the "Discourse," pp. 112–124, giving an account of these operations. Cf. also a paper by Dr. Kenrick in the " Transactions of the Lancashire and Cheshire Historic Society," Vol. 4 (1852), p. 18. The attack is said to have begun at four o'clock in the afternoon and lasted till dark. One account states that the Earl of Derby declared that he would set fire to Warrington rather than surrender it, and that Sir William Brereton thereupon ordered a retreat in order to save the town. This was the Parliamentarian way of explaining away their defeat. There is no Moot Hill now, though Dr. Kenrick states that military relics have been found on the site by excavation.

near Clayton-le-Moors were their only forces in the
neighbourhood, and these retreated to Padiham, after
sending to warn Colonel Shuttleworth, who was at his
house at Gawthorpe. Shuttleworth received the message during the night, but he at once sent out summonses to the countryside, and next morning one
additional troop of horse and about 500 foot had
collected (Ap. 20). The Earl of Derby instead of
continuing his march had occupied Whalley, and early
on the same morning he drew up his troops on the east
side of the river Calder, apparently waiting to be
attacked. Derby himself had quarters in Whalley
Abbey, Sir Ralph Assheton's house. The royalists
made a great mistake in not at once advancing in force.
After some delay, however, they advanced and the
scouts of both sides approached each other near Read
Hall, half way between Padiham and Whalley. The
royalists were so overwhelmingly superior in numbers
that Shuttleworth and his captains refused to engage with
them, and ordered a general retreat towards Padiham.[1]
But the soldiers took matters into their own hands and
"being resolute men replied to the Captains boldly
bidding them take what course they pleased for their
safety, yet they would adventure themselves, see the
enemy and have one bout with them, if God will."
Shuttleworth, therefore, drew out his men to await the
royalists' advance.

About a mile from Whalley on the high road to
Padiham a bye-road turns up the hill to the left; after
passing a further turn to Sabden it leaves on the right
hand a farm house called Easterley, crosses Sabden
Brook, skirts the grounds of Read Hall, and descends
again to join the main road. There seems no doubt
that in this now secluded and very beautiful lane, the
decisive encounter of the Civil War in Lancashire

1. Mr. Ormerod appears to assume that Colonel Assheton was in
command, and it is true that one of the accounts ("C. W. T.," p. 97)
does mention a Captain Ashton; but as he is not mentioned anywhere
else he was probably not present.

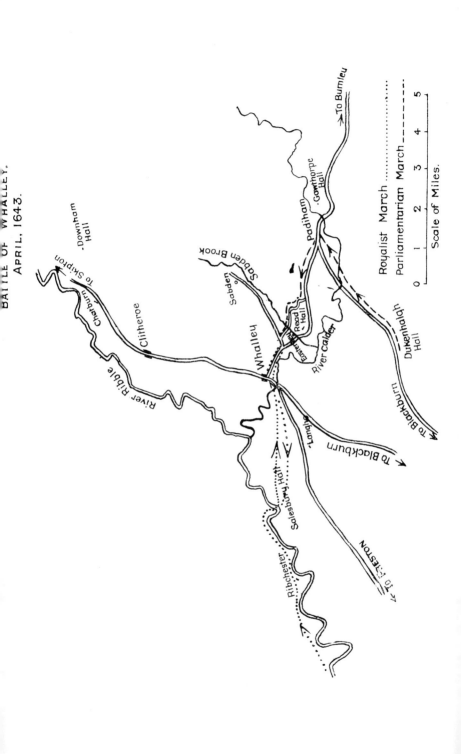

BATTLE OF WHALLEY.
APRIL, 1643.

To Skipton
Downham Hall
Chatburn
Clitheroe
River Ribble
Sabden Brook
Sabden
Whalley
Easter Read Hall
River Calder
Langho
To Blackburn
Salesbury Hall
Ribchester
To Preston
Padiham
Gawthorpe Hall
To Burnley
Dukenhalgh Hall
To Blackburn

Royalist March ....
Parliamentarian March - - - -

0   1   2   3   4   5
Scale of Miles.

began.[1] The Parliamentarian troops awaited the royalist advance just above Read Hall, hiding their musketeers behind the stone walls on either side of the lane. Presently they saw the advance guards descending the hill by Easterley to the Brook. As the royalists mounted again out of the hollow they were surprised by a well-directed volley which threw them into disorder; and the Parliamentarians followed up their advantage so well that the royalists broke and fled back towards Whalley pursued by the Parliamentarian foot. Tyldesley himself was with the advance guard and joined in the flight. Gaining confidence as they proceeded, Shuttleworth's men pressed the royalists hard, and by the time they had reached Whalley the retreat had become a rout. The royalists remaining in Whalley, being taken by surprise, were not able to make any stand, but joined the flying troops, who were now pursued along the way they had come through Langho towards the River Ribble. The chase extended over about five miles; and the Parliamentarian troops as they followed found the country strewn with arms which the royalists had cast away in their flight. The Earl of Derby himself with difficulty maintained some sort of order in the rearguard. Arrived at Salesbury, horse and foot plunged into the water without waiting for the boats, and waded the river up to their necks. Once across they were safe from attack, but the flight continued to Preston, and Derby did not draw rein until he reached Penwortham Hall near Preston, where he stayed the night.[2]

1. The narrative in the "Discourse," p. 33, is very minute, being evidently that of an eye-witness. He says that the first sight of the royalists which their opponents had was "mounting out of a Hollow dingle between Ashterley and Reed-head." This hollow dingle must certainly be the depression through which Sabden Brook flows; the roadway now crosses it by a bridge. The farmhouse on the right descending to the brook is still called Easterley.

2. "Discourse," pp. 31–34. "A True Relation of a great and wonderfull Victory, etc." ("C. W. T.," p. 95). The latter is largely reprinted in "Continuation of Certain Speciall and Remarkable Passages," May 4–11. The Ribble at Salesbury takes a wide curve, and is therefore somewhat shallower. There is no 'boat' there now, but a bridge at Ribchester.

This was the most remarkable victory of the war in Lancashire, and it was decisive. The royalists had been successful at Warrington; and on this occasion their army must have outnumbered their opponents by at least four to one. The Parliamentarians were quite unprepared, and in all probability if Derby had advanced directly on Padiham the result would have been very different. As it was the defeat showed the real weakness of the royalist cause in Lancashire. The Earl of Derby left the county a few weeks later to join the Queen in Yorkshire; and he never led an army in Lancashire again until the ill-fated expedition of 1651. After this the supremacy of the Parliamentary cause was never in real doubt.

Assheton was not slow to follow up the victory at Whalley. Two days later he marched on Wigan (April 22), which was occupied by Colonel Tyldesley with 9 troops of horse and 700 foot; Assheton had 2,200 horse and foot mostly belonging to the Manchester garrison, and the royalists were in no condition to resist superior numbers. They fell back on Lathom without fighting, and Assheton demolished all the out-works and fortifications at Wigan, burnt the new gates and posts, and made the townsmen swear not in future to bear arms against "King and Parliament."[1] Derby himself seems to have been at Prescot, but on Assheton advancing against him he retreated to Lathom, and then the Parliamentarians gradually moved northwards and westwards, driving the enemy before them. On hearing of the loss of Wigan, the Queen sent a message to Lord Derby not to engage the enemy again until she sent him reinforcement; but having waited for a fortnight in vain he was persuaded by Molyneux and Tyldesley to endeavour to hasten it in person. There is no doubt that the Queen at this time intended to invade Lancashire. She writes from York to the King on April 23

1. "Speciall Passages," May 6 ("C. W. T.," p. 98).

"my proposition is this—to detach from the body of the army 2000 footmen and 1000 horsemen, 200 dragoons and some cannon and to send them at once into Lancashire to join with Earl Derby and to clear out that county, which I hope can be done in ten or twelve days, and then come to join me at Newark"; and three weeks after this she writes again that the army was to march directly on Leeds, Bradford and Halifax. Derby was to return, to collect what troops he could, and remain on the defensive until "the army can march to Manchester which I hope will be soon; for I believe that Leeds being taken, the other two places will be inconsiderable, and so Manchester will come into play; which if we take it all Lancashire is yours." [1]   These plans were, however, frustrated by the royalist defeat by Sir Thomas Fairfax at Wakefield in May; and there was no longer any hope of reinforcements to the Lancashire royalists from the Queen's army. Derby returned to Lancashire; and a rumour having come of a Scotch invasion by means of the Isle of Man, he was persuaded to sail thither to prevent it. Returning to Lancashire about the end of May, he hastily crossed the county with a very small following, and rode to Whitehaven, whence he took ship to the Isle of Man, landing there on June 15. The Countess of Derby and her children remained at Lathom House.[2]

It is difficult to understand why Derby should have left Lancashire just at a time when it appeared that the presence of a leader was most necessary there; unless indeed he had already given up the cause as hopeless. This explanation of his joining the Queen and of his departure for the Isle of Man is his own, and is probably the true one though the Parliamentarians put a much

1. Marlet, "Charlotte de la Tremoille," pp. 88, 89.   "Letters of Queen Henrietta Maria," edited by Mrs. Everett Green (1857), pp. 190, 195.
2. Seacome, p. 82. The Earl reached the Isle of Man on June 15; he evidently found the island in a very turbulent state. The Queen wrote to Newcastle: "Lord Derby is here. He is no longer capable of defending himself or of raising troops."

less favourable construction on his movements. They hinted that his leaving Lancashire was due to cowardice. And even his enemies at the Court made it an occasion of maligning him by suggesting that he had more care for his own property in the Isle of Man than for the royal cause in England. But at best he was sacrificing the royalist interests in Lancashire. Three days after landing in the Isle of Man Derby summoned a meeting of his tenants at Peel; but no great eagerness was shown in response to his request for aid.

Meanwhile things had gone from bad to worse for the royalist cause in Lancashire. After the capture of Wigan, Assheton had chased Molyneux and Tyldesley from Ormskirk to Preston, and thence across the Ribble into the Fylde. The royalists quartered at Kirkham for two days, but on Assheton's approach made practically no resistance; they marched northwards across the Wyre and through Cockerham to Hornby. Assheton followed as far as Lancaster; he took from there 14 of the Spanish guns and leaving the remainder to fortify the Castle, returned back through Preston to Manchester. On the return march his men took advantage of his temporary absence to make a detour through the Fylde, where they plundered Royalists and Parliamentarians alike. After Assheton's return Tyldesley crossed into Yorkshire to join the Queen; Molyneux proceeded southwards again, and taking on his way a few prisoners whom he left at Lathom went over Hale Ford into Cheshire.[1]

Warrington was the victors' next objective. On May 20, the Manchester garrison marched out against it, and three days later met at Warrington Sir William Brereton with a considerable force of Cheshire men, who had left Nantwich on May 21. Next morning the besiegers' cannon were placed in position and opened fire on the town. There was, however, no close fighting,

1. "Discourse," p. 39.

as the royalists had very little provision for a siege;
and on the following Saturday, May 27, a parley was
called by Col. Norris, the royalist Governor. During
the week a garrison had been dislodged from Winwick
Church, three miles away, and the position of Warrington had been rendered hopeless by the certainty that
no help could be looked for from the Queen. Accordingly Norris surrendered, his officers being allowed their
horses and pistols, while the men were suffered to depart
without their arms. Next day (Trinity Sunday, May 28)
Sir George Booth, lord of the manor, entered the town
again. Only six men were reported to have been killed
in the last siege, four of the besiegers and two royalists.[1]

Sometime before this Liverpool had been occupied for
the Parliament, apparently without opposition.[2]

The work of reducing the county was not yet, however, quite complete. The royalists in North Lancashire, taking advantage of Assheton's preoccupation in
the south-west, laid siege to Lancaster. The castle,
however, held out for three weeks, and the other places
being reduced, Assheton marched to its assistance.
The royalists did not wait for his approach, but retreated
and disposed some of their forces for the defence of
Hornby and Thurland Castles, the remainder marching
to join the Queen. Assheton immediately set out to
effect the capture of these places.

Hornby Castle is about nine miles north-east of Lancaster, Thurland four miles further away. Approaching
Hornby first, three companies of foot were sent on
before to reconnoitre; they fell into an ambush but
suffered little loss, though the royalist reports magnified
it into a great reverse. The castle was found to be very

1. Newspapers in "C. W. T.," pp. 100–101; *vide* also "Perfect
Diurnall" (Cook), May 15–22. There is a tract in "C. W. T.," p. 102,
which professes to give an account of the surrender of Warrington, but
it is exceedingly unreliable.
2. "Valley of Achor" ("C. W. T.," p. 138). Contradictory statements
are, however, made about a ship from the Earl of Warwick's fleet which
appeared in the Mersey at this time.

difficult of access, being on a steep hill, and the building itself rising gradually from its lowest point at the gate-house. The besiegers, however, captured a soldier escaping from the Castle, and from him learnt that it was possible to enter by some windows high up on the east side of the building at the end of the hall. This adventurous effort succeeded. Under cover of a frontal attack on the gatehouse, a party armed with ladders, ropes, and combustible materials, effected an ascent of the windows, and set the Castle on fire; attacked thus in two places the garrison surrendered at discretion.[1]

Next day the Parliamentarian troops marched on to Thurland, which was given up at their summons with little or no fighting. Sir John Girlington himself was taken prisoner, and also many royalist ladies who had found a refuge in this last stronghold. Much spoil of money and plate was also made.

Thus by June, 1643, practically all Lancashire was for the first time in the hands of the Parliament; Lathom House and Greenhalgh Castle being now the only places where the royalist flag was still flying. Many of the Parliamentarian soldiers returned to their homes. "Now the whole county being cleared of all the King's forces way was made that all such as had fled out of any part thereof might return to their wives, children and friends and have what their enemies had left them."

1. "Discourse," p. 40. Hornby Castle has been largely re-built, the lower portion of the lofty central tower being the oldest remaining part. The Castle stands on an isolated hill, occupying a very strong natural position. The hill on all sides is steep, and especially so on the north-east side where its base is encircled by the River Wenning. It was evidently on this quarter that the surprise attack was delivered; but it is hardly possible now to judge of the danger of the enterprise. The descent down to the Wenning, partially levelled at the top to make a garden, is not an arduous climb; and the present buildings on that side do not approach very near to the edge of the descent. On July 6 the House of Commons ordered that Hornby Castle should be demolished in order to avoid the expense of keeping a garrison there; and two days later Assheton was directed to send the order down to Lancashire, although no answer had been returned by the House of Lords ("C. J.," Vol. 3), pp. 158–159.

CHAPTER VI.

Remaining Events of 1643 ; and the First Siege of Lathom House.

It was a sign of the complete victory of the Parliamentarian party in Lancashire that now for the first time
troops from this county began to be sent into Yorkshire
and Cheshire. In the middle of June, 1643, before the
surrender of Hornby and Thurland Castles, 2000 men
from Manchester were reported to have joined Lord
Fairfax in Yorkshire, and a month or two after this we
find Lancashire troops taking part in the war in Cheshire.[1]

Fairfax at this time had need of all the help that he
could get, for Newcastle was pressing him hard. The
royalists took Leeds, Halifax and Wakefield in succession. In the last few days of June the Fairfaxes marched
from Bradford against Newcastle, who left his quarters
at Howley and drew up his army on Adwalton Moor,
some three miles from Bradford, to await their attack.
The Parliamentarian force consisted of 1,200 men from
Leeds, 500 from Halifax, Pontefract and other places,
7 companies from Bradford, together with 12 companies
from Lancashire under the command of Colonel Assheton and Colonel Holland. All these were foot; and
there were also 13 troops of horse of which 3 had come
from Lancashire. The royalists on the other hand had
8,000 foot of their former army, and 7,000 recently raised
by Commission of Array, with perhaps 4000 horse.
Newcastle drew up his men on Adwalton Moor, also
occupying some houses in the enclosed ground in front
of his position. The Parliamentarian 'forlorn' was
under Captain Milday; the van under Major-General
Gifford consisted of the 1,200 Leeds foot, and the main
battle was formed by the Lancashire foot and the 500

1. Newspapers in " C. W. T.," pp. 152, 153.

from Halifax under Lord Fairfax himself; in the rear
were the Bradford soldiers under Lieutenant-Colonel
Forbes.   Sir Thomas Fairfax commanded all the
cavalry.   At first the battle went in favour of the
Parliamentarians; they attacked vigorously, their ' forlorn' driving back the enemy, and their van then faced
the royalists' right wing, while their rear attacked in
the centre.   All Newcastle's line began to give ground,
but the Parliamentarians incautiously advanced too far
into the open moor; and Newcastle, who greatly outnumbered them, sent forward a detachment along a lane
to the left of his position which took the enemy in the
rear.   Most of the Yorkshire troops had been used only
to garrison duty, and caught thus between two fires,
they were unable to execute an orderly retreat, but began
to run.   The loss in killed was not very great, but a
large number were taken prisoner, and two of the four
guns were lost.   The Parliamentarian centre being
strengthened by the Lancashire troops, was brought off
safely by Sir Thomas Fairfax.   Lord Fairfax could only
be persuaded to leave the field when the royalists had
intercepted his retreat to Bradford, and he reached the
town with difficulty.   Sir Thomas was forced to seek
refuge in Halifax for that night, and joined his father
in Bradford the following day.[1]

The defeat was a serious blow to the Parliament's
cause in Yorkshire, and its moral effect was greater still.
Moreover the Lancashire troops at once returned home,
with the exception of 200 foot and 20 horse, who were
persuaded to remain on promise of prompt pay.   The
Fairfaxes were unable to retain Bradford, and were
forced to retreat to Hull, which was soon practically the
only place in Yorkshire in the hands of the Parliament.
It was indeed only by good fortune that they kept Hull,
for Sir John Hotham had declared that he would shut

1. "Portland MSS.," Vol. 1, p. 717.   T. Stockdale to Wm. Lenthall.
This is a very minute description of the battle.

the gates against them; but the discovery of the Hothams' plot and their arrest gave Fairfax a place of retreat when he most needed it.

On July 5th, Newcastle dated from Bradford a summons to the town of Manchester. He offered the townsmen protection and pardon if they would lay down their arms. But it was not likely that having already driven the royalists out of their own borders the Manchester garrison would listen to a summons sent from 30 miles distant; and a defiant answer was returned two days later. "Sir we are nothing dismayed at your force, but hope that God who hath been our Protector hitherto, will so direct our just Army that we shall be able to return the violence intended into their bosoms that shall essay the prosecution of it." This is, however, very different language from the urgent letter to Lenthall written the day before,[1] in which they refer to their loss of men and arms at the battle of Adwalton Moor, the encouragement which that defeat had given to the royalists at home, and the great danger in which they were placed by the retreat of Fairfax to the extreme east of Yorkshire. Newcastle, however, soon had too much on his hands in Yorkshire to do more than send a summons into a neighbouring county. But the Lancashire leaders took the precaution of guarding the frontier against him. They sent 1200 men to Rochdale, and 800 more to Blackstone Edge, four miles further on, over which passes the main road into Yorkshire. The garrison was attacked once at least; and it was kept there most of the winter, being maintained out of the several Hundreds of the county from sequestered Roman Catholic estates. Colonel Tyldesley's estate at Myers-

1. "A Declaration and Summons sent by the Earl of Newcastle, etc." ("C. W. T.," p. 143): "I cannot but wonder while you fight against the King and his authority, you should so boldly offer to Professe yourselves for King and Parliament, and most ignominously scandalize this army with the title of Papists, when we ventured our Lives and Fortunes for the true Protestant Religion, established in this Kingdom." The Lancashire letter to Lenthall is in the "Tanner MSS.," Vol. 62, fol. 152.

cough was one of the first to be sequestered (Oct.).
The defences at Blackstone Edge were constructed under
the direction of Rosworm, who was sent from Manchester for that purpose. The newspapers report that
in the middle of July Newcastle sent 200 horse to break
through, but without success. A few were killed and
many taken prisoners, and the rest retreated; "because
it is naturally so strong that 500 men can keep 1000
neither is that way fit either for carriages or ordnance."
Indeed the nature of the ground, which is very rough
and covered with heather, is such as to make it exceedingly difficult for the movements of cavalry.[1]

The newspapers also mention royalist defeats in July
at Colne, where 40 prisoners were taken, and also at
Clitheroe, and at Thornton. It would appear from this
that Newcastle continued his attempts to break through
the Lancashire defences. Evidently it was necessary to
keep a watch upon the eastern border of the county
during this winter, and it was fortunate for the Parliamentarian party that the Moors formed such a strong
natural defence. Some troops for a time were kept at
Colne and even at Emmott Lane Head, which is three
miles further on just on the border of the county.[2]

Lancashire forces were also sent to fight under the
command of Sir William Brereton and Sir Thomas

1. Newspapers : Rosworm's "Good Service" ("C. W. T.," pp. 146, 147,
228). The border of Lancashire and Yorkshire about Blackstone Edge is
formed by high moors. The main road over the Edge is 1,269 feet
above sea level; and the summit of the moor 1,553 feet. The next
summit to the south, Bleakedgate Moor, is 1,663 feet; Rosworm says
that this too was fortified. The descent on the Lancashire side is
rather steeper than that into Yorkshire, but the latter is steep enough
to make attack very difficult. Blackstone Edge is 18 miles from
Manchester, 6 from Rochdale, and 11 from Halifax; Rosworm calls
Halifax "distant about 16 mile from us"; but actually it is 28 miles
by the nearest way, and over Blackstone Edge 29. In spite of the
fortification of the border, it was thought advisable to send away the
royalist prisoners at Manchester to some more distant place ("C. W. T.,"
p. 146).

2. During these operations the Parliamentarian troops were supported
out of sequestered estates, the Order for Sequestrations being now for
the first time put into force. Tyldesley's estate at Myerscough was
sequestered in October, the first in Amounderness Hundred ("Discourse,"
p. 44).

Fairfax in Cheshire. They do not seem to have taken part in any very important engagements in that county; but they assisted at the siege of Halton Castle which fell on July 22, and they also fought at Chester. Some time in June, 1643, Alexander Rigby arrived in Lancashire with a Colonel's commission to raise forces in Leyland and Amounderness Hundreds. Rigby was not the man to remain idle, even though the fighting seemed over. He appointed 15 or 20 captains in Amounderness to raise foot companies and one troop of horse; and a few also in Leyland. The Order of Parliament for impressing troops was not passed until the end of October, 1643, but it was easier to raise men now that they could be provided for out of sequestered estates.[1] With the troops which he had raised Rigby at once set himself to reduce Thurland Castle, which had been re-occupied by Sir John Girlington, and well stored with ammunition and provisions; and early in August he marched against it. This second siege proved much harder than the first, and lasted seven weeks. The position of Thurland Castle is a strong one, and it was surrounded, as it still is, by a moat which made a close approach to the walls impossible.[2] The Parliamentarian main guard was at Canstfield, which is only half a mile from the Castle, but is hidden from it by a small hill; on the east side of the building in the field between Thurland and Cantsfield the ordnance was placed in position. Some of the besiegers lay at Tunstall on the north-west side; and Rigby himself stayed at Hornby Castle, which is four miles away, and rode over daily to the siege. The Parliamentarian horse were quartered up and down the country. During most of the time in

1. "L. J.," Vol. 6, p. 279. Order for pressing 3,000 soldiers in Lancashire, with so many gunners, trumpeters, and surgeons, as the Committee may think fit.

2. Thurland Castle is still of much the same extent as formerly, but the old building only remains in the lower part of the walls. Two pictures in Philips' "Lancashire Halls," 1822–24, show a very dilapidated building. The moat is three or four yards wide and seven feet deep, and is still only crossed by a single bridge.

which the siege was in progress the Westmoreland royalists harassed the besiegers. They were under the command of Colonel Huddleston of Millom, and of two Lancashire refugees, Roger Kirkby and Alexander Rigby of Burgh. After several false alarms Rigby heard that Colonel Huddleston had collected a force of 1,600 men in Furness and was about to march to the relief of Thurland. Without waiting to be attacked Rigby left only as many men before the Castle as were quite necessary to maintain the blockade, and himself started with 500 foot, 3 troops of horse and 2 guns to meet them. Marching 30 miles in one day "over mountains and through sea sands and waters," he found the royalists on Sunday, October 1, at Lindale, three miles from Cartmel. The Parliamentarian word was "God with us," and they charged with such vigour that the enemy began to retreat almost before the battle was joined, and in a quarter of an hour the royalists fled in confusion. Few were killed, but the cavalry in pursuit captured Colonel Huddleston, two of his captains and an ensign, 400 men and the magazine, which was large enough to take eight oxen to draw it. Hardly stopping to take food Rigby returned to Thurland as hurriedly as he had come to find the small force there menaced by the Westmoreland royalists; but on hearing of his victory at Lindale Sir Philip Musgrave, who was in command, made negotiations for the surrender of Thurland Castle. The defenders were to have free passage, but the building was ordered to be demolished. Rigby says that he endeavoured to save the combustible materials from fire but without success. In the middle of October he returned to Preston. Notwithstanding the disorganisation of the royalists the battle of Lindale was admirably planned and carried out, and proved that Rigby was a man of considerable military skill.[1]

1. "Discourse, p. 41. "A True Relation of the great victory, etc." ("C. W. T.," p. 148). "The British Mercury," No. 5, November 27. "The Weekly Account," No. 7, October 18. Rigby's letter to the

Shortly after this Colonel Moore came down to
Lancashire, and considerably strengthened the defences
of Liverpool by erecting fortifications and gates, and
planting guns in position. He also raised a few troops
of foot in West Derby Hundred. These preparations
turned out to be very necessary, for shortly before
Christmas, 1643, seven or eight royalist warships sailed
up the Mersey and lay in the river for many days; they
did not, however, offer to put into the harbour. Cheshire
was at that time mostly royalist, and Sir Thomas
Tyldesley kept some troops at Birkenhead which it was
thought were intended for an attack on Liverpool.
Rigby, hearing of this, summoned Captain Pateson
from the Fylde, and called for volunteers to accompany
him. There was no lack of response, and leaving
Preston on Christmas Eve they joined some other
troops at Wigan and marched as far as Prescot. The
danger was, however, over; all the ships had gone save
one, which put into Liverpool harbour and surrendered
to the Parliament. After remaining five or six days
in Liverpool the Parliamentarian troops returned to
Preston.[1]

The Lancashire troops also took part in the critical

1. "Discourse," p. 45. Cf. also "Hist. MSS. Comm.," Vol. 10,
app. 4, p. 66, where is given a petition from the town of Liverpool that
Colonel Moore might be Governor in place of Venables, who had been
ordered to Ireland (March, 1643–4). Moore was Governor later in the
same year when the town was taken by Prince Rupert.

Speaker was read in the House of Commons, and on November 18 he
was formally thanked, and the destruction of Thurland Castle approved
("C. J.," Vol. 3, p. 315). It is evident that in spite of statements to the
contrary, the common soldiers on both sides were alike in the matter of
plundering. There are two places in Furness named Lindale, one near
Cartmel, and one near Dalton. As Rigby says that the royalists were
driven into the sea, it must have been the former of these places where
the battle was fought.

In some resolutions agreed upon at a meeting of the Deputy-Lieutenants
of Lancashire at Preston on October 12, 1643, it was decided that
Hornby Castle should be destroyed according to the Order of Parliament;
so that the Order had evidently not yet been carried into effect. It was
also decided to maintain the garrisons of Warrington and Liverpool
("Hist. MSS. Com.," Vol. 10, app. 4, pp. 67, 68).

events in Cheshire in December, 1643, and January, 1644. The general royalist position was at this time far other than it was in Lancashire.   The King was master of about two-thirds of the country; and so evenly balanced was the issue in the summer of 1643, that both sides had summoned outside help, Parliament the Scots, and Charles the troops from Ireland, which had been set free by the Cessation. The King's negotiations with the Irish had been marked by his usual duplicity, for he could have no hope of keeping the promises he made.

In March, 1643, the Irish had demanded a free Parliament, on promise of which they would send over 10,000 men.   Charles authorised Ormonde to treat for 12 months Cessation of arms, and at length conceded the demand for a Parliament.   In spite of divisions among the Irish leaders, the Cessation was concluded on September 15.   News of the coming Irish landing brought back the Lancashire forces from North Wales where they had marched as far as Wrexham, and the hope of the Lancashire royalists revived.   They secured the King's warrant for the march of the new army into Lancashire.   "I am desired by the Lancashire gentlemen," writes Abraham Shipman to Ormonde on October 28, "to acquaint your Lordship that those forces that are to come from Dublin are assigned by His Majesty for their county, which they are preparing to receive. My lord, the extreme necessity of that county craves speedy succours and therefore humbly desire your furtherance"; and Sir Gilbert Hoghton was ordered to Chester to await the arrival of the troops.   The Lancashire plan was that the Irish regiments should march at once to attack Liverpool, which was not strongly defended, and was situated in the royalist part of the county and near Lathom House.   It was thought that some troops could be raised in Lancashire; there were said to be 2000 men ready to invade the county from the north, and help was expected from Newcastle in Yorkshire. Thus it was expected that the advance of the Scots would be checked.[1]

These hopes were, however, destined not to be fulfilled. The Irish troops, to the number of about 5000, landed in North Wales in the middle of November, and for a time they carried all before them. First they took Hawarden Castle and then marched on Chester; leaving there on December 12 they proceeded to Northwich in order to cut off communications between Manchester and Nantwich, and afterwards summoned Beeston Castle, which was speedily surrendered. The Parliamentarian Governor was executed for cowardice. The Cheshire Committee summoned help from Lancashire, and Colonel Assheton marched to their assistance with 1500 foot. He had reached Sandbach, when Byron being warned of his approach detached 4000 men to intercept him. The Parliamentarians began to retreat towards Middlewich, but the royalists came up with them at Booth Lane, north of Sandbach, and a retreat against such superior numbers soon became a rout. The Lancashire men were chased along the road to Middlewich three miles away, with heavy loss and many prisoners. At Middlewich 300 of them took refuge in the church and were given quarter; the rest of them fled through the town and were scattered.[2]

But the tide now turned against the royalists. Byron laid siege to Nantwich which under the circumstances was a place of very great importance. Clarendon says "it cannot be denied the reducing of that place at that time would have been of unspeakable importance to the King's affairs, there being between that and Carlisle no one town of moment (Manchester only excepted) against

1. "Carte MSS.," Vol. 7, fol. 287. Bridgeman to Ormonde, *ibid*, Vol. 7, p. 638.
2. "C. W. T.," pp. 152–154. Colonel Robert Byron to Ormonde, January 9, 1643–4. "Carte MSS.," Vol. 8, fol. 464, 465. Byron says that 800 of the Parliamentarians were killed, and 274 taken prisoners. His own regiment bore the brunt of the fighting, and he himself was wounded.

H

the King; and those two populous counties of Cheshire
and Lancashire (if they had been united against the
Parliament) would have been a strong bulwark against
the Scots."[1]   Realising its importance the garrison held
out resolutely, and Sir Thomas Fairfax was sent in
haste from Yorkshire to raise the siege.   While he was
on his way a royalist force under Sir Richard Willis,
coming from Shrewsbury with ammunition, were
defeated by a much smaller number of Parliamentarians;
and several attacks on Nantwich were beaten off.   Sir
Thomas Fairfax left Manchester on January 21 with
2,500 foot and 28 troops of horse.   His first encounter
with the royalists was near Delamere where he took 30
prisoners; and about six miles further on another force
appeared which was, however, dispersed after half an
hour's fighting.   Having reached Acton Church, a mile
from Nantwich, Fairfax found a large detachment of the
royalists drawn up; and he at once attacked these before
they could be reinforced.   The royalist troops had
besieged Nantwich on both sides of the river, and a
flood had separated their forces.   Byron, however, came
up before the issue was decided, and Colonel Holland's
and Colonel Booth's regiments were faced about to meet
the attack.   The fight lasted for two hours, and Assheton
was particularly praised for his part in it.   The Parliamentarian cavalry were once hard pressed, but being
nearest to the town they were assisted by a sortie of the
garrison, and at length both divisions of the royalists
were driven into Acton Church and obliged to surrender.
A large number were taken prisoners, including their
Major-General, four Colonels, many other officers and
1,500 common soldiers.   Colonel Monck was one of
those captured.   More than half of the prisoners took
service in the Parliamentary army.   (January 25, 1644.)
The battle of Nantwich had a decisive effect not only on
the war in Cheshire but to some extent on Lancashire

1. "Clarendon" (Macray), Vol. 3, p. 315 (bk. 7, par. 401).

also. If the town had been taken all Cheshire would have been over-run by the Irish troops, and there is no reason why they should not have carried out their plan for an invasion of Lancashire. But the victory won by Fairfax and the Lancashire troops restored at one blow the Parliamentarian cause in Cheshire.[1]

In Lancashire the way was now open for the siege of the last royalist strongholds. Only two places still held out to the King, Lathom House and Greenhalgh Castle, and of these the former was much the more important.

The Earl of Derby was still in the Isle of Man, but Lathom under the able direction of the Countess of Derby, assisted by such Lancashire royalists as still remained in the county, had been gradually prepared for resistance. It being almost the only place of refuge left, many of the militant royalists had gathered there. The House had been summoned as far back as May, 1643, after the capture of Warrington; but nothing had been done towards reducing it. The royalists had been, however, practically confined to the Park at Lathom, and Rigby sent what troops he could spare to harass them at intervals. The garrison on their part plundered all they could. Early in February, 1644, the royalists had the better of a skirmish with some Parliamentarian horse under Captain Hindley; and when the danger in Cheshire was over the troops from Cheshire were at liberty to begin the reduction of Lathom.

The first siege of Lathom House is quite the most picturesque incident of the Lancashire war. More has been written about it, and it is probably better known than any other event. This has rather served to disguise the fact that the siege was not very important from a military

1. Magnalia Dei ("Cheshire Civil War Tracts," C. S. new series 65, p. 97). Great care must be taken in using this volume, as it is exceedingly badly arranged. No notice is taken of the fact that in the seventeenth century March 25 was reckoned as the first day of the year, the Tracts for January, February and March of each year being placed at the beginning of the year, instead of at the end as they ought to be. Cf. also " C. W. T.," pp. 152–154; "Discourse," pp. 44, 45, and notes.

point of view. There was no great issue depending upon its capture as in the case of that of Manchester in October, 1642, or of Warrington in April, 1643; its resistance for a few months more or less did not affect the general position. It was a centre of hostile influence, but its garrison was bound to be only on the defensive and could never hope to be strong enough to make Lathom the starting point for a re-conquest of Lancashire for the King. Thus the defence was in the nature of a forlorn hope, and derived from this greater interest; when it is added that the defence was directed by a woman after the Earl of Derby and lesser royalist leaders had been driven out of the county, it easily became 'ever memorable' to the royalists. The attempt to save a splendid and historic mansion from the destruction which afterwards unhappily overtook it makes a further appeal to the imagination; and that the attempt was successful owing to the appearance on the scene of the chivalrous figure of Prince Rupert, supplies the last touch of sentimental interest.

Nothing now remains of old Lathom House and no picture of it is known to exist. Its situation and appearance was accurately described by Seacome, but it is impossible now even to identify the site.[1] Lathom House in those days was strong not only from its situation but from its structure. It stood upon marshy ground in a hollow surrounded by small hills which made it very difficult to effect an approach to the walls. The wall itself was six feet thick, and the whole was surrounded by a moat twenty-four feet across and six feet deep; a palisade between the walls and the water provided a further defence. On the wall were nine towers upon each of which were planted six guns, three turned one way and three the other, and in the centre of the building was a higher tower called the Eagle

1. *Vide* note at the end of the chapter.

Tower. The gate house, which was a strong and lofty building, stood at the entrance to the first court.

On Saturday, February 24, 1644, it was decided at a meeting of the Committee at Manchester that Colonels Assheton, Rigby and Moore should undertake the siege of Lathom House.[1] News of this came to Lathom on Sunday, and the Countess of Derby at once sent out to obtain information from a friend which she had in the enemy's camp, while hastening on the reinforcement and provisioning of the garrison. The messenger returned on the following day with the news that the Parliamentarian troops had already marched as far as Bolton, Wigan and Standish. On Tuesday, February 27, they had taken up their quarters round the house at a distance of from one to three miles from it. The rest of the week was spent in negotiations. A formal summons of surrender was first brought on Wednesday by Captain Markland from Sir Thomas Fairfax, who further promised that he would use his influence with Parliament if the Earl of Derby would submit himself to their mercy. Lady Derby asked for a week's delay in which she might send a message to the Earl to know his opinion. This was refused, and Fairfax then requested her to come in her coach to New Park, a house about a quarter of a mile from Lathom, in order to have a personal interview with himself and his Colonels. But the Countess remembering her birth, returned a haughty refusal, "conceiving it more knightly that Sir Thomas Fairfax should wait upon her than she

1. The main authority for the first siege of Lathom is a "Journal" by someone in the House (usually supposed to have been Archdeacon Rutter, Lady Derby's chaplain), of which two MSS. copies exist, one being "Harleian MSS.," No. 2074, the other preserved in the Ashmolean Museum at Oxford. They differ only slightly. The former is printed in "C. W. T.," pp. 159–186. *Vide* also "Discourse," pp. 46–49; "Seacome," pp. 86–93. Cf. also "Victoria County History of Lancs.," Vol. 3, p. 252. There is an account of both sieges of Lathom by Mrs. Colin Campbell in "Memorials of Old Lancashire" (1909), Vol. 1, pp. 107–129 : it is not of much historical value, being apparently based chiefly on Seacome.

upon him." After two more days of messages Assheton and Rigby entered Lathom with propositions, which as might have been expected were severe. The House and all arms and ammunition were to be delivered up, the garrison having leave to depart to Chester or elsewhere; Lady Derby was to reside at Knowsley, being allowed 20 musketeers for her protection, or she was to join the Earl in the Isle of Man. These conditions were refused "as in part dishonourable in part uncertain." On Monday, March 4, Assheton came again alone in order to receive the royalist proposals. These required a month's delay for the removal of Lady Derby and her family to the Isle of Man, during which time the royalist garrison was to be kept at Lathom; but afterwards none of the arms were to be employed against the Parliament. After her departure none of the tenants of the Earl were to be molested. It was evident, however, that all negotiations were useless. On their own confession the royalists did not believe that Fairfax's promises were genuine, nor did they intend to keep their own. The Parliament referred to in their proposals was understood by them to mean the King's Parliament at Oxford. The only object of allowing negotiations at all was in order to gain time to put the House into a better state for defence. The besiegers, however, made one final offer which was brought by Colonel Morgan, the assistant engineer, "a little man short and peremptory";[1] they allowed the time which had been asked for to

1. Seacome calls this officer Major Morgan. It is somewhat remarkable that the writer of the "Discourse" does not mention him at all, but states that the chief engineer was named Brown (*vide* p. 109). Morgan was afterwards one of the foremost engineers of his time. He was the second son of Robert Morgan of Llanrhymny; had served in the Low Countries before the Civil War broke out, and became Governor of Gloucester for the Parliament. He was with Brereton when the last royalist force was defeated at Stow-in-the-Wold in 1646. Later he was closely associated with Monck; was knighted by Richard Cromwell in 1651, and continued in the army after the Restoration ("Discourse" note, p. 133). "Dictionary of National Biography," art. by Prof. C. H. Firth.

evacuate Lathom, but the cannon were to be left for its defence and not removed with the rest of the arms and goods. By 10 o'clock the following day all the royalist garrison was to be disbanded and 40 Parliament soldiers to be received as a guard. The royalists, however, seeing that there was now no more time to be gained, formally broke off all negotiations. The defiant answer was at length given which had been kept in the background for a week. The Countess of Derby refused all their articles, and declared "That though a woman and a stranger, divorced from her friends, and robbed of her estate, she was ready to receive their utmost violence trusting in God both for protection and deliverance."

Seacome states that at some point in the negotiations Sir Thomas Fairfax himself visited the House, and that Lady Derby drew up all her garrison in an imposing array, from the main guard in the first court to the great Hall where she herself received him. This ruse had its desired effect; so impressed was Fairfax with the strength of the garrison that he dissuaded the other leaders from making an immediate attack, which was just what the garrison most feared.[1] The besiegers now moved their lines nearer to the walls. But even now all treaty was not at an end. Nothing much was done during the rest of the week; but on Sunday, March 10, a deputation of tenants was persuaded to enter Lathom to plead with Lady Derby to surrender; but once inside the gates their royalism was apparent and the pleading was not very powerful. Yet once more, however, on the day following (Monday, March 11) Captain John Ashhurst, whom the royalists praise for his courtesy, came in with a last proposal from Fairfax. All former conditions were to

1. Cf. however, "Martindale's Life," p. 44 : "Had Lathom beene only blocked up at a distance by small garrisons and forts at considerable passes (for which there was spare forces enough) and not closely besieged, perhaps that great storme had not fallen upon Lancashire (especially Bolton and Liverpool) by Prince Rupert's forces in their march to York."

be waived; the Countess, all the garrison and all the household were to have liberty to depart wherever they pleased with all their arms, ordnance and goods, yielding up the house to Sir Thomas Fairfax. The arms, however, were never to be employed against the Parliament; and everyone must leave the house at once excepting a hundred people who might remain ten days. This was of course refused, and all negotiations were now at an end.

The siege now began to be pressed with more vigour. The royalist garrison consisted of 300 men. Lady Derby was called Commander-in-Chief, with Mr. Farington as her chief adviser; and the Captains were Farmer, Ogle, Molyneux, Radcliffe, Chisenhale, Rawsthorne, Charnock, and Fox. Farmer, who was made Major of the House, was a Scotchman who had seen service in the Low countries. He was afterwards killed at Marston Moor. Rawsthorne, then Colonel, was in chief command during the second siege. The garrison was divided equally among all the Captains, who had therefore not quite half a company each. Half the garrison was on duty every night, and 16 marksmen from the whole number kept watch all day on the Towers.

The Parliamentarian soldiers before Lathom were drawn out of each Hundred by turns, their whole number being between 2,000 and 3,000. At first the troops seemed to have come from South Lancashire, those from the Fylde being called up at the end of a fortnight. The soldiers were on duty every third day and night, their provision and pay being levied on the towns in which the companies were raised.[1] Sir Thomas Fairfax, who conducted the negotiations, left the siege early in March, and after his departure the chief command seems to have devolved upon Colonel Rigby, who

1. "Discourse," p. 47.

stayed at Ormskirk, three miles away, and came over daily to the siege.

The first advance of the Parliamentarians drove out the royalists from the Stand in the Park which they had occupied; but the besiegers seem at first to have greatly underrated the difficulty of their task, not decause they expected to take the House by storm, but thinking it was so poorly provisioned that it might be easily starved into surrender. As a matter of fact, however, Lathom was well stocked with food, and for a time at least the blockade was so incomplete that supplies could easily be brought in. Moreover the difficulty of the ground for siege operations soon became apparent, and the nearer the lines were drawn to the walls the more danger was incurred from the marksmen on the Towers. The garrison was not content merely to look on at the attack but soon began to make sorties which greatly harassed the besieging force. On Tuesday, March 12, Captain Farmer led out 100 foot and the 12 horse which was all the garrison possessed, attacked the besiegers' works, and slew several of them, taking six prisoners. The following Sunday night, Captain Chisenhale sallied out from the rear gate with 30 men, and put the Parliamentarians to ignominious flight. The accounts of these sorties are probably exaggerated, and the number of the besiegers who were killed is certainly placed much too high; but the attack was not pressed with very much resolution. Much of the firing against the House was wild, and large amounts of ammunition were wasted;[1] though it is evident that a good deal of damage was done to the buildings by cannon shots. The besiegers' most successful weapon was a large mortar which was loaded with grenades or with eight pound stone bullets and did considerable execution. One shot falling into

1. "There was needlessly spent against it in shot and powder an infinite quantity. Some was alwaies shooting at nothing they could see but the walls" ("Discourse," p. 47).

an old court destroyed most of the buildings which surrounded it; and another struck one of the Towers and broke down a large clock.

Towards the end of March a message came from the Earl of Derby to Sir Thomas Fairfax, desiring free passage for his Lady and children from the House; but the garrison realising that Lord Derby knew nothing of the provision which had been made for a siege, or of the successful defence which was being carried on, resolved to take no notice of it. A formal acknowledgment was sent to Sir Thomas Fairfax, and a messenger was sent to Lord Derby who was then at Chester, to acquaint him more exactly with the state of things in Lancashire.

The besiegers still continued their bombardment of the House but without much effect; and the garrison continued to have much the best of the sorties. On the morning of Wednesday, April 11, Captain Farmer and Captain Radcliffe led out about half the garrison from a postern gate and drove the Parliamentarians from most of their works, which had now been formed all round the walls, Radcliffe showing especial bravery. The retreat was secured by Captain Ogle and Captain Chisendale. The royalists declared that they had spiked all the besiegers' guns, but as the bombardment continued after this without any intermission the statement must be false. They were evidently obliged to take great precautions against the cannon shot, and men were constantly on the watch with damp cloths to prevent the buildings from catching fire. Towards the middle of April a chance shot entered the window of Lady Derby's room "but was too weak to fright her from the lodging"; ten days afterwards, however, two larger cannon bullets broke into the room, and she was obliged to remove to another part of the building. The royalists were most in fear of the large mortar piece; and their next expedition was made with the object of effecting its capture. About 4 a.m. on April

26th,[1] a sortie in force was made. The walls and gates were well guarded, and a reserve told off to assist a retreat if necessary; Captain Chisenhale then issued from the eastern gate, surprised the besiegers and after severe fighting drove them from their trenches. The great cannon was placed upon a sledge which had been kept in readiness and drawn within the walls. The Parliamentarians must have suffered considerably in this skirmish, and they lost still more in prestige. Inside Lathom there were extravagant expressions of joy at the capture of the dreaded mortar; and the royalists boasted that the very day of its capture Rigby had invited a number of his friends to witness the surrender of the House. The besiegers were proportionately discouraged by its loss; and many of their other guns were now removed in order to prevent their capture.

The Parliamentarians now endeavoured to cut off the water supply from Lathom and to drain the moat. The first was impossible, as the springs that supplied the well inside Lathom were drawn from higher ground east of the House. A trench was begun in order to empty the moat, but it does not seem to have been proceeded with. The country people of the neighbourhood were pressed into service, and many weeks' work was spent in vain. The fidelity of the chief engineer, whose name was Brown, was by no means above suspicion, and he was at any rate incompetent if not treacherous. In one of the sorties by the garrison an assistant engineer was taken prisoner, and he explained the design of the trench.

Colonel Assheton had been called away from the siege early in April. After the sortie of April 26, the discouragement of the Parliamentarian troops was great, and Rigby wrote in much depression to the Committee

1. This is the date given in the Earl of Derby's Diary, "Stanley Papers," part 3, Vol. 3, p. 3 (C. S. 70), ed. Raines.

at Manchester. "We are obliged to repel them five or six times in a night. These constant alarms, the numbers of the garrison, and our great losses, compel our men to mount guard every other night and even two nights in succession. For my part I am spent with anxiety and fatigue."[1] It is therefore surprising to find that summonses for surrender were still being sent into Lathom. The very day before the capture of the mortar a demand was sent to the Countess "to yield up Lathom House, all the persons, goods and arms within it to receive the mercy of the Parliament, and to return her final answer the next day before 2 o'clock." It was to this summons which Lady Derby returned her famous answer—

" Tell that insolent rebel, he shall neither have persons, goods nor house; when our strength and provision is spent, we shall find a fire more merciful than Rigby, and then if the providence of God prevent it not my goods and house shall burn in his sight; myself, children and soldiers rather than fall into his hands, will seal our religion and loyalty in the same flame."

This heroic declaration roused the garrison to wild enthusiasm, and they broke out into loud exclamations "we will die for His Majesty and your honour. God save the King."[2]

After this very little was done before Lathom for some weeks, though skirmishing continued at intervals with varying success. The Parliamentarians now confined themselves to a blockade of the House, and even this was not very effective. For five or six weeks before the

1. Quoted in Marlet, "Charlotte de la Tremoille," p. 117. The "Mercurius Aulicus" tells a story about one sortie, that "the rebels held up a shoulder of mutton on a pike, and called to the defenders to come and dine." The garrison therefore sallied out on them as they were at dinner and scattered them.
2. "A Briefe Journall of the Siege against Lathom" ("C. W. T.," pp. 176, 177).

end of the siege there seems to have been practically no fighting. The besiegers continued at work in their trenches, but a heavy fall of rain which caused some of the earth to fall in and killed three men, interfered with this undertaking. The royalists stated, and probably with some truth, that the besiegers were so disheartened that they could not prevent their men from deserting in large numbers.

At a meeting of the Committee in Manchester on April 23rd, it was resolved to raise additional troops for the siege at Lathom, and to assess a weekly amount of £4,627/6/4 on the whole county, except Lonsdale Hundred and Garstang Parish, which were already being taxed to maintain the siege of Greenhalgh Castle.[1] It is improbable, however, that these resolutions were carried into effect, for the attack showed no more vigour than before; and it had little prospect of success long before the approach of Prince Rupert effected a complete change in the position of affairs. It was not till towards the end of May that news came of Rupert's march, and Colonel Rigby again sent a summons to Lathom to surrender. This was of course refused; and the same day a messenger arrived from the Earl of Derby with news of the Prince's approach. This was, as a matter of fact, only two days before Rupert crossed the Mersey, and as soon as this was ascertained, the Parliamentarian troops marched away from Lathom with all haste. (May 27.) The royalists claimed that the besiegers had lost 500 men during the siege.[2]

1. "Stanley Papers," part 3, Vol. 1 (Chet. Soc. 66), p. ci note
2. This is the estimate of the "Journall" ("C. W. T.," p. 186. The numbers in the "Mercurius Aulicus" seem to be considerably more exaggerated even than are parliamentary figures of royalist losses. The only reference to numbers on the part of the besiegers is in a letter written by Colonel Moore to the Lords Commissioners for England and Scotland, on April 16 : "They sallied forth of the House upon Wednesday last, and we lost five and they fower. They likewise sallied forth last evening, but we beat them in without losse, and they lost two." (Stewart MSS., "Hist. MSS. Com.," report 10, app. 4, p. 472.)

NOTE ON THE SITE OF LATHOM HOUSE.

Almost incredible as it seems, not only has old Lathom House completely disappeared but it is impossible to decide with any certainty where it stood. The present house is not large and was evidently all planned at the time it was built, which was early in the eighteenth century. It is said that it stands on a part of the former site, and certain parts of it, of darker stone than the rest, are supposed to have come from the former building; moreover a hundred yards or so before the house (which faces south) and drawn round it for about three hundred yards is a shallow depression which is said to be the old moat. This has been filled in at the back of the present house to make a garden. Excavations near the present site are said to have discovered human remains.

All this may sound conclusive, but it is impossible to reconcile the surroundings of the present house with the exact description given by Seacome. In spite of his usual inaccuracy in recording events it seems impossible that such a description as he gives, evidently that of an eye witness, can be incorrect except perhaps in one or two details. His exact words may be quoted:—

"As to the situation of Lathom House it stands upon a flat, upon a moorish springy and spumous ground, and was encompassed with a strong wall of two yards thick; upon the walls were nine towers flanking each other and in every tower were six pieces of ordnance that played three one way and three the other; without the wall was a moat eight yards wide and two yards deep; upon the back of the moat between the wall and the graff was a strong row of palisades around. Besides all these, there was a high strong tower, called the Eagle Tower, in the midst of the house surmounting all the rest; and the gate house had also two high and strong buildings with a strong tower on each side of it . . . . . Besides all that has hitherto been said of the walls, towers, moat, etc., there is something so particular and romantic in the general situation of this house as if nature herself had formed it for a stronghold or place of security; for before the house to the south and south-west is a rising ground so near it as to overlook the top of it, from which it falls so quick that nothing planted against it on those sides can touch it further than the front wall; and on the north and east sides there is another rising ground, even to the edge of the moat, and then falls away so quick, that you can scarce, at the distance of a carbine shot, see the house over that height; so that all the batteries placed there are so far below it as to be of little service against it: and let us observe by the way that the uncommon situation of it may be compared to the palm of a man's hand, flat in the middle, and covered with a rising round about it, and so near to it that the enemy, during the siege, were never able to raise a battery against it, so as to make a breach in the wall practicable to enter the house by way of storm." ("House of Stanley," p. 90.)

Either Seacome invented all the above, or the present Lathom House is not only not on the old site, but it is not anywhere near to it. For it is impossible to suppose that the nature of the ground can have changed so entirely. The soil round the present Lathom House is not marshy but sandy, and it is not hilly but flat. There is a very slight slope away from the front of the house to the south, and also to the north, but on no side is there any place which can possibly be supposed to answer to Seacome's description. Moreover the so-called moat is by no means convincing. It is conceivable that a moat may have been considerably filled in since the seventeenth century, but the wall which now supports the bank is not high and the stone looks new; Seacome's eight yards wide and two yards deep could hardly have so shrunk.

In the woods recently planted, which began about half a mile south of the present house, is an evidently artificial ditch, some 250 yards in length, bending slightly in the middle and running roughly E. and W. and N.E. and S.W.   This is known as Cromwell's Trench, and the tradition is said to be an ancient one; there is also at some distance a large block of stone containing on its upper surface two hollows which are said to have been used for casting bullets; this is locally known as Cromwell's Stone.   It may be noted that Roby's reference to the site, though he evidently visited it, is not quite accurate.   He says "It is said that the camp of the besiegers was in a woody dell near what is now called the ' Round O Quarry ' about half a mile from Lathom.   This dell is still called 'Cromwell's Trench'; and a large and remarkable stone, having two circular hollows or holes on its upper surface, evidently once containing nodules of iron, is called 'Cromwell's Stone,' the country people supposing these holes were used as moulds for casting bullets during the siege." ("Traditions of Lancashire," 5th ed., 1811, vol. i, p. 315.)

Actually the trench is rather more than half a mile from Lathom but the Stone is a quarter of a mile from the Trench, and the Quarry is at least a mile further off again.   But Roby evidently thought that the old house was at a considerable distance from the present one, for his imaginary view[1] is taken "from a hill above the valley or trench where it is said the main army of the besiegers was encamped."   The present house cannot be seen from the edge of the woods.

Roby's view seems to the present writer to give approximately the site of the old House.   Accepting the Trench tradition as correct, it fixes the position of the House somewhere in the immediate vicinity, for 17th

1. This view is given in "Traditions of Lancashire," 3rd ed., 1843, Vol. 1, p. 170.

century siege guns were so poor that the besiegers' camp must have been quite close to the walls. It is of course possible that the Trench is that made during the second siege which the "Discourse" says was a good distance from the walls, but even so there would be no point at all in having it more than half a mile away. Moreover the character of the ground at this point is both hilly and marshy just as in Seacome's description. It seems, therefore, most reasonable to suppose that the site of old Lathom House was somewhere in the woods, but on account of the undergrowth it is not possible to determine its exact position.[1]

In the gardens at Lathom are many pieces of cut stone which have come from the old building, and in one place has been pieced together the upper tracery of a large window, perhaps from the chapel.

1. Cf. "Victoria County History of Lancs.," Vol. 3, p. 252, note 3.

CHAPTER VII.

Prince Rupert in Lancashire.

IN the months of May and June, 1644, Lancashire for the first time became involved in the general course of the war, and for some weeks it was the centre of most important events. So much of other than merely local interest had the first siege of Lathom House, that it influenced the course of Rupert's march north, which was made in order to effect a junction with the Earl of Newcastle to check the Scotch army which was now on its way to the assistance of the Parliament. The Scots, 21,000 strong, under Alexander Leslie, Earl of Leven, had crossed the Tweed on January 19, 1643-4. Newcastle at once summoned Rupert to come to his aid, and marching northwards occupied the town of Newcastle; but he was soon obliged to fall back on Durham. Meanwhile Sir Thomas Fairfax, after the battle of Nantwich on January 25th, had rejoined his father in Yorkshire, and the two soon began to recover the county for the Parliament. On April 11th they stormed Selby, taking among other prisoners Lord Bellasis, whom Newcastle had left in command during his absence. This defeat obliged Newcastle to retreat still further southwards, and he shut himself up in York which was blockaded by Fairfax and the Scots on April 22nd.[1]

In January of this year Rupert had captured Aylesbury, and early in March he set out to relieve Newark which had been invested by the Parliament. The siege was raised, and the besiegers, who were commanded by Sir John Meldrum, were forced to capitulate; but Rupert

1. "Cambridge Modern History," Vol. 4, pp. 320, 321; "C. S. P.," pp. 35, 39.

had to return his troops to the garrisons from which he had borrowed them, and almost without an army he marched back to the Welsh border, where he occupied himself with raising fresh troops to go to the assistance of the Earl of Newcastle.

As soon as his intentions for the north were known, the Earl of Derby endeavoured to persuade him to march by way of Lancashire in order to relieve Lathom House. The besieged Countess must have written to her husband in a very different tone from that of her defiant answers to Rigby; indeed if the Earl of Derby did not unduly exaggerate the position of the garrison, they must have been in imminent fear of being compelled to surrender. The petition was, however, seconded by the Lancashire royalists, and the Earl of Derby promised that if Lathom were relieved he would aid Rupert's further march with 2,000 men and a considerable sum of money. It was pointed out that the towns of Liverpool and Warrington were but weakly garrisoned, and that the reconquest of Lancashire would be a great gain for the King's cause in the north of England, " the rebellion in those parts being wholly supported from there." Liverpool would be of immense use as the port towards Ireland, and Derby and Prince Rupert had already discussed over the map the possibility of reducing it.[1]

Sir John Byron, the royalist Governor of Chester,

1. Derby to Rupert, Chester, March 7, 1643–4 : "I have received many advertisements from my wife of her great distress and imminent danger, unless she be relieved by your Highness, on whom she doth more rely than any other whatever, and all of us consider well she hath chief reason so to do" ("Rupert MSS.," Add. MSS. 18980, fol. 81). Derby's information was that there were only 50 men each in the towns of Liverpool and Warrington, the garrisons having been withdrawn to the siege of Lathom.

Sir John Byron to Rupert, Apr. 7, describes Lathom as in danger of being lost : "The constant intelligence from that county every day is that if your Highness only appear there, the greatest part of the rebels' forces will desert them and join you, and that county being once reduced, all this part of England will presently be clear." "Rupert MSS.," fol. 137; "Clarendon" (Macray), Vol. 3, p. 339 (book 8, par. 17).

was persuaded to support the scheme; and the Earl of
Derby having personally written to the King urging its
desirability, Charles' approval was given. The prospect
of invasion had caused great consternation among the
Lancashire Parliamentarians as early as the middle of
March;[1] but it was two months after that before Rupert
was able to move. Drawing his forces together he
began his advance towards Yorkshire about the middle
of May. On the 18th the royalists moved from Holt,
Malpas, and Whitchurch, to a more easterly position
at Market Drayton; and next day they crossed the
River Weaver, and advanced to Audlem and Bruerton
which are just over the Cheshire border. A thousand
Parliamentarian troops marched out of Nantwich as far
as Hatherton, but Rupert was not anxious to fight and
fell back to Audlem. (Monday, May 20th.) It was
feared that he would lay siege to Nantwich, but he
passed to the east of that place, and on Tuesday, May 21,
his troops were quartered about Haslington and Sandbach, while Rupert himself stayed at Betley. On
May 24th the march to Lancashire began, and the
royalists lodged at Knutsford, which is only ten miles
from the Lancashire border; the following day they
advanced to Stockport, only seven miles distant from
Manchester. Prince Rupert's forces were estimated at
8,000 or 10,000 men, mostly cavalry, and they were said
to have 50 guns. At Stockport Colonels Mainwaring
and Duckenfield were posted with about 3,000 men to
oppose his advance, but they seem to have made very
little resistance, and after a short skirmish they broke

1. Assheton to Moore, March 18 (Stewart MSS., "Hist. MSS. Com.,"
rep. 10, app. 4, p. 71). He has heard that the Princes are joined, and
fears that their objective may be Lancashire by way of Hale Ford or
Liverpool. In the meantime Derby continued to address urgent appeals
to Rupert. He has not been able to raise the regiments which the
Prince had required in order to raise the siege, "and the time is now
past, for the enemy is so close to the House that it is impossible for
that design to take effect which might have been some relieving of a
distressed woman whose only hope, next to Almighty God, is in your
Highness's help." ("Hist MSS. Com.," report 9, app. 2, p. 437.)

and fled towards Manchester, leaving 800 prisoners. The royalists occupied Stockport, and were joined there by some of Newcastle's cavalry from Derbyshire. Rupert left some of these to garrison Stockport, and moved on into Lancashire with the main body of his army.[1]

The Parliamentarian leaders before York thought that Rupert ought to have been stopped at Stockport.[2] There were two ways by which the royalists might have entered Lancashire, either at Stockport or at Warrington; probably the passage of the river Mersey at Warrington was too strongly guarded for Rupert to attempt it, for he must have preferred that way if he could have chosen. Not only was it the most direct way to Lathom but it passed through country which was much better affected to the King's cause than East Lancashire. But no doubt the resistance offered at Stockport was very feeble. Rupert had certainly not more than 10,000 men, and there should have been almost an equal number available to oppose him. For the Lancashire leaders had refused in April to send 2,000 men out of the county for the relief of the Earl of Denbigh on account of the necessities of their own county.[3] Lathom House, they said, was still unsubdued; the Earl of Derby threatened invasion from Wirrall, and the Westmoreland royalists from the north. It is true that some troops which had marched into Yorkshire had been kept there to assist in the siege of York; but the two Committees of Lancashire and Cheshire ought to have had far more than 3,000 men at Stockport to

1. Newspapers in " C. W. T.," 187; " C. S. P.," 173, 174.
2. " C. S. P.," 1644, pp. 206, 207. They urged that there were only two ways for Rupert to go, either through Warrington or Stockport; and that both should be well guarded.
3. Lancashire Committee to the Earl of Denbigh, May 16 : " They profess willingness to send some troops, but that if the older soldiers are withdrawn the new recruits are not to be trusted " (" C. S. P.," 1644, p. 164). The regiments intended for Denbigh were Holland's and Booth's (*ibid.*, pp. 111, 123). Cf. also H. L. Calendar, " Hist. MSS. Com.," report 6, p. 13.

oppose the royalist advance. Perhaps one reason for their failure was the acute differences which had broken out among the Lancashire leaders. Complaints were made against Colonel Dodding, Colonel Holland and others, and there was even insubordination shown to Sir Thomas Fairfax. There seems to have been no ground for the suspicions of Dodding. He had suffered considerably for the Parliamentarian cause, and he continued to serve it faithfully. As regards Holland the complaints were probably justified; he had always been a rather lukewarm supporter of his party.[1]

As soon as Rupert had entered Lancashire his forces were considerably increased, the local royalists flocking to him in large numbers. The Earl of Derby joined him with all the forces he could raise. The royalists had now to decide whether they would attack Manchester or march straight for Lathom. On the day after Rupert's victory at Stockport, Manchester was secured by Sir John Meldrum with one Scotch regiment and one of Fairfax's consisting of Lancashire men.[2] Apparently Meldrum had intended to arrive in time to prevent the royalists' advance from Cheshire, but he was too late. Rupert, however, had not much time to waste in sieges, and it was evident that Manchester could not be taken except after a long investment. Rosworm describes an attempt which was made by the royalists to induce him to betray the town by promise of a large sum of money and advancement under Prince Rupert. The intermediary was Peter Heywood. There may be some truth in the account, but Heywood's plot to betray Manchester seems to have been made about a month before this time, and Rosworm's narrative is here very

1. "C. S. P.," pp. 173, 200. Cf. Rosworm's "Good Service," "C. W. T.," pp. 230–232. Some action of Fairfax's, it does not appear what, had evidently provoked resentment. Dodding afterwards marched with his regiment into Yorkshire, and fought at the battle of Marston Moor, where he lost many of his men ("Discourse," p. 50).

2. "Perfect Diurnall," June 3 ("C. W. T.," p. 188).

inaccurate. For instance he places Rupert's advance after the siege of Liverpool in August, in which he himself was engaged.[1] Whether or not the royalists attempted to gain Manchester by treachery, they certainly made no approach on the town but keeping to the west they moved by way of Barlow Moor and Trafford Park about three miles distant from Manchester. Rupert's objective was now Bolton, the second Puritan stronghold of the county.

When the news of Rupert's coming reached the camp of the besiegers before Lathom House the only doubt was where they might escape. The terror of Rupert's name was worth a great deal to the royalists. Colonel Rigby showed great indecision; he could not make up his mind whether to stay in Lancashire, or to cross into Yorkshire. His troops were first removed to Eccleston Green, and they would then probably have been marched to Manchester but for the fear of meeting Rupert on the way. Rigby's own family were in Preston, and they at once escaped into Yorkshire. In Preston also there were about 50 royalist prisoners guarded by Captain Pateson and Captain Swarbreck; and they twice received orders which were afterwards contradicted to join Rigby at Eccleston. Finally they were directed to convey their prisoners to Lancaster Castle. Leaving Preston on the same day that Prince Rupert took Bolton they quartered one night at Myerscough Lodge; next day they were attacked by a troop of royalist horse, and but for the timely assistance of Colonel Dodding, who was quartered at Garstang on his way towards Manchester, the prisoners would probably have been released.[2]

Rigby finally made up his mind to go to Bolton,

1. Rosworm's "Good Service," "C. W. T.," p. 229. But cf. "C. S. P.," 1644, p. 205, where a reference is made to a letter from Col. Moore before Lathom on May 9, stating that Heywood's plot had then been discovered and that he had fled. Rosworm says that Heywood was captured, but released through Holland's influence.

2. "Discourse," p. 49. The details are probably correct, though all the dates in this narrative during May, 1644, are a fortnight too early.

thinking that Rupert would march either to Blackburn, or to Preston and Lancaster; but as it turned out the Parliamentarians only reached Bolton on the day before the royalists. Rigby occupied the town on May 27th, and next morning Rupert appeared before the town; and finding Rigby and his men in possession they determined on an assault.

The chances were obviously in favour of the royalists. They were quite three to one in numbers, and were commanded by the dreaded Prince Rupert and by the Earl of Derby. Their opponents were disheartened by an unsuccessful three months' siege; moreover they were mostly newly raised troops, and as there had been no garrison kept in Bolton for almost twelve months the defences were considered out of repair. Nevertheless the fight was very fierce and for a time undecided. The royalists approached the town about 2 o'clock in the afternoon from the south-west, and at once delivered an attack at several quarters; but after about half an hour's hard fighting at close quarters the first assault was beaten off. The royalists state that they lost 200 men in this repulse. Colonel Rigby sent out of the town a troop of horse to stave off the second attack, but these were defeated. The Earl of Derby in person led the second attack, having requested Prince Rupert to allow him for this purpose two companies of his own soldiers then under the command of Colonel Tyldesley. After a quarter of an hour's desperate fighting the royalists effected an entrance, the Earl being the first man to enter. Some cavalry were admitted to another part of the town through the treachery of one of the townsmen, and caught between the two forces the Parliamentarian troops were routed. Each man saved himself as he might, but against the overwhelming superiority of the royalist horse in an unwalled town the defenders were helpless and the slaughter was great.[1] Little mercy was

1. "C. W. T.." pp. 183, 188; "Seacome," p. 93; "Discourse," pp. 50, 51.

shown by the infuriated royalists, Prince Rupert having, on their own confession, at first forbidden quarter to be given to any in arms. Seacome states that 2,000 Parliamentarian soldiers out of a total of 3,000 were killed, and another royalist account puts the slain at 1,600 with 700 prisoners. Both these estimates are probably too high. It does not seem probable that Rigby had more than 2,500 men, and large numbers of these certainly escaped, while more than 200 were taken prisoners. A more reasonable estimate by a Parliamentarian writer places the total loss on both sides at 1,200 to 1,500, which is more likely to be correct. The Parliamentarians would not be likely to over-estimate their own losses. Of this 1,200 or 1,500 no doubt the larger number would belong to the town. Supposing the royalists to have lost 200 men in the first attack and 200 more during all the rest of the engagement, it would still make the losses of the town three or four times as numerous, which is credible enough; for the Parliamentarian troops would have lost very heavily in their flight, Rupert having a large number of cavalry who could be of service in the pursuit. Colonel Rigby's cleverness alone secured his own escape. Being on horseback he mingled with the royalists as they entered the town, learned their password, and posed for a time as one of their officers; then taking advantage of the general confusion he rode away with one attendant into Yorkshire.

The capture of Bolton, or "Bolton Massacre" as the Parliamentarian writers called it, was the saddest incident of the whole war in Lancashire. Nowhere else was the naturally bitter character of an intestine struggle so unhappily illustrated; nowhere else were such furious passions aroused; nowhere else was the slaughter so terrible. The account by a townsman, "An Exact Relation of the bloody and barbarous Massacre at Bolton in the Moors in Lancashire," etc., is without parallel in all the contemporary authorities for the vivid horror of its descriptions. Against the otherwise moderate conduct of the Lancashire war this terrible incident stood out in sharp contrast. It is of course easy enough for the historian, surveying it impartially at a long distance of time, to explain why this was so. No one could call Prince Rupert's methods of war merciful at any time; and in the present instance he was in haste to relieve York, and would be sure to make short work of any obstacles in his way. For the local royalist troops engaged, it was the first experience of victory after many months of defeat, and the garrison opposed to them was the same force which had besieged Lathom House, against whom naturally the Earl of Derby and his followers had a particular grudge. They were commanded by the hated Rigby, and Bolton, 'the Geneva of the north,' was especially detested by the opponents of Puritanism. All these considerations served to make the capture of Bolton more than usually terrible. It is probable, however, that the stories related by both sides of the outrages committed by their opponents, are exaggerated if not invented. The royalists assert that after their first attack had been beaten off, some prisoners taken were put to death in their sight upon the walls of the town; and they attribute their unrestrained slaughter on gaining the victory to this act of cruelty. The statement is, however, made by Seacome, who is notoriously inaccurate; and as it is quite unsupported by any other testimony, it is impossible to believe it. On the other hand, horrible stories of barbarity are related by the Parliamentarian writers as having been committed by the victors, in some cases on defenceless townsmen, and even on women and children. These are much more likely to be true than the other, but they are probably exaggerated. The gravest charge is that made against the Earl of Derby himself, that one Captain Bootle, formerly in his service,

was taken prisoner and brought before the Earl at his
own request to ask for mercy; and that Derby thereupon
drew his sword and ran him through the body in cold
blood. This story may be equally discredited.[1] Bootle
was certainly killed during the siege; and the royalists
state that he was killed by the Earl of Derby during the
fighting, which is most probably true. Before his
execution Derby denied the charge; and it seems quite
incredible that a man so highminded and chivalrous,
should have committed such an act even in the excitement of victory. There was perhaps great cruelty
shown by the royalists, but not by Derby personally;
and we must attribute the story of the manner of Bootle's
death to party malice.

Prince Rupert sent all the twenty-two colours taken
at Bolton to Lady Derby at Lathom House, by the hand
of Sir Richard Crane, but he did not immediately march
there himself. The Earl of Derby presented to Rupert
a ring worth £20 as a token of his gratitude; and at
Lathom there were great rejoicings. No garrison was
left in Bolton, and the prisoners were taken away bound
two and two together, and sent over Hale Ford into
Cheshire where they were distributed between Chester,
Shrewsbury, and other places.[2] After this success the

1. For a full and thoroughly sound discussion of this incident, *vide*
"Discourse" note, pp. 134–142. The only possible doubt of Derby's
innocence of the crime is that the charge is made with great detail by
the author of the "Discourse," who is an unusually impartial writer,
and had, moreover, a high opinion of Derby.
2. Arthur Trevor to Ormonde, June 29 : "My Lord of Derby is now
sending over to your excellency to barter for or buy arms and ammunition. I shall, on his lordship's behalf, desire he may pay well. I
promise he is well able to do it, for upon the relief of Lathom he
presented the Prince with a ring worth twenty pounds sterling at most;
Sir Richard Crane, who carried the 22 colours to be left as trophy in
his house, a ring price 40 shillings, and W. Legge with four candlesticks
worth £10 in all." ("Carte MSS.," Vol. 11, fol. 315.) The rather cynical
tone of this letter may be taken as an example of the Earl of Derby's
unpopularity with the royalist leaders. The ford at Hale was for a
long time the principal pass over the Mersey between Liverpool and
Warrington. It ceased to be generally used about 150 years ago; but
almost within living memory horses were taken over by this way for
hunting in Cheshire. It is now impossible to get across.

county came in very fast to the royalists, and Derby soon had 5,000 men under his command.

The Parliamentarians never forgave the massacre at Bolton. Wrongly accused as he was, Derby's share in the engagement was in part at least responsible for the implacability with which his enemies pursued him to the scaffold. From this time onwards the Parliament placed his name among the list of those who were to be excepted from pardon in case peace was made with the King. Bolton market place was chosen as the place of his death in remembrance of the royalist victory there. As regards the Prince, they delighted to ascribe his subsequent disaster to the vengeance of Heaven for his cruelty in Lancashire. "The blood of Bolton would not let him rest till all the glory he had got was lost in one hour" [1] writes Baillie on July 12. At Marston Moor, though the royalists were nearly successful, it was the ever victorious Rupert who was driven off the field at the first encounter.

A collection for the relief of Bolton was made in Manchester Church and Salford Chapel in June, and reached the total of £140, a large sum considering the general distress which prevailed. [2]

When the Committee of both Kingdoms heard of Rupert's advance, they wrote to the Earl of Manchester before York urging him to send a considerable force to resist the Prince in Lancashire. (June 1st.) It was urged that Rupert might secure Lancashire, capture the passes so that he could send out troops into the neighbouring counties as he liked, and by means of Liverpool take in supplies from the sea; by which the war would be indefinitely prolonged. Similar letters were sent to Fairfax and to Leven. But the Parliamentarian generals in Yorkshire, rightly objected to dividing their forces; deciding that it was impossible for them to deal with

1. "Baillie's Letters" (ed. Laing, 3 vols., 1841–2), Vol. 2, p. 203.
2. "C. W. T.," p. 199.

an enemy who was yet so far away, and that for the present the West must look after itself. The Committee in London were urgent, and letters passed daily during the month of June; but their ignorance of the situation sufficiently illustrates the absurdity of endeavouring to direct a campaign by votes of a Committee distant 150 miles from the seat of war. The Earl of Denbigh, the Parliamentarian general in the Midlands, defended himself at length and with some heat from the charge that he was to blame in not being able to check Prince Rupert's march by falling upon his rear.[1] At length Sir Harry Vane was sent down to York to consult with the generals there; but on arriving early in June he was speedily convinced that it was impossible to divide the army as the Committee suggested. Assheton and Rigby, who were in Yorkshire. naturally seconded the Committee's opinion; but until the Earl of Manchester's foot had been brought to the siege, progress had been very slow, and it would have been very unwise to weaken the besieging force; as it was, York was closely beset on all sides and might soon be expected to capitulate. The Committee were evidently wrong. To divide the Parliamentarian army would have been dangerous, to raise the siege of York would have played into the enemy's hands. Rupert was in fact wasting time in Lancashire. His best chance would have been to gather all the troops he could after his capture of Bolton and to march straight on York; but he spent four precious weeks before he left Lancashire. "I hope you will not have cause to apprehend Prince Rupert's strength," wrote Manchester, "for excepting plundering, at which his army is expert, no considerable places have been taken possession of by his army."[2] The Committee of both Kingdoms indeed over-rated Prince Rupert's ability. He was no great general though a splendid

1. " C. S. P.," 1644, pp. 192, 200, 207, 223–225.
2. " C. S. P.," 1644, p. 217.

cavalry officer. The plan which they sketched for him of securing Lancashire and using it as a base was beyond his powers, even if it had been possible under the circumstances. And the Lancashire royalists had been so scattered before Rupert came, that they were not able to give him any very substantial help. As long as it continued to be impossible for the King to march north, Rupert might be left to himself.

After a few days rest at Bolton, the royalists marched at once to Liverpool. They stated that Newcastle had sent word that he could still hold out for a few weeks. The Liverpool of that day was a small town situated on a ridge of land east of the Mersey, and sloping on the west towards the river and on the east towards the country. It was strongly fortified and held by Colonel Moore, who was the Parliamentarian Governor. At the north end of the town was a high mud wall, and a ditch 12 yards wide and 3 yards deep was drawn round most of the landward side. At the south end was a castle also protected by a ditch which could be filled with water from the river; all the streets facing the river were blocked up, while those on the other side of the town were palisaded and defended with cannon. When Rupert first looked down on the town from the higher ridge which overlooked it on the east he likened it to a crow's nest which might easily be robbed; but before he had taken it he said it might better be called an eagle's nest or a den of lions. Flushed with their victory at Bolton, the royalists delivered a furious attack expecting to overcome as they had done the other town; but at Liverpool the fortifications were much stronger, and they were beaten off with the loss of many men. They then established a blockade, Rupert's main camp being placed at the Beacon, a full mile from the town, from which he relieved his trenches and batteries twice daily. Day after day a furious bombardment was directed against the defences, Rupert's natural impatience being increased by urgent appeals which now began to come from York. But for a fortnight the town continued to hold out, and at least two attempts to storm were beaten off with loss. The failure of the bombardment was partly due to an unusual defence which was resorted to. The refugees from Ireland, of whom there were a great many in the town, had brought over among other effects many bags of wool, and the tops of the walls were lined with these bags, which proved of great service in deadening the force of the enemy's shot. The Parliamentarians also had command of the river, and a reinforcement of 400 English and Scotch troops from Manchester were marched to Warrington and from thence sent to Liverpool by water. At length the royalists gained an entrance at the north end of the town by a night attack during Whit-week (June 12 or 13), and carried the town by storm. There was some slaughter and much plundering; but there were still some ships in the river, and when the royalists entered the town Moore embarked as many of his soldiers as he could and himself escaped. He was afterwards much blamed for deserting the town, and it was suggested that he had yielded the northern works by treachery in order to ingratiate himself with Rupert and save his own house, Bank Hall, which was on that side of the town. But this suggestion seems to have been without foundation; and it was afterwards stated in Moore's defence that when the royalists entered Liverpool his soldiers refused to follow him, and that he himself only retreated when resistance was hopeless, and embarked under fire.[1]

1. *Vide* p. 37. "Discourse," p. 52; "C. W. T.," p. 199; "Seacome," p. 95. Ramsay Muir, "History of Liverpool (1907), chap. 9, p. 16. Legge to Trevor, June 13 : "And now Liverpool is in our hands, I hope we shall have a freer intelligence from Ireland than before we had. I assure you that was the end we stopped ther for." In spite of this advantage, the siege of Liverpool was not worth while, and the royalists admit that the 100 barrels of powder which it cost, left Rupert but ill provided. ("Carte MSS.," Vol. 11, fol. 184, 313.) "Seacome," p. 96, says that the siege lasted nearly a month, but this is evidently an error, for it cannot have begun before May 30.

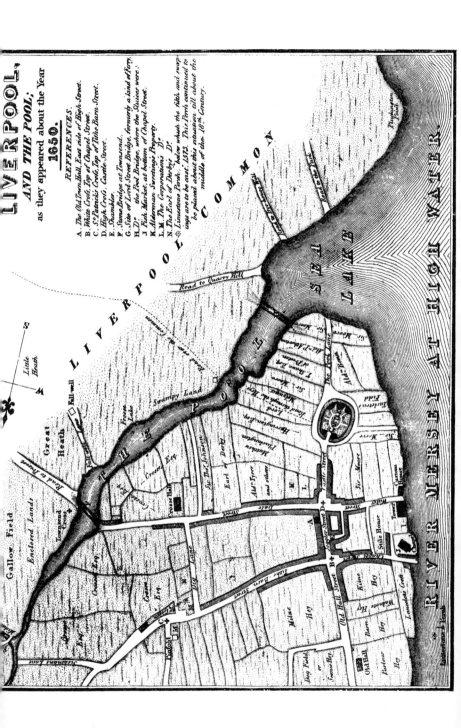

LIVERPOOL,
AND THE POOL;
as they appeared about the Year
1650.

REFERENCES.

A. The Old Town Hall, East side of High Street.
B. White Cross, Top of Chapel Street.
C. St Patrick's Cross, Top of Tithe Barn Street.
D. High Cross, Castle Street.
E. Shamble.
F. Stone Bridge at Townsend.
G. Site of Lord Street Bridge, formerly a kind of Ferry.
H. Do. the Pool Bridge, where the Sluices were.
J. Fish Market, at bottom of Chapel Street.
K. Alderman Sweeting's Property.
L. M. The Corporations' Do.
N. The Earl of Derby's Do.
✳ Limestone Pools: below which the filth and sewings are to be cast 1573. This Pools continued to be placed about this situation till about the middle of the 18th Century.

LIVERPOOL COMMON

Road to Quarry Hill

SEA LAKE

Little Heath

Fall-well

Swampy Land

Great Heath

Enclosed Lands

Gallow Field

Road to Prescot

Townsend

Road to ye Park

RIVER MERSEY AT HIGH WATER.

Prince Rupert left Sir John Byron as Governor of
Liverpool, and himself marched to Lathom House whose
fortifications were considerably strengthened under his
direction. He promoted Captain Rawsthorne to the
rank of Colonel, and appointed him Governor of the
fortress; Captain Chisenhale was also made Colonel and
accompanied Rupert into Yorkshire. The Countess of
Derby and her children had removed after the raising of
the siege to the Isle of Man.[1] Liverpool was garrisoned
by Colonel Cuthbert Clifton's regiment, newly raised in
the Fylde.[2]

The Committee of both Kingdoms still persisted in
its design of having Rupert opposed on his march into
Yorkshire; which might have been sound policy provided no troops were withdrawn from the siege of York
for that purpose. On June 13, they directed the Earl
of Denbigh to march into Cheshire with all his forces
and to keep in touch with the garrison at Manchester
which now numbered 5,000 men; and Colonel Hutchin-
son at Nottingham was also told to be ready to march
with 200 horse and 300 foot.[3] Later a general rendezvous
was appointed, at which these forces were to be joined
by Lord Grey with 200 horse and 300 foot, and by Sir
John Gell from Derby with 500 horse and 500 foot.
Apparently the generals before York were at last prevailed upon to promise some troops for Lancashire. By
the end of June, Denbigh was said to be on the march;
but before the preparations were completed they were no
longer needed.

Early in June Rupert was joined by Lord Goring with
reinforcements of cavalry, which brought his army up
to nearly 15,000 men; but even still there were delays.
Disquieting rumours reached the Prince of the oppor-

1. "Seacome," p. 97. "July 30, 1644: My wife landed in the Isle of
Man." Derby's Diary, "Stanley Papers" (C. S. 70), ed. Raines, pt. 3,
Vol. 3, p. 4.
2. "Discourse," p. 52.
3. "C. S. P.," 1644, pp. 231, 248, 272, 292.

tunity which his enemies at court were making in his absence to accuse him to the King. It was "the common discourse of the Lord Digby, Lord Percy, Sir John Culpeller, and Wilmot, that it is indifferent whether the Parliament or Prince Rupert doth prevail." Naturally Rupert was so enraged "that he was once resolved to send the King his commission and get to France. This fury interrupted his march ten days." At last, however, the Prince set out on his way to York. He stopped at Preston, where a banquet was prepared for him, but he refused it saying "Banquets were not fit for soldiers," and instead carried the Mayor and Bailiffs prisoners as far as Skipton Castle where he left them.[1] He probably used both the roads out of Lancashire by Clitheroe and Colne; and his march was harassed by Colonel Shuttleworth. Several skirmishes took place, which were not to the royalists' advantage. Garrisons were left in Clitheroe and Skipton Castle. On June 25th Rupert was said to be still in Lancashire, and the Cheshire royalists were still hoping to catch him on his march; two days later his advance guard was at Skipton; but after this he marched more swiftly. On Monday, July 1st, the Parliamentarian armies raised the siege of York on hearing that Rupert had passed Knaresborough; and the battle of Marston Moor was fought on the following day.

Marston Moor was the most important battle of the whole civil war, and the importance of the coming engagement was fully realised before it took place. Both sides as usual invoked the Divine aid. "If God help us to take York and defeat him (Rupert) the business is ended in England," wrote Baillie on June 9th, and in the same strain Colonel Robert Byron wrote to Ormond after the battle but before its result was known : "And doubtless it is the greatest business that hath been since

1. Trevor to Ormonde, Chester, June 26, 1644 (" Carte MSS.," Vol. 11, fol. 312, 313 ; " Discourse," p. 52.

the war began. God Almighty give the Prince good success." [1] Perhaps nowhere was the event of the battle awaited with greater anxiety than in Lancashire. Rupert's coming had changed again the whole state of affairs in that county. "Half of the county at this time was under their power, viz., Derby, Leyland, and Amounderness Hundreds from the taking of Bolton, May 14th, till the 20th August." While the Prince was in Lancashire the royalists showed great activity so that they might hold out after he had gone. On the result of Marston Moor depended whether or not this state of things should remain; but with the defeat of the royalists the tables were turned again. Instead of having to fight on the defensive against the victorious enemy the Lancashire Parliamentarians had now only fugitives to deal with. After the battle Rupert stayed one night in York, then made his way back by the Yorkshire Dales into Lancashire; but while his first appearance in the county had been a progress of victory, at his second coming he headed only fragments of a defeated army, which were anxious to escape without further fighting. Indeed what fighting there was took place with his lieutenants. The Prince himself was at Hornby Castle on July 8th; from there he marched hastily through the Fylde to Preston and then down the western coast and so over Hale Ford into Cheshire. His forces, however, remained in Lancashire for a month afterwards. The Committee of Both Kingdoms were still in great fear of what Rupert might do, and urged Fairfax to send forces after him; but Rupert was anxious to get out of Lancashire as fast as he could, and the forces which he left were in a scattered condition and without ammunition. They were under the command of Goring, Molyneux and Tyldesley, and they remained in Amounderness Hundred, until at length Sir John Meldrum was

1. Baillie to Spong, June 9 ("Letters," Vol. 2, p. 193). Col. R. Byron to Ormonde, July 5 (" Carte MSS.," Vol. 11, fol. 495).

despatched from York with 1,000 horse to clear the county. Reinforced with Lancashire foot, he set out in search of the enemy about August 10th, and the royalists on hearing of his approach retreated again over the Ribble into the Fylde. Some of them, however, under Lord Ogleby and Colonel Huddleston of Millom attempted to reach Lathom House and were encountered near Walton by Colonel Dodding. The royalists, consisting of 400 horse, outnumbered Dodding, but word being sent to Colonel Nicholas Shuttleworth who was near Blackburn, he hastened up and thus reinforced, Dodding routed the royalists and captured 40 or 50 prisoners, including Huddleston and Ogleby (Aug. 15). The remainder escaped to Lathom, but few of them could get through the lines there, the siege having been renewed. There seems to have been a further skirmish at Ribble Bridge a few days later.

Colonel Dodding then joined Sir John Meldrum, who reached Preston late on Friday, August 16th, and quartered there on the following Saturday and Sunday. On August 17th Goring joined the other royalists who were encamped about Lytham and Kirkham, plundering greatly; they now numbered about 2,700, nearly all cavalry. A rendezvous was appointed on Freckleton Marsh on Monday, August 18th; and on the same day Meldrum drew up his forces on Penwortham Moor, south of Preston, intending to attack them. But he seems to have been ignorant of the country. Intending to cross the Ribble below Preston, he found the passage impracticable on account of the tide; and having wasted much time he was forced to return to Preston and to march along the north bank of the Ribble by way of Greaves Town and Lea Hall. From the latter place the royalists were discovered across Freckleton Marsh crossing the river some three miles away. Meldrum at once gave chase as fast as possible, the horsemen each taking up a musketeer behind him for greater speed; but when they reached the water the tide had again risen too high for them to cross, and they were only in time to send a parting shot or two after the royalists. Meldrum waited for the rest of his foot, and the same night returned to Preston. Next day (Aug. 19th) he again set out in pursuit, marching south-westward; and in the evening he encountered the royalists near Ormskirk. They had been forced to make a detour on reaching the southern bank of the Ribble in order to avoid Colonel Assheton who lay with some troops near Hesketh Bank, and so had been unable to escape further. Though it was 8 o'clock in the evening when Meldrum came up with the royalists, he at once ordered an attack. Colonel Booth's foot regiment opened fire and the royalists made very little resistance; their defeat was completed by a charge of cavalry who pursued as long as the light would allow. The royalists were quite scattered. Their chief men managed to escape, but most of the officers and 300 men were taken prisoners. The few who escaped fled south-wards and over Hale Ford into Cheshire. Prince Rupert was said to be on the southern bank of the Mersey waiting for a chance to invade Lancashire again; but this defeat made it impossible for him to do so.[1]

1. "Discourse," pp. 57, 58; "C. W. T.," p. 204; "Denbigh MSS.," Vol. 1, p. 275. It seems evident that if Meldrum had been better informed of the fords across the Ribble below Preston, he might have caught the royalists a day before he did. In the Parliamentarian newspapers the number of prisoners taken was placed as high as 1,000 men. On July 15, Sir George Booth at Dunham was informed that Prince Rupert was still at Preston with 6,000 horse and some foot.

CHAPTER VIII.

The End of the First Civil War.

THERE was now no longer a royalist army in Lancashire; the only places which still held out were Liverpool, Lathom House and Greenhalgh Castle. Clitheroe Castle had been deserted by its garrison a few weeks after the battle of Marston Moor; but Skipton, over the Yorkshire border, was for some time longer a source of apprehension to the Parliamentarians in Blackburn Hundred. After the defeat of the royalists at Ormskirk, Meldrum at once laid siege to Liverpool; but the fortifications were strong, and the town resisted for ten weeks, being at last surrendered on Friday, November 1st. Colonel Rosworm directed the ordnance at the siege, and Colonel Moore commanded some ships from the river. But Meldrum was called away for service in North Wales, and during his absence the siege was not conducted with any vigour. "I have had much ado," he wrote to the Committee of Both Kingdoms from Liverpool on October 2nd, "to bring back the Lancashire foot to their quarters before Liverpool, in regard to their want of obedience even to their own officers, the unseasonableness of the weather, and the time of harvest. They have had no pay for 18 weeks, and have been much pinched for want of victuals ever since they have been under my charge, the country being so wasted and spoiled by Prince Rupert's two journeys through Lancashire . . . . . During my being abroad the enemy has taken divers of our men while sleeping upon their guard, and by what is intercepted I find them reduced to great extremities by inviting the garrison of Lathom House, consisting of 200 horse and 300 foot under Colonel Vere, who since the rout at Ormskirk hath been there, to fall upon some of our quarters upon Thursday next and in the meantime those within the town resolved to fall desperately upon some of our quarters and to make their retreat to Lathom House." [1]   The Earl of Derby was also reported to be gathering troops in Cheshire for the relief of the town; but he was defeated by Sir William Brereton, and the intended attack from Lathom House never took place.   But no breach could be made in the walls of Liverpool, and in the end it was starved into surrender.   The circumstances were peculiar.   In the last days of October 60 English soldiers of the garrison escaped, driving away with them some of the cattle, and surrendered to the besiegers, many of them taking service under the Parliament.   The officers in the town realising that resistance was useless after this occurrence, attempted to make their escape by sea as Colonel Moore had done when Liverpool was captured by Prince Rupert.   But the remainder of the garrison, who were Irish troops, feared that they would be excepted from quarter; they therefore secured their officers, and opened the gates to the Parliamentarians on promise that their own lives should be spared.   Colonel Clifton and 20 other officers with many arms were captured; Clifton was taken to Manchester and afterwards died.   The capture of Liverpool was important enough to be made the occasion of a public thanksgiving on November 4th. [2]

Differences, however, again broke out among the Lancashire leaders, and it was difficult to find a Governor for Liverpool who would be generally acceptable. Meldrum himself was in favour of leaving the town in

1. "C. S. P.," 1644-5, p. 5.

2. "C. W. T.," p. 208; "Discourse," pp. 59, 60; "C. S. P.," 1644, p. 485. At Oswestry, where Meldrum was also engaged, there were taken prisoners Tyldesley and other Lancashire royalists, who had taken refuge there after being driven out of their own county.   For the royalist defeat in Cheshire, vide Verney MSS., "Hist. MSS. Com.," report 7, p. 445.   "C. J.," Vol. 3, pp. 686, 688. Parliament had intended to give no quarter to the Irish, but as it had been granted before their instructions had been received, the quarter was allowed.

the hands of Colonel Moore, of whose ability he had evidently formed a high opinion. Moore seems to have acted as Governor for a time, but in May, 1645, John Ashhurst, now Major, was appointed. There was at first some doubt about the continuance of the garrison. The Committee of Both Kingdoms were of opinion that the works had better be demolished on the ground of expense, though it would be necessary to keep a small vessel to guard the harbour. But the position of Liverpool as a port forbade its being left without a garrison, and a force of 300 foot and 1 troop of horse was ordered to remain there. In March, 1646, the House of Commons ordered that the Liverpool garrison should consist of 600 foot.[1]

The siege of Greenhalgh Castle was entrusted to Col. Dodding and Major Joseph Rigby, younger brother of the better known Colonel Rigby. It was garrisoned by a number of royalist refugees, the Governor being Mr. Anderton, probably Christopher Anderton of Lostock. The castle stood on a little hill about half a mile southeast of Garstang; it was very strongly built, and having only one entrance was difficult of approach. Probably only a few troops were told off for the siege, for the garrison could sally out to plunder the countryside, and for a time at least had the better of the Parliamentarians. The sandy nature of the soil made mining operations difficult, and on one occasion the garrison countermined and captured five barrels of powder. At length Anderton died, and the garrison surrendered on promise of their liberty. The Castle was demolished and all the timber sold; only a part of one tower now remains.[2] (June 10th, 1644).

1. Meldrum to the Committee of Both Kingdoms, Nov. 2, 1644: "The partialities and divisions among the gentlemen here are so great that I cannot but leave Liverpool in the hands of Colonel Moore." ("C. S. P.," 1644-5. Cf. also pp. 129, 168. "C. J.," Vol. 5, p. 101. "Carte MSS.," Vol. 12, fol. 107.)

Meldrum afterwards served in Yorkshire, where he lost Scarborough Castle in Feb., 1645. He died later in the year.—D. N. B.

2. Derby to Ormonde, April 5, 1645 ("Carte MSS.," Vol. 14, fol. 357;

During the autumn of 1644 negotiations were opened with the Earl to induce him to surrender. These were conducted by Sir John Meldrum, who employed as his agent Major Ashhurst, the only Parliamentarian officer at the first siege of Lathom House for whom the royalists had a good word to say. In October Meldrum wrote twice to Derby, and early in the following month William Farington and John Greenhalgh came into Lancashire under safe conduct to discuss terms. What exactly the propositions were is not stated, but Meldrum told the Committee of Both Kingdoms that he would only begin to treat on condition that Lathom and Greenhalgh were surrendered. In spite of this, however, he was of opinion from notes of a private interview which Ashhurst had with the Earl, that Derby would be "found inclinable to any course which may give the Parliament contentment." A fortnight later he writes more decidedly :

" I find the Earl inclinable to give all satisfaction to both Houses of Parliament, if he may have the least testimony under the hands of the Earls of Pembroke and Salisbury that upon demolishing the fortifications and removal of the garrisons of Lathom House and Greenhalgh Castle, he may expect to have fair and noble dealings." (Nov. 21st, 1644.)

Later still it seemed as if an agreement had nearly been reached. Meldrum writes :—

" I desire to know your pleasure whether the Earl after the full accomplishment of the Treaty may not begin his journey to London, and stay at St. Alban's till he shall receive an order from both Houses or from your Lordships to come to London." (Dec. 16th, 1644.)

"Discourse," p. 60). The date of surrender is given only in a tract entitled "Memorable Dayes and Works of God, etc., etc.," containing a list of the places given up during 1645; but in this tract the date of the surrender of Lathom House is stated to be Dec. 7, which is incorrect, E. 314 (6).

Greenhalgh Castle is often incorrectly identified with the village of that name, 3 miles north-west of Kirkham.

It is not quite clear what led to the breaking off the negotiations; but the Parliament would be almost sure to ask more than Derby was willing to yield, and the longer the strongholds in Lancashire held out the more severe might the Parliament terms be expected to become. Twelve months later they made a proposal which could only have been intended as an insult. He was required as the price of his reconciliation to give up Lord Digby, the Earls of Nithsdale and Carnwath, Sir Marmaduke Langdale, Sir William Huddleston, and other royalists who had found refuge in the Isle of Man when the King's cause in England was entirely lost, "otherwise your Lordship is not to expect from us any further invitation." As might have been supposed, Derby returned an indignant refusal.[1]

The defeat of Rupert at Marston Moor completely destroyed the King's chances of victory in the Civil War, but less than two months later his triumph over Essex at Lostwithiel, where all the Parliamentarian foot were obliged to surrender, gave his cause a new lease of life in the south of England. The winter was passed in fruitless negotiations; when they had broken down the New Model Ordinance was passed through Parliament,

1. For Meldrum's negotiations with Derby, *vide* his letters to the Committee of Both Kingdoms in "C. S. P." 1644–5, pp. 109, 137, 191. On March 15, 1647, the House of Lords sent a message to the Commons suggesting that the Earl of Derby should be admitted to compound. ("C. J.," Vol. 5, p. 498.) The suggestion to Derby that he should give up the royalists with him was made on Nov. 29, 1645. ("C. S. P.," 1645–7, pp. 242, 243.) But it is evident that this did not entirely close the negotiations, for the Earl petitioned to be allowed to compound on January 22, 1648–9, and drew up particulars of his estate, showing a yearly income of £4,324. 10s. 8d. ("Royalist Composition Papers." Vol. 2, pp. 122–5.) The lists and petitions occupy 120 pages of this volume; among them are several from merchants whose ships had been seized at sea by vessels from the Isle of Man. Derby claimed deductions amounting to £600 a year, and for a debt of £1,520, and his fine was eventually calculated as £15,572. 16s. 5d. How far the negotiations went, and exactly the reason for breaking them off, does not appear. Whitelock ("Memorials," 1732 edition, p. 432) says that Parliament ordered the proceedings with regard to the composition to be stopped because Derby continued to hold the Isle of Man; but this is not a very satisfactory explanation.

and in the spring of 1645 the toils began to close round the King who left Oxford and marched northwards with Rupert.

Thus once more Lancashire was brought into the general course of events. It was feared that Charles would try to break through to join the Earl of Montrose in Scotland; instead of advancing Leven retreated, notwithstanding remonstrances from Sir Thomas Fairfax. The Fairfaxes themselves were at York, and thus Lancashire was left completely undefended. The leaders were in great consternation. Already in the middle of March, 1645, it was feared that the King would march on Shropshire and Cheshire, and the Committee of Both Kingdoms wrote to Sir George Booth to be careful to guard Warrington.[1] Two months later the danger was acute; if the King could enter Lancashire he might indefinitely increase his forces. Charles penetrated into Cheshire in May, and obliged Sir William Brereton to raise the siege of Chester and draw his men into garrisons. Fairfax promised to send 1,500 men in order to hinder the King's advance, and the Lancashire leaders were urged to keep careful watch over all the passes into that county, and to have 200 horse and 1,000 foot ready to send to any rendezvous which Fairfax and Leven might appoint. Colonel Assheton's regiment was recalled in haste from Cheshire. The ford at Hale was guarded by 1,100 foot and 4 troops of horse, and the general rendezvous was appointed at Barlow Moor, near Manchester, on Thursday, May 19th. The Lancashire troops, however, attended in small numbers. They were greatly disorganised and the county much wasted by three years of war; and they complained of the place chosen for the rendezvous as being too near to plague-stricken Manchester. Lathom was still a thorn in the

1. Committee of Both Kingdoms to Sir George Booth, March 18. They refer to Warrington 'as being the principal pass into Lancashire.' (" C. S. P.," 1644–5, p. 354.)

side of the Parliamentarians of the county, and they were obliged to leave some troops at Ormskirk to continue the siege; there remained only one company of foot to defend both Liverpool and Warrington, and one of Egerton's regiments flatly refused his order to march. On May 22nd the Lancashire Committee wrote to London that they had obeyed the orders regarding the disposition of troops, "but it is more difficult to defend the country near Manchester, the river being shallow, and the Scots and Cromwell both marching further off than was expected." Next day Sir William Brereton wrote from Manchester, giving a very gloomy picture of affairs. "The forces assigned for the passes are inconsiderable, the passes many and indefensible." All the men he could spare were on the borders of Cheshire but they were quite inadequate to oppose the King if he should try to enter Lancashire. A few days before the Earl of Callander had sent a letter to the Scotch Commissioners in London to the same effect. "If we should abandon Yorkshire to go into Lancashire, this county would lie open to the King, and York will probably be lost; if we stay here the King is at liberty to enter Lancashire and increase his army, because of the many disaffected persons in that county. It is impossible to defend both places which is a line of 80 miles, at once, the ways and passages also between those counties being such as the forces in one county cannot without very great difficulty and marching a long way give assistance to the other." [1]

1. There are a large number of letters dealing with these movements in "Brereton MSS." (Additional MSS. 11331), ff. 136–163; and also in "C. S. P.," 1644–5, p. 482–545. The Lancashire Committee wrote to Brereton on May 19 for the return of Col. Assheton's regiment, and Brereton made the required order on the same day. The Committee complained about the place chosen for the rendezvous on the following day, but apparently their complaint was neglected; or perhaps it was too late, for the order of Fairfax, Leven and Brereton for the muster was issued on May 20. The Lancashire foot ordered to be present were Col. Assheton's and Col. Holland's regiments except Major Radcliffe's company; and of horse the troops of Col. Nicholas Shuttleworth, Capt. Butterworth, Col. Dodding, Major Robinson, and Capt. Hindley. Callender's letter is given in "Portland MSS.," Vol. 1, pp. 223, 224.

All this may have been exaggerated, but there is no doubt that Lancashire was in a state of great distress. Fortunately for the Parliamentarian party, however, the King's position was even worse than their own. Weak as they were, he was in no condition to force an entrance into hostile territory. The resistance offered may have been inadequate, but the appearance of force was enough to turn him in another direction. On May 21st he was at Whitchurch, 'not 24 miles from Hale Ford'; but he came no nearer to Lancashire than Market Drayton, but turned eastwards into the Midlands, and on May 31st took Leicester by storm.[1]

There were further fears of Charles in September when he was in Cheshire; but his defeat at Rowton Heath disposed of that danger. Even in October when he was at Welbeck, it was feared that his plan was to march northwards to relieve Skipton and Lathom, and to recruit his foot in Lancashire, "where Manchester will be as easily entered as attempted"; but the defeat of Langdale, near Pontefract, removed this danger too.[2]

Meanwhile the siege at Lathom House dragged on. During the winter of 1644 the garrison was practically unmolested, so that they were able to make little plundering expeditions, riding out after nightfall and returning to the house before daylight. Sometimes they even ventured further afield into the Fylde country. So great was the nuisance occasioned by their plundering and that of the royalists at Greenhalgh, that in December a local "cessation" was effected; but the Parliament promptly annulled it. At length the Committee at Manchester decided to re-form the siege, and Colonel

1. On May 25 Brereton wrote to Fairfax from Stockport that the King's army was at Uttoxeter, and was making for Newark. He had sent a troop of horse to follow. ("Brereton MSS.," fol. 155.)

2. Brereton to William Ashhurst, Oct. 18, 1645, "Brereton MSS." (Add. MSS., 11332), ff. 5, 16. The Committee of Both Kingdoms directed Col. Vermuyden to march towards Nottingham and Leicester in order to guard the country of the Eastern Association. ("C. S. P.," 1644-5, p. 528.)

Egerton was chosen for command. (January, 1644-5.) Troops were provided out of all the county, but no serious attempt was made to storm, the object being rather to starve out the garrison. In the House were a numerous garrison under Colonel Rawsthorne and Colonel Vere, who had with them Charnock, Key, Molyneux Radcliffe, Farington and other Captains who had taken part in the first siege. There seem to have been three divisions of the royalists, the main guard being in Lathom itself, and others at New Park; while the third division consisting of the Irish troops who had been at Liverpool during the previous summer occupied the Lodge.

The Parliamentarian engineer was Colonel Morgan, who had also taken part in the first siege. No trenches were made close to the house, but under his direction a deep ditch was drawn round the wall at some distance, and the attacking force lay on the outer side of that. There would only be fighting when the garrison sallied out for stores. The siege made very slow progress. On March 25, 1645, Egerton writes very despondently to the Speaker concerning the state of the siege and the discipline of his troops. It was now nearly three months since he had first advanced, and in spite of promises his force was so small that he dared not approach nearer than four or five miles from the House. Most of the troops had been got together by his own efforts. He had at first advanced to within two miles, but finding that he could not stop the garrison plundering, he had retired again and spread out his men, who only numbered 100 foot and 400 horse. Even these were constantly deserting, and trying to take their colours with them.[1] Some months before this Meldrum had written

1. Egerton to Lenthall ("Tanner MSS.," Vol. 60, fol. 5). He says that he cannot punish the offenders without the assistance of some of the M.P.'s of the county, most of whom had been called away. For the second siege of Lathom *vide* "Seacome," pp. 98–103; and "Discourse," pp. 61–63; "C. W. T.," pp. 209, 210. The information concerning this siege is much less detailed than in the case of the first.

that the Colonels of three regiments "told me plainly that if I should press the soldiers to an approach which would require them to lie in the trenches without shelter, where there was neither money nor victuals, they would all be gone do what we could to prevent it." [1]

By the middle of July, however, the Parliamentarian troops had made a considerable advance, for they carried the Lodge by storm, forty of the defenders being killed and sixty taken prisoners; and soon afterwards the garrison at New Park also surrendered, after which the royalists were confined to Lathom itself. In August, two of the Earl of Derby's servants named Sharples and Moreau, came over from the Isle of Man, and were captured in trying to get through the besiegers' lines. Sharples was sent into the House that he might explain the hopelessness of resistance, but in vain. The garrison refused to be convinced, and Sharples was allowed to return to the Earl of Derby. For three months more the royalists held out. But it was an unnecessary display of courage, and was bound to have disastrous results for Lathom House. This second siege was very different from the first. The glamour of Lady Derby's presence was gone. Instead of a numerous garrison well armed and provisioned, making successful sorties at intervals, and hopeful of release from without, there were only a few irreconcilables being gradually starved into submission. And they had nothing to gain by prolonging the war, for after the Battle of Naseby the royalist cause was dead.

After the defeat of Charles at Rowton Heath in September, 1645, he sent word to Lathom that there was no longer any prospect of relief from him, and the garrison had better therefore surrender. It would appear, however, that negotiations had already been

1. Meldrum to the Committee of Both Kingdoms, Nov. 17, 1644. ("C. S. P.," 1644–5, p. 129.)

entered into. Very favourable terms were at first offered. The House with all its contents were of course to be surrendered; but the garrison might freely depart, and Lady Derby and her children were to be allowed to live at Knowsley House with one-third of the Earl's estate for their support. Seacome states that these terms were freely offered by Egerton, and were only broken off by the obstinacy of one of the royalist Commissioners, who absolutely refused to agree unless the cannon were allowed to remain at Lathom for its defence. Actually, however, it would seem that the Committee of Both Kingdoms interfered, and forbade the conclusion of the negotiations. If suitable terms should be proposed, they professed to be willing to consider them.[1]

By the middle of November the shortage of provisions of the garrison had become so great that another parley was requested. A place was appointed, and the two sides again met; but even now they could not agree, the royalists refusing to accept any terms except those which they themselves proposed. The conference was broken off and they returned outwardly confident to Lathom; but their action was really just as much a piece of bluff as Rigby's last demand for surrender during the first siege in May, 1644. The tables were now turned, and it was Rigby's shrewdness which perceived how desperate the condition of the garrison was. When they were gone, Colonel Alexander Rigby said to the rest of the Colonels and Commanders then present that "he was persuaded that notwithstanding their seeming stoutness and highness of stomacke they could not hold

---

1. "Seacome," p. 100. Cf. however, a letter from the Committee of Both Kingdoms to the Lancashire Committee, Sept. 27, 1645. They consider the terms for surrendering Lathom very unreasonable, Lady Derby's coming to Knowsley and enjoying her lands, paying the ordinary assessments, and the Earl's not being required to come to London and submit to Parliament; and that Lathom should remain in possession of the Earl's servants. They will, however, consider any reasonable terms. ("C. S. P.," 1645–7, p. 162.) It seems that the local men were ready to make easier terms than Parliament would agree to.

out long, the smell and taste of their garments bewraied it." [1] Nevertheless the garrison did hold out for three weeks longer, and it was the beginning of December before the great House was at last starved into surrender. The final agreement was made between Colonel Booth on one side, and Colonel Nowell, Colonel Vere, and two others on behalf of the royalists. The terms were as follows:—The House with all its plate and furniture, and all the horses and arms of the garrison were to be delivered up to the Parliament; only the Governor might take his horse and pistols and £10 in money. Officers above the rank of Lieutenant were allowed their swords, but all below that rank and all the common soldiers were to depart unarmed. Convoy was to be provided for them to Aberconway, which was the nearest royalist garrison not besieged.[2]

There were said to be about 200 common soldiers still remaining in Lathom, but few of them took advantage of the opportunity to lay down their arms 'being old blades and mercenaries.' Some 15 guns and 400 smaller arms were captured, with some ammunition and stores of provision of several kinds. It was chiefly the deficiency of bread which had compelled the garrison to surrender. Lathom was finally given up to the Parliament at 3 p.m. on December 3rd, 1645, and the King had now no garrison left in Lancashire.

" This evening," says the "Perfect Diurnall" of December 6th, "after the House was up, they came letters to the Speaker of the Commons House of the surrender of Lathom House in Lancashire belonging to the Earl of Derby." All the newspapers for that week

---

1. " Discourse," p. 62.

2. Bradshaw, Hoghton and Booth to Sir William Brereton, Ormskirk, December 4, 1645, the House having been surrendered on the previous day. " Brereton MSS." (add. MSS. 11332), f. 122. The actual date of the surrender and the terms agreed upon are variously stated, but this letter appears to put the particulars beyond question.

are full of references to the event.[1] At Castle Rushen, when at length the news reached the Isle of Man, there was great distress. Lord Derby's " Book of Private Devotions" contains *A Meditation which I made when the Tidings were brought to me of the Delivering up Lathom House to the enemy,* which consist of a long series of texts chiefly from the book of Job and from Jeremiah.

" Oh that I were as in months past, as in the days when God preserved me." (Job 29, v. 2.)

" But now they that are younger than I have me in derision, whose fathers I would have disdained to set with the dogs of my flock." (Job 30, v. 1.)

" Oh how sits the city solitary which was full of people? How is she become a widow? She that was great among the nations, and princess among the provinces, how is she become tributary." [2] (Lam. 1, v. 1.)

It is impossible not to fully share his grief for the destruction of this magnificent fortress, "a little town in itself." "It was the glory of the county," wrote one who fought against the Earl in the civil war. This great House, whose Lords had enjoyed almost royal power for centuries was now a ruin. Splendid in loyalty, supreme among the nobility of the North of England, generous to their tenantry, the Lords of Lathom had a great record of honour and service. This was now at an end. The demolition of their House was complete. Everything moveable and saleable was stripped off and sold, the walls were cast down into the ditch; and it was

1. The above quetation is given in "C. W. T.," p. 211; but other papers contain more particulars. *Vide* "Kingdom's Weekly Intelligencer," Dec. 2-9; "Scottish Dove," Dec. 3-10; and "Moderate Intelligencer," Dec. 4-11. The first of these contains the statement of the deficiency of bread being the final cause of surrender, adding also, "Those in the House had for about six weeks past drunk nothing but water." The details of capture of arms and ammunition are variously given.

2. "Stanley Papers" (ed. Raines, C. S. 70), pt. 3, Vol. 3, pp. 31-34.

never rebuilt.[1] And with old Lathom House departed
much of the glory of the House of Stanley. Before the
end of the civil war the Earl of Derby was beheaded at
Bolton, and his descendants never recovered the state
which had been his. In the following century the direct
male line of his House died out, and the title passed to
another branch.

This ended the fighting in Lancashire for the present;
but the King's standard still floated over a few isolated
towns and fortresses, and one of these was Chester,
which had long been invested by Sir William Brereton,
but still held out. The Cheshire Committee appealed
to the neighbouring county for assistance in the autumn
of 1645, but there was little help to spare from Lancashire then. In October, however, when there was a
prospect of a royalist attempt to raise the siege of
Chester, 200 horse and all the forces of Lonsdale
Hundred were sent to Brereton's help. But he still
appealed for more men (Oct. 27), and on November 7th
more troops of horse were despatched under Major
Clarkson and Major Robinson. Five hundred men had
recently gone out of Lancashire to assist in the blockade
of Skipton Castle, and the siege of Lathom House was
still a heavy drain on the resources of the county. When
Lathom fell, the troops there were set free for other
service, but so wearied and insubordinate were they that
they would not move without a fortnight's pay, and pay
Brereton had none to give. Protests were of no use.
At length Colonel George Booth was sent to Bolton to
negotiate with the Lancashire Committee and succeeded
in persuading their troops to march by promising them

1. Apparently there was some delay about the destruction of the
House. On December 10, 1645, the Committee of Both Kingdoms
passed a resolution to write to the Lancashire Committee asking for
their opinion as to what was to be done with Lathom House, "whether
to be kept or dismantled." On January 5, 1645–6, the request was
repeated; but what answer was returned is not recorded. ("C. S. P.,"
1645–7, p. 297.)

'the same pay as other auxiliaries.' On December 11th the Lancashire Committee issued an order for all the available men to march, the horse under Colonel Nicholas Shuttleworth, Colonel John Booth and Colonel Assheton to command their own regiments of foot; and companies of foot not in either of these regiments might choose in which they would serve. The commanders at Chester, however, had still to endure some delay. Colonel Assheton had only just returned from London, and his regiment was very late in starting. Shuttleworth, with nine troops of horse, reached Tarporley about December 21st, and the others followed soon after.[1] The Lancashire horse were kept before Chester to strengthen the siege, and the foot, together with the Cheshire foot, were sent out to Whitchurch to intercept a possible royalist advance. When the royalists retreated all were brought back to the siege. Loud complaints were made by the Cheshire Committee of the insubordination of the Lancashire troops, but as they were paid more than any of the other auxiliaries they were probably more valuable. Brereton, however, continued to send appeals for help into Lancashire until nearly the middle of January, but on February 3rd, 1645-6, Chester was finally surrendered. The Lancashire troops returned home and were mostly disbanded; there were now no soldiers in arms in the county excepting the garrison at Liverpool.[2]

1. "Brereton MSS." (Add. MSS. 11332), ff. 23, 33, 36, 110 (Add. MSS. 11333), ff. 5, 8, 11, 14, 17, 44). Much was made by the Cheshire Committee of the prospects of royalist relief for Chester. Booth (who was a nephew of Sir William Brereton) was afraid lest he had promised too much; but it took great persuasion to accomplish even so much, and he expressed the hope that the agreement was 'restrained and loose enough.' Assheton was in London on December 2.

2. "Brereton MSS." (Add. MSS. 11333), ff. 69, 92, 97, 100, 107. Brereton urged that the Lancashire troops should not be deprived of their share of the plunder from Lathom, because they had left the county. "It should not be expected that they should remain upon duty here, if those that remain at home and disobey orders should be better paid and rewarded than those that obey orders and perform their duty cheerfully." On January 7 he wrote that Chester was still confident of immediate relief from the royalists.

There was now some years' quiet in Lancashire, and the stricken county was able to recover slowly from its devastation and misery. The general course of affairs was briefly as follows. After Sir Thomas Fairfax had beaten Goring at Langport in July and Rupert had surrendered Bristol in September, the royalist resistance was practically at an end though Raglan Castle held out until August, 1646. The King surrendered to the Scots at Southwell in May, 1646, and was sent to Newcastle; and there then began the long series of negotiations in which Charles showed all the duplicity and untrustworthiness and lack of judgment which was the worst side of his nature. First the joint offer of the Scots and Parliament was refused because the King would not abandon episcopacy; when the Scots went home in January, 1646-7, he continued to play off the Independents against the Presbyterians. Circumstances favoured him to an extraordinary degree, but it was only a waste of time because he never really desired to come to any agreement, but continued to believe that he could regain his position by refusing all the terms which were offered. Then followed the open breach between Parliament and the army, the carrying off of the King from Holmby House, and the extremely moderate demands made by the Army in the Heads of the Proposals. These provided by far the best solution of the difficulty if only both sides could have accepted and kept them. In all this Lancashire had no part. The leaders were interested, particularly in Ecclesiastical affairs, but the people in general cared less about the negotiations than about the recovery of their own position. There can never be war, and especially civil war, without much misery; and though the Civil War in England was on the whole conducted with moderation, it inevitably brought in its train, want, loss of trade, and the dislocation of ordinary modes of life. The proportion of the population who actually fought in the war was very small, but in counties where fighting was carried on there can have been few if any of the inhabitants who were not indirectly affected by it. The graphic account of Adam Martindale of the disaster which it brought upon his family may be quoted.

" Things were now woefully altered from the worst from what I had formerly known them. My sister was married to a noted royalist, and going to live about two miles from Lathom which the Parliament forces accounted their enemy's headquarters, they were sadly plundered by those forces passing along the road wherein they dwelt. The great trade that my father and two of my brothers had long driven was quite dead; for who would either build or repair a house when he could not sleep a night in it with quiet and safety? My brother Henry, who was then about 24 years of age, knew not where to hide his head; for my Lord of Derby's officers had taken up a custom of summoning such as he and many older persons upon pain of death to appear at general musters, and thence to force them away with such weapons as they had if they were but pitchforks to Bolton, the rear being brought up with troopers that had commission to shoot such as lagged behind; so as the poor countrymen seemed to be in a dilemma of death either by the troopers if they went not on, or by the great and small shot out of the town if they did." [1]

This is probably not an isolated but a typical case. If the families of the gentry were divided among themselves, so also would be those of the yeomen and the villagers. Royalists in Parliamentarian country, and Parliamentarians in the royalist districts, would have an unhappy time. The royalists in Manchester would no doubt be liable to plunder. The estates of Parliament-

1. "Life of Adam Martindale" (C. S., No. 4), p. 31.

arian partisans which lay in the west of the county, as that of the Ashhursts' near Lathom, and of Rigby near Preston, were fair game for the royalists, and became quite worthless to their owners. In addition to local burdens there came, as the war proceeded, pressure from headquarters. The royalists' estates were sequestered, and for the Parliamentarians the Assessments became a growing burden. As a local means of raising resources the most obvious was the levying of contributions on estates, and this was the means first resorted to. The Order authorising it in Lancashire was made by the House of Lords on January 26th, 1642-3. Twelve of the leaders were named assessors, any three of whom had power to assess the inhabitants of the county at a sum not greater than that of one-twentieth of their estate; resistance might be met by the sale of the objector's goods, and if necessary by the use of force.[1] In the following August an Order was for the first time passed for raising money for the payment of the army by a weekly assessment on the whole country. The list is composed of 52 counties and towns in England and 12 in Wales, Lancashire being assessed at £500 weekly, Yorkshire at £1,060/10/- (York £62/10/- in addition), and Cheshire at £175 (Chester £62 in addition). The weekly sums were to be paid for two months "unless the King's army shall be disbanded in the meantime."[2]

In February, 1644-5, an Ordinance was passed for the maintenance of the Scotch army at £21,000 per month for four months, to begin on March 1st. This time Lancashire was assessed at £730 and Cheshire at £255; on August 15th the Ordinance was continued for four months dating from the 1st July. The reason for this assessment of the money was that the Sequestra-

1. "L. J.," Vol. 5, p. 573.

2. "L. J.," Vol. 6, p. 165. On Sept. 6 the Lancashire Committee were ordered to appoint a Treasurer, and elected Humphrey Chetham.

tions, on which it had originally been charged, were quite unable to bear their share. [1]

By the time that the fighting in Lancashire was over the financial exhaustion of the county was extreme. "That country (England) is in a most pitiful condition, no corner of it free from the evils of a cruel war. The case is like the old miseries of the Guelphs and Ghibellines. Every shire, every city, many families divided in this quarrel, much blood and universal spoil made by both armies where they prevail," wrote Baillie.[2] And in the same strain a letter of Egerton's to the Speaker may be quoted :—

> " Sequestrations which are looked upon to bring great things are well known to us to be of no considerable respect, for the sequestered estate which was heretofore worth £600 per annum is now scarce sufficient to discharge those lays and taxations which are imposed upon it according as those estates are managed. So that from them we expect very little. The whole country is extremely exhausted, and they have been plundered of horse and cattle by both sides; and land is so cheap by the great quantity of sequestered land untilled and unstocked that the well affected from whom we receive our greatest relief can make very little of their estates." [3]

The Lancashire Committee protested bitterly against the new assessments in 1645. They declared that they could not possibly bear any more levies, and complained that after their stand for the Parliament's cause and all the help which they had sent into other counties, it was unreasonable to impose a fresh tax upon them. If they even attempted to raise it all the troops would disband; and instead of paying, they urgently demanded a large

1. This order was passed by the House of Lords on February 20, 1644-5. ("L. J.," Vol. 7, pp. 224, 341.)
2. "Baillie's Letters," Vol. 2, p. 57.
3. "Tanner MSS.," Vol. 60, fol. 5.

contribution from Parliament which they hope would not be long delayed. "'This (however strange reports have been or may be made of our condition by such as know little of it) is nothing but real truth."[1] Parliament did have some consideration for Lancashire, for on September 11th, 1644, the House of Commons ordered that on the following day which was a Fast, half the collections in the churches of London and Westminster should be devoted to the relief of that county.[2]

As the commercial centre of the county, and the base of the Parliamentarian operations, Manchester naturally suffered severely. After the siege in 1642, Parliament ordered a fund to be opened for its benefit, any one who would make subscriptions to have public faith for repayment at the then usual rate of interest of 8 per cent. (October 24th). In addition to its other miseries, the town was in the summer of 1645 visited by plague, which was very severe, and reached its height in August and September of that year. In July 172 persons were buried at the Parish Church, in August 310, and in September 266; the numbers in ordinary months ranging from 6 to 30. Moreover in August and September there were no christenings, and in September no marriages "by reason of the sickness being so great." All those who could left Manchester, and the Committee of Both Kingdoms became concerned for the safety of their headquarters in Lancashire. The outworks had been defended chiefly by volunteer soldiers from the country adjacent, and now no one would go near the town for fear of infection. The country people declared that "they would rather be hanged at their own doors than enter such an infected town." As Manchester had been the place of meeting of the Lancashire Committee there

1. Letters from the Lancashire Committee to Lenthall ("Tanner MSS.," Vol. 58, fol. 469; Vol. 60, fol. 111.)
2. "C. J.," Vol. 3, p. 625.

had never been any Governor there, and as the Committee had now removed elsewhere there was no one left to direct affairs. The Committee of Both Kingdoms wrote to the Deputy-Lieutenants to ask their opinion about appointing a Governor, and also whether they thought it desirable to keep a garrison in Manchester any longer, and if so "by what means a constant maintenance may be had for them in regard of the decay of trade, and the impoverished condition of the town and parts adjacent." It was suggested that the works might be reduced and so kept with fewer men. Under the circumstances it was feared that the store of arms and ammunition in Manchester might be in considerable danger. The town was once more indebted to the engineer Colonel Rosworm, who had refused to leave his post when so many of the richer people had departed, even though Warden Heyrick had tried to persuade him to withdraw with the others. Though only in command of 12 musketeers, the other soldiers having removed some distance from the town, he was able to frustrate a plot made to seize all the valuables in Manchester.[1]

With the approach of winter, however, the plague slackened, and the inhabitants began to return to their homes. On December 9th Parliament directed that a collection should be made on the following Sunday, December 11th, in all the churches and chapels in London and Westminster for the relief of Manchester, "one of the first towns in England that in this great cause stood for their just defence against the opposition and attempts of a very powerful army, and hath for a long time been so sore visited with the pestilence that for many months

---

1. The figures of mortality are given by Rev. Richard Parkinson, editor of the "Life of Adam Martindale" (note, pp. 53, 54), from extracts from the Church registers. The statement of the attitude of the country people is Brereton's. "Brer. MSS." (11331), f. 168. The Committee of Both Kingdoms wrote to the Deputy-Lieutenants, Committee and Commanders in Lancashire on July 24, 1645. ("C. S. P.," 1645-7, pp. 28, 29.) For Rosworm's account, *vide* "Good Service" ("C. W. T.," p. 231). As usual, he rates his own services very high.

none were permitted either to go in or to come out of the said town, whereby most of the inhabitants (living upon trade) are not only ruined in their estates, but many families like to perish for want, who cannot be sufficiently relieved by that miserably wasted country." In the following May, Heyrick, preaching before the House of Commons on a Fast Day, referred to Manchester as "the only town untouched by the enemy, the only town stricken by God." [1]

In 1646 Presbyterianism was set up by the Parliament. A petition had been presented to Parliament on August 31st of that year by more than 12,500 "of the well affected gentlemen, ministers, freeholders, and others of the County Palatine of Lancaster," in favour of Presbyterianism, "against sectaries, heretics and schismatics." The petition was urged for the reason that the petitioners, who numbered 12,578 in all, were those who had won the county of Lancaster for the Parliament; more than 6,000 of the signatures came from Salford and Blackburn Hundreds, which out of the six Hundreds of the county had been mainly active in the Parliament's cause. Many of them were among those who had also signed the Petition to the King at York in 1642 to return to Parliament, "which evidenceth that the petitioners attend a golden mediocrity." No malignants had been allowed to sign, and the names of some who were in favour of the Covenant were removed because they rested under a suspicion of royalism.[2]

Parliament promised to take the Petition into consideration, and the Ordinance for division of Lancashire into nine classical Presbyteries was brought before the House of Commons on September 15th, 1646, though it was not finally sanctioned until December. As is well known, Lancashire furnished the most completely

1. Both the above are quoted in "C. W. T.," p. 213.
2. "A True Copie of the Petition of 12,500 Gentlemen, Ministers, etc. . . . of Lancashire," E. 352 (3).

organised system of Presbyterian government in the whole country; and the system continued in force until the Restoration.

A year or two after the surrender of Lathom House, however, things had returned to a more normal condition in Lancashire. "Some malignant enough were fled where they could get to be safe. Others that had been abroad were come home again and glad to live quietly though in a meaner condition. So that the county was in a reasonable quiet posture for a long space corn and all things plenty and cheap." [1] But a new storm now appeared on the horizon.

1. "Discourse," p. 63.

CHAPTER IX.

The Second Civil War. The Scots in Lancashire ; Battle of Preston.

THE Second Civil War was fought under a strange re-arrangement of the old parties in the struggle, the all-supreme Army having aroused against it a variety of otherwise conflicting interests. Presbyterians and Anglicans, Royalists and the Scots, all had their share, and there were outbreaks of one kind or another in half a dozen counties. That part of the war which concerns us here is the Scotch Invasion which passed through Lancashire, and was defeated within the borders of this county. "Though this was not any of the Lancashire wars yet was it acted in this county and God's goodness therein is to be kept in remembrance." The campaign of Preston was not a part of the Lancashire Civil War in that the causes which led up to it concerned the general history of the country; but local troops were engaged both on the side of the Parliament, and among the English royalists who joined the Duke of Hamilton. And the royalists were probably disappointed that Lancashire did not rise much more decidedly in their favour.

When Charles I. had refused all the propositions of the Army he turned once more to the Scots, and accepted from them the terms which he had previously refused, making with them the Engagement by which he bound himself to establish Presbyterianism for three years. When the Duke of Hamilton, the leader of the party of the nobility, secured a majority in the Scotch Parliament he procured a vote to the effect that the agreement between the two Kingdoms had been broken, and urged an invasion of England to assist the King to carry out the Engagement by force of arms. Though his army was very much less numerous than he expected, he made preparations to cross the border, hoping to be joined in England by large numbers of the old royalist party, and by a detachment of Scots from Ulster under Sir George Munro.[1] In preparation for his coming, Langdale surprised Berwick, and Sir Philip Musgrave occupied Carlisle. When the news of this reached Lancashire the leaders there were in considerable difficulty. They were Presbyterians of the Scotch type, and were therefore averse to fighting against Hamilton; they were by no means in accord with the direction of affairs in London and feared the consequences of openly joining either party. Yet they could not remain neutral. Their dilemma is illustrated in a Declaration made by the officers and soldiers in the county on the 9th May, 1648, which was directed to the Ministers of the county. They expressed their adherence to the Solemn League and Covenant, and declared that they stood "for the fundamental government of the Kingdom by King Lords and Commons, according to the laws of the land, and the declarations of this present Parliament before our first engagement; that we love desire and should much rejoice in the regal and regular Government of His Majesty that now is." It is evident that the Revolution had already gone too far for the Presbyterians in Lancashire. A private letter written at the same time as this Declaration, and printed with it, further expresses the same difficulty, "our soldiery apprehend themselves in great straits; for if the Army come down, and they join with them to suppress the Cavaliers, they fear and are very jealous that the Army will afterwards fall upon them and suppress them." It was evidently thought that unless Parliament got the better of the Army, there was little prospect of a peaceful settlement. "For should the Presbyterian party and the Sectaries joyn to suppresse the common enemy, it is very much to be feared that they would afterwards

1. "Political History of England," Vol. 7, p. 339.

clash one with another; for when those that adhere to the Covenant are put into a posture of defence, they will never lay down arms to become tame slaves to the Sectaries, who for all their specious pretences and flattering proposals, have not hitherto really acted one thing whereby our distractions may be removed, and truth and peace, which is the desire of all good men, may be perfectly accomplished." It is sufficiently apparent that though they were unwilling to join a foreign invader, and especially one who was assisted by the old royalist party which they themselves had helped to overthrow, the Lancashire Presbyterians were very apprehensive of what would happen if the Army should gain still more power than it already possessed. This Declaration was not signed by any of the Lancashire Members of Parliament, but among the 17 names attached to it were those of Nicholas and Ughtred Shuttleworth, Richard Radcliffe and John Ashhurst.[1]

The inhabitants of Lancashire were dismayed by the prospect of another war, and many persons fled from their homes; though some returned again when it became apparent that the invasion was not so imminent as at first appeared. Eventually the leaders made up their minds to assist the Parliament. Colonel Rigby, who was not a very fervent Presbyterian, but who was decidedly a man of action, was the first to move. On May 5th he had called a meeting of the Deputy-Lieutenants, but only Holland, Bradshaw, Birch and himself and his son attended. However, they decided to call a general meeting of the Committee and Deputy-Lieutenants for the following Monday at Bolton, and sent out warnings of musters throughout all the county. Five hundred of Rigby's old soldiers, both horse and foot, assembled without orders, and he encouraged them to remain in arms. Owing to the Orders of Parliament for disbanding, and against the free quarter of troops,

1. "C. W. T.," pp. 248–251.

the officers were uncertain as to how far their action was permissible, and Rigby wrote to the Speaker for further instructions.[1] By the end of the month, however, both Rigby and Dodding had their men still in the field, and the newspapers reported that "the common soldiers of Lancashire are exceeding forward to fight the enemy." On May 17th the House of Commons desired Colonel Assheton to go down to Lancashire and take control of the recruiting, and when once the raising of troops was begun it was pushed on without delay.[2] By the middle of June the Lancashire troops consisted of four regiments of foot and two of horse. Colonel Assheton was appointed Commander-in-chief, with Rigby, who commanded one regiment of horse, as his Lieutenant-Colonel; the other regiment of horse was under Colonel Nicholas Shuttleworth. The Colonel of the foot regiments were Dodding, Standish (who commanded his own and Rigby's foot), Assheton and Ughtred Shuttleworth. The total number seems to have been 1,500 foot and 10 troops of horse, so that the regiments of horse were not quite full, and the foot regiments only at half strength. On July 20th the Committee of Both Houses wrote to Assheton praising his forwardness in raising men, and ordering him into Westmoreland to join with Colonel Lambert, who had been sent forward to intercept Hamilton's advance.[3]

Delayed by a difficulty of transport, and by bad weather, the Scotch army had moved very slowly. Although they had occupied Carlisle in April it was nearly three months afterwards before their general advance really began. The Lancashire troops who had

---

1. Rigby to the Speaker, May 6, 1648 ("Tanner MSS.," Cary, Vol. 1, pp. 407–410). May 5 was a Friday, and the following Monday was therefore May 8. Rigby says that May 6 had been appointed for a general royalist rising in Lancashire.
2. "Letters from Scotland, etc.," No. 11. "C. J.," Vol. 5, p. 563.
3. "Letters from Scotland, etc.," No. 13. "C. S. P.," 1648–9, p. 237. At the same time the Deputy-Lieutenants were directed to carefully guard the passes out of Lancashire into that county.

been raised in May and June encamped about Lancaster on June 15th, and the following day crossed the border of the county and advanced to Kirkby Lonsdale. A few days later they reached Kendal, having heard that a party of 200 royalists were in that neighbourhood. Colonel Rigby advanced with three troops of horse, and the royalists retreating before him he occupied Kendal. On the same day Colonel Assheton sent out a party of foot to occupy Bentham House in Westmoreland. The first summons was refused, but afterwards the garrison, which only consisted of 30 or 40 men, surrendered and were allowed to march away to join Langdale; two barrels of powder and 10 muskets were, however, taken by Assheton; the House itself was made untenable.

In the first few days of July, the Lancashire troops having joined Colonel Lambert near Carlisle, had a skirmish with the enemy at Stanwix Bank, and encamped at Brunstock; but they were largely outnumbered by the invaders, and Lambert was forced to fall back in order to wait for the army with which Cromwell was marching with all speed to his assistance. On July 5th they were at Penrith again, and on the 14th at Appleby.[1] It was uncertain whether Hamilton would march straight forward to Lancashire or would turn south-eastwards through Wensleydale in order to relieve Pontefract Castle. Lambert thought the latter course was more

1. "Letters from Scotland, etc.," No. 15. Diary of Captain Samuel Birch, from May 15, 1648, to March 29, 1649 in "Portland MSS.," Vol. 3, p. 173. Birch raised his troop at Manchester on May 15, and gives a detailed itinerary of his March through Wigan, Lancaster and Kirkby Lonsdale, to the general rendezvous at Halton. He afterwards accompanied Lambert into Yorkshire, reaching Ripon on August 3, and Knaresborough on the 7th. His dates agree with those given by Cromwell for the subsequent movements; he was quartered on August 14 at Carleton, near Skipton, and on the following night at Downham. At the battle of Preston "I had charge of our Lancashire brigade's folorn; my lieutenant had charge of my division of musquettiers; my ensign by command of General Assheton lead the pykes and collours up against the defenders on Ribble Bridge and beat them off. Allmost all my officers markt, none killed, divers souldiers shott and hurt, some very dangerously, most performed very well. Blessed be God for his great deliverance." Birch then remained in Preston in charge of the prisoners and magazine.

probable and retreated that way; but Hamilton, who had
on July 31st seized Appleby Castle and on August 2nd
Kendal, decided to push on through Lancashire. By
August 9th he was at Hornby, where he remained for
some days. On August 10th he directed a letter to the
Ministers of Lancashire who, on his approach, had
withdrawn from the northern parts of the county and
assembled at Lancaster. He declared that the object of
his coming was "for settling Presbyterian government
according to the Covenant, liberating and re-establishing
his Majesty, and for other ends conducing to the good
and peace of the Kingdom," and he denied that any
harm was intended to the Ministers or their families.
But they refused to be conciliated, or to believe his
promises of safety and freedom, " knowing our old
Enemies of Religion and the Kingdom's peace are with
your Excellency."[1]   They preferred to believe that the
English Parliament were more to be trusted for the
establishment of Presbyterian government. Hamilton's
assurances of protection were the less to be depended
upon because his army plundered most unmercifully
while on the march. The Scots had no regard for either
party in the north of England, and provided themselves
from the goods of both roundheads and cavaliers alike.
They are said to have cleared the whole district of sheep
and cattle, and even Sir Thomas Tyldesley was unable
to protect the royalists from his oppression.[2]

About the middle of August Hamilton marched slowly
southward, his army covering many miles of country.
The Earl of Callander, his Lieutenant-General in command of the cavalry, was far in advance of the main body

1. " C. W. T.," pp. 252, 253. Probably all the Lancashire ministers
were by no means of the same mind. In Feb., 1648-9, one Thomas
Smith preached two sermons in Lancaster Church and was imprisoned
for the views he expressed. Smith thought " We should have no peace
till the Scotts came to suppress that army of Sectaries, and being
asked what he intended to do if they came he replyed that he would
joyne with them." " Clarke Papers," ed. Prof. C. H. Firth, Camden
Soc. (N. S., 49, 54), Vol. 2, p. 188.
2. " The last Newes from the Prince of Wales, etc." " C. W. T.,"
pp. 254, 255.

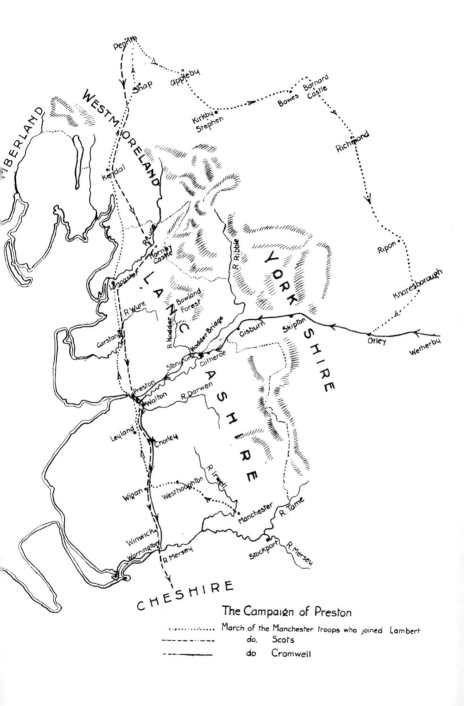

Penrith
Shap
Appleby
Kirkby Stephen
Bowes
Barnard Castle
Richmond
Ripon
Knaresborough
CUMBERLAND
WESTMORELAND
Kendal
R. Lune
Hornby Castle
R. Ribble
YORKSHIRE
Lancaster
Bowland Forest
Gisburn
Skipton
Otley
Wetherby
Carstang
R. Wyre
R. Hodder
Hodder Bridge
Stonyhurst
Clitheroe
L A N C A S H I R E
Preston
Walton
R. Darwen
Leyland
Chorley
R. Irwell
Wigan
Westhoughton
Manchester
R. Tame
Winwick
Warrington
R. Mersey
Stockport
R. Mersey
CHESHIRE

The Campaign of Preston

.... March of the Manchester troops who joined Lambert
– – – – – –   do.   Scots
– — – — –   do   Cromwell

of the Scottish infantry under Hamilton himself, while
Monro with the Ulster Scots was far in the rear. Langdale with the English royalists marched on the west of
the main body. By this time Cromwell was hotly in
pursuit, and as usual his rate of march was very different
from the leisurely progress of the Scots. He had reached
Leicester when Hamilton was at Kendal, and Nottingham on August 5th. Advancing northwards he waited
for three days at Doncaster for his ammunition to come
from Hull; and on August 13th he was joined near
Wetherby by Lambert, who had quartered there with
5,000 men to cover the siege of Pontefract. Next day the
combined armies marched to Otley, sending on their
guns to Knaresborough in order to march more swiftly.
Advancing along the Ribble Valley, Cromwell reached
Skipton on August 14th, and on the 15th quartered his
men round Gisburn; next day they advanced to the
Bridge over the Ribble, at Clitheroe.[1] Here a council
of war was held to decide whether to cross the bridge,
there being no other between that place and Preston,
and so march along the north bank of the Ribble, or
to turn south-westwards through Whalley in order to
intercept Hamilton's march further on. Cromwell,
however, was determined to fight as soon as possible,
though he had less than 9,000 men to 24,000 of the
Scots; and believing that Hamilton would make a stand
at Preston his army crossed the Ribble and marched
swiftly along the northern bank. The 10,000 men with
whom Hamilton had entered England had been increased
by reinforcement; Langdale's detachment numbered
about 4,000 and Munro's not quite 3,000 men. But
their superiority in numbers was entirely discounted by
the disordered condition of their line of march, which

1. "Lieutenant-General Cromwell's Letter, &c." "C.W.T." p. 259. Cromwell's
narrative is here not quite correct. He states that the council of war was held at "Hodder
Bridge over Ribble." But Hodder Bridge is not over the Ribble, but over the Hodder,
near Mitton. The old bridge which Cromwell used still stands. Obviously, however, the
council of war was held before crossing the Ribble. The army must first have crossed the
bridge at Clitheroe, and afterwards Hodder Bridge over the Hodder in order to reach
Stonyhurst. It would appear that Cromwell when writing his narrative, forgot that there
were two bridges, and wrote Hodder Bridge instead of Clitheroe Bridge.

stretched from Wigan to Kirkby Lonsdale, a distance of nearly 50 miles. Moreover they were evidently quite ignorant of Cromwell's approach until the very day before he burst upon them.[1]

On the night of August 16th Cromwell had quartered his army in Stonyhurst Park, nine miles from Preston, the General staying at the Hall. Next day he sent forward an advance party of 200 horse and 400 foot under Major Smithson and Major Pownall, who encountered Langdale's royalists who were some miles to the north-east of Preston about Ribbleton and Fulwood. The main body of the Scotch foot were then marching through Preston, and the undecided Hamilton was persuaded to countermand his order for them to return; they therefore hurried on their retreat, leaving Langdale to his fate. "It was reported that when word came to the Duke that General Cromwell was in the rear of Sir Marmaduke Langdale's army fighting and killing them, his answer was—'let them alone—the English dogs are but killing one another.' So little care had he of them."[2] Langdale was thus left with his 4,000 men to resist the whole attack of Cromwell's army; and his men fought with the utmost bravery for four hours against overwhelming numbers. The royalist position was very well chosen at the end of a deep lane leading towards the town, his men being sheltered behind hedges. Two regiments of cavalry, Cromwell's and Harrison's, were set to charge along the lane supported

1. The authorities for the campaign of Preston are : "Lieutenant-General Cromwell's Letter concerning the Total Routing of the Scots Army, etc." ("C. W. T.," p. 255); "Lt.-General Cromwell's Letter to the Honourable William Lenthall, etc." ("C. W. T.," p. 258); "An Impartiall Relation of the late Fight at Preston " . . . . . by Sir Marmaduke Langdale ("C. W. T.," p. 267); "Discourse," pp. 64–67; and "Autobiography of Captain John Hodgson" (1882 edition), pp. 28–35. The first of Cromwell's letters was written to the Committee at Manchester. The second was largely reprinted in the "Perfect Diurnall," No. 265, August 21, 28; *vide* also Whitelock's "Memorials" (1732 ed.), pp. 331, 332. There is a map of the campaign in Gardiner's "Great Civil War," Vol. 3, p. 431.

2. "Discourse," p. 65.

on either flank by infantry, by the regiments of Colonel
Read, Colonel Dean and Colonel Pride on the right,
and Colonel Bright's and Fairfax's regiments on the
left. Assheton and the Lancashire foot were in reserve,
and there was a reserve of horse at each point. The
royalists fought desperately and the ground was very
heavy owing to the recent rains. "Such a wet time
this time of the year hath not been seen in the memory
of man," wrote one of the Lancashire Captains who took
part in this campaign. The Parliamentarian foot on
the right wing outflanked the enemy, but there was a
very severe struggle in the lane and on Cromwell's left
wing. The Lancashire men came into action here. At
length, after four hours fighting, the royalists broke and
fled towards Preston, pursued by Cromwell's horse.
Four troops of his own regiment entered the town first,
and being seconded by Colonel Harrison, they charged
along the streets and cleared the town of the royalists.
Colonel Assheton's regiment was specially praised by
Cromwell for its bravery in the action, and the Committee of Both Houses directed a special letter of thanks
to him.[1]

Most of Hamilton's foot were by this time marched
across Ribble Bridge, three-quarters of a mile south of
Preston; this they barricaded, and another fierce engagement took place between them and Fairfax's and Assheton's foot regiments, whom Cromwell sent forward in
pursuit. After severe hand-to-hand fighting the Scots
were dislodged from Ribble Bridge and chased across
the bridge over the river Darwen, and up the hill to
Walton, when night put an end to the engagement.
The Parliamentarians guarded both the bridges, and

1. "C. S. P.," 1648–9, p. 265. Cromwell wrote to the Manchester
Committee : "In this service your countrymen have not the least
share." He also especially mentioned Assheton's regiment in the letter
to Lenthall ("C. W. T.," pp. 257, 261). Cf. "Hodgson," p. 33 : "The
Lancashire foot were as stout men as were in the world, and as brave
firemen. I have often told them they were as good fighters and as
great plunderers as ever went to a field."

Cromwell himself returned to Preston for the night. He places Hamilton's losses at 1,000 killed and 4,000 prisoners; and 4,000 or 5,000 arms had been captured.

There is no reason to suppose that Cromwell had any decided plan of campaign, but he had been very fortunate in taking the Scotch army on the flank, and his bold attack had been completely successful. The invaders' forces was now completely cut in two; moreover the English royalists who had been defeated and almost annihilated were probably Hamilton's best troops, and Monro's men, who were also veterans, were now too far north to be engaged. The cavalry which should have returned to his assistance had also taken no part in the action; and Hamilton's foot were largely newly raised men, the old soldiers of the Covenanting army having refused to follow him. Thus though he still largely outnumbered the Parliamentarian army his forces were more disorganised than ever, and his men were dispirited. Cromwell lost no time in following up his victory. The same night (Aug. 17th) he sent off a letter to the Committee at Manchester describing his victory and directing them to oppose Hamilton's further advance; while next morning he himself hastened after the Scots, leaving the Lancashire troops in Preston to guard the prisoners. During the night Hamilton had marched three miles on the road to Wigan. Colonel Thornhaugh was sent in advance with three regiments of horse in order to bring them to bay, while his foot followed as fast as possible. Thornhaugh came up with the Scots at Chorley, and he himself was killed in the engagement. Hamilton had still 7,000 or 8,000 foot and 4,000 horse to the 3,000 foot and 2,500 horse with which Cromwell was pursuing him; but the Scots attempted to make no stand, except so much as was necessary to protect their retreat. On Standish Moor, near Wigan, they drew up as if for resistance, but on the advance of the Parliamentarians, they retreated into the town. The pursuers were too weary to go further after their forced marches and two days' hard fighting. The weather was still against them, "having marched 12 miles of ground as I never rode in all my life, the day being very wet," writes Cromwell of this day's pursuit. That night the Parliamentarians encamped in the open country close to the Scots; but during the night there was skirmishing at intervals, and about 100 of Hamilton's men were taken prisoners, including some officers of note.

After the capture of Preston some of the royalist horse who had escaped rode northwards toward Lancaster. Cromwell sent a regiment of horse in pursuit, which followed the flight for some 10 miles, killing some and taking 500 prisoners. There was therefore no longer any danger to be feared from this part of the army. The remaining fugitives scattered into the Fylde district and dispersed.

On Saturday, August 19th, the Scots continued their retreat southwards toward Warrington, still hotly pursued by Cromwell. The most determined stand they made was at Winwick, three miles from Warrington, in a narrow lane on the road from Newton. Here for some hours they beat off all the attacks of the pursuers, until some country people showed the Parliamentarians a way round through the fields, and the Scots then retreated towards Warrington. They stood at bay for some little time on the green on the south side of Winwick Church; but at length their resistance was broken, 1,000 being killed and the remainder driven into the church and made prisoners.[1] The remnant of the army reached Warrington, and marching through the town attempted to hold the bridge over the Mersey. But the Scots were now thoroughly beaten. They were almost without ammunition, and many of them had

1. "Discourse," p. 66, and note, p. 145. Mr. Beamont is especially an authority on the neighbourhood of Warrington. The site of this skirmish at Winwick may still be seen.

thrown away their muskets in the pursuit; Baillie, who was in command, sent to Cromwell for terms of surrender. Considering the difficulty of crossing the Mersey elsewhere, and the strength of the bridge, Cromwell agreed to give quarter if they would surrender as prisoners of war. About 4,000 of the Scots capitulated at Warrington, their whole losses during the three days fighting being 2,000 killed and between 8,000 and 9,000 being taken prisoners.

After the first engagement at Preston Sir Thomas Tyldesley, who was still in command of some horse, laid siege to Lancaster, and was on the point of taking it when news of further defeats arrived. Thereupon he joined Monro, and attempted to persuade him to advance and attack Cromwell's rear, as they had still an equal number of troops. The proposal was an illustration of Tyldesley's bravery, but it was too rash for Monro to accept, and if carried out would probably have effected little.

Weariness alone prevented the victors from completing the ruin of the Scots in Lancashire. Cromwell's men were too exhausted to follow up the main body of the cavalry under Hamilton himself, which had crossed the Mersey into Cheshire. "If I had 1,000 horse that could trot 30 miles," Cromwell wrote on August 20th, "I should not doubt but to give a very good account of them; but truly we are so harassed and hagled out in this business, that we are not able to do more than walk an easy pace after them." As it was Cromwell himself did not follow the Scots into Cheshire, but left Colonel Lambert to continue the pursuit, and wrote to Lord Grey, Sir Henry Cholmondeley, and Sir Edward Rhodes to intercept Hamilton. Indeed the Scotch army might now almost be left to melt away of itself. They marched to Malpas and from there to Drayton, and then to Stone and Uttoxeter, where the Parliamentarian forces fell upon their rear and captured many prisoners, including

Lieutenant-General Middleton. But Hamilton himself was too ill to continue his flight any further and surrendered with most of his men. A remnant of the force under the Earl of Callander and Sir Marmaduke Langdale endeavoured to escape northwards to return to Scotland, and reached Ashbourne in Derbyshire; but here Callander's men mutinied, and Langdale, escaping with three other officers was discovered, though they had tried to pass themselves off as Parliamentarians. They were all seized and lodged in Nottingham Castle. The Duke of Hamilton was executed in March, 1649.

On August 23rd, 1648, letters were read in the House of Commons from Cromwell, giving an account of the fighting in Lancashire. The total number of prisoners was stated to be 10,000, including many of the Scottish nobility; 3,000 of the invading army had been killed, and much ammunition, together with 150 colours, had been taken.[1] September 7th was appointed as a public thanksgiving day, and Warden Heyrick was named as one of the preachers before the House of Commons. Cromwell returned at once to Lancashire, where he stayed one night at Stonyhurst; and then summoning all his troops which had been left in Lancashire to follow him, he marched after Monro into Scotland, where he remained for some months, returning to London in December. There was, however, still a little to be done in the way of reducing the royalists still in arms in the north of England, and this was entrusted to Assheton. But they were so disorganised that little or no fighting was necessary. Assheton and his Lancashire troops dislodged them from Cockermouth, whence they marched to Carlisle, but they were refused admittance to the

1. "C. J.," Vol. 5, pp. 680, 685. On September 25 the Committee at Derby House was asked to grant a Commission to Assheton as Major-General in Lancashire, and for him to have 40 shillings per diem as pay in addition to his pay as Colonel of horse and Colonel of foot. The Lancashire Committee were also to be asked to recommend to the House of Commons some way of paying the arrears due to the soldiers. "C. J.," Vol. 6, p. 32.

town, and scattered in various directions; the main body
of cavalry, about 1,000 in number, retreated to Appleby.
Here Assheton followed them, and as the royalists had
no spirit for further fighting terms were soon agreed
upon.   The inferior officers and common soldiers were
to lay down their arms and have liberty on promising
to observe all the Ordinances of Parliament; the
Colonels were given six months in which to leave the
country.   Appleby Castle was surrendered on Oct. 9th
together with 1,000 arms and 5 pieces of ordnance.
Most of the 1,200 horses of the royalists were bought at
low rates by the Parliamentarians before the actual
surrender.   The chief officers were Sir Philip Musgrave, Sir Thomas Tyldesley, Sir Robert Strickland,
Sir William Huddleston; the whole list included 15
Colonels, 9 Lieutenant-Colonels, and 65 inferior officers.[1]

So once more the fighting in Lancashire was over,
and the stricken country had again a few years more in
which to recover from its distress.   Its condition was
now even more pitiable than before.   Trade was
destroyed, life disorganised, and everyone suffered
indirectly if not directly from the Scotch Invasion. The
care of the wounded soldiers scattered up and down the
county was an added burden.   Parliament had ordered
that voluntary offerings made in all the churches and
chapels of England and Wales on the Thanksgiving
day, September 7th, should be devoted to the relief of
Lancashire, one half to the care of the wounded soldiers,
and one half for the relief of the general distress.   The
London treasurer of this fund was Henry Ashhurst,
brother of William Ashhurst, M.P. for Newton, and of
Major John Ashhurst.   But the sum subscribed was not
very large.   Probably people's intentions were generous
enough, but they had little to give.   In the following
May a pitiful appeal was issued by the Major and

1. "A Great Victory at Appleby, by Col.-General Ashton, etc."
"C. W.T.," pp. 273-276. Whitelock's "Memorials" (1732 edition),
p. 390.

Bailiffs of Wigan, and four well known Lancashire Ministers, describing "the lamentable condition of the county of Lancashire and particularly of the towns of Wigan, Ashton and the parts adjacent." These two towns were perhaps worse off than the average, having been visited by pestilence; but the description given would apply in a less degree to the whole county. "In this county," the appeal runs, "hath the plague of pestilence been ranging these three years and upwards occasioned chiefly by the wars. There is a very great scarcity and dearth of all provisions, especially of all sorts of grain, particularly that kind by which that country is sustained, which is full six-fold the price that of late it hath been. All trade, by which they have been much supported, is utterly decayed; it would melt any good heart to see the numerous swarms of begging poore and the many families that pine away at home, not having faces to beg. Very many now craving almes at other men's dores, who were used to give others almes at their dores—to see paleness, nay death appear in the cheeks of the poor, and often to hear of some found dead in their houses, or highways, for want of bread."[1]

During the next few years, great events were being enacted in London, but in these Lancashire had no part. The county was full of unrest, which found its outlet in disturbances and riots. Two years later the Council of State was much concerned with disturbances which broke out at Preston, Ormskirk, Manchester, and Rochdale, in resistance to the imposition of the Excise. Large numbers of people were put in prison; and three troops of horse under Major Mayer were commissioned to remain in Lancashire until further orders to assist Colonel Birch and the Sheriffs to preserve the peace of the county. The Act for bidding the proclamation of a King was duly published in Lancashire from Feb. 5-10,

1. "C. J.," Vol. 5, p. 680. "C. W. T.," p. 277.

1649, but it evidently provoked no enthusiasm in the
county, for the remnants of the royalist party began to
carry themselves with much more boldness than formerly.
In July, a party of them well armed and mounted, even
dared to proclaim Charles II. as King at Manchester
Cross. They then rode to Wigan and to Kendal with
the same object; and it was only after some days that
meeting with a troop of Parliamentarian soldiers they
were dispersed.[1]

The same spirit of unrest was shown in the difficulties
encountered in enforcing the Ordinance for Disbanding
the militia. Four thousand of Colonel Assheton's troops,
being zealous for the Covenant, at first refused to
disband. On February 10th the House of Commons
ordered that Assheton's and Shuttleworth's troops were
to be disbanded by Major-General Lambert, who was
authorised to use force if necessary; but some months
at least elapsed before the order could be carried into
effect. It was not altogether zeal for the Covenant but
also the fact that their pay was largely in arrear, that
caused the opposition among the Lancashire soldiers.
The matter was considered important enough to receive
the attention of Cromwell himself, and on February 27,
1648-9, the Council of State requested him to urge on
the House of Commons the necessity of providing a
further sum of money for disbanding the Lancashire
forces. On March 4th, accordingly, the Committee at
Goldsmith's Hall were ordered to pay the sum of
£1,444/14/10 which had been voted for this purpose.
A month later practically all the soldiers were dispersed
except one or two free companies, who gathered all the

1. Sir Gilbert Ireland, Sheriff of Lancashire in 1649, wrote to the
Speaker giving a full list of the times and places at which the Act
forbidding the Proclamation of a King was published in the county
("Tanner MSS.," Vol. 57, fol. 522).
    "C. S. P.," 1650, pp. 40, 44, 50, 75, 78. Complaint is made of
'pulpit incendaries' who "have endeavoured for the setting up of an
interest of their own, destructive of that of the people, to stir up the
people to disobedience, and again to embroil us in new troubles, and
enflame the nation into another war."

disorderly spirits in the county and lived by plunder. One of these under Captain Bamber was ordered to be disbanded by force by Major General Assheton, their horses and arms being restored to those from whom they had been stolen. They gave out that they were appointed for service in Ireland, but they had no commission. Bamber seems to have preyed upon the county for two months longer before he was actually subdued by Colonel Duckenfield.[1]

This was probably the last service which the Parliament ever asked Assheton to undertake. He and the other leaders who had subdued the county seven years before were now entirely out of sympathy with the existing government of the country. When the militia was further re-organised in 1650, the matter was taken out of their hands altogether. Assheton, Shuttleworth, Rigby, Colonel Richard Standish, and Sir Richard Hoghton, were formally dismissed from employment in connection with the Militia; and the commissions which were granted in the following summer to Lancashire officers, were nearly all given to new men. Joseph Rigby became Lieutenant-Colonel, and there one or two names which had previously appeared in the records of the war; but for the most part those previously best known are absent. Colonel Thomas Birch seems to have been the only one of the former leaders who still enjoyed the confidence of the Parliament, and he was for the next few years largely entrusted with the direction of affairs in Lancashire. [2]

1. Whitelock's "Memorials" (1732 edition), p. 390; also quoted in "C. W. T.," p. 277. "C. S. P.," 1649–1650, pp. 70, 98, 139, 163.

2. "C. S. P.," 1650, p. 34. For the reorganisation of the Militia, ibid., pp. 308, 509, a list of the Commissions being given.

CHAPTER X.

The Last Stand. Battle of Wigan Lane. Trial and Death of the Earl of Derby.

DURING the last five years the Earl of Derby had been in the Isle of Man. Since the failure of the former overtures made to him by the Parliament through the agency of Sir John Meldrum, he had been living in retirement at Castle Rushen. It was the life which he liked best, and had it not been for the recollections of the events of the preceding years, he might have been happy in the leisure afforded for the exercise of the literary tastes in which he delighted. He composed, during this period, his Commonplace Books and several Books of Devotions which manifest his deeply religious nature. But confinement and reflection only deepened the natural melancholy of his nature, and increased his hatred for the enemies who had deprived him of his position and his estates. In 1644 Meldrum had found him willing to listen to reason; proposals made a few years later were rejected with contempt. In 1649 Derby was summoned to surrender the Isle of Man, being offered the enjoyment of half his estate if he would do so. He had apparently petitioned to compound in the ordinary way and particulars of his estate were furnished by himself, upon which his fine was estimated at £15,572; but when matters had gone so far the Earl changed his mind, and he refused to "forfeit his allegiance and sell his loyalty for £15,000."[1] Apparently there would have been opposition on the other side.

1. *Vide* note on p. 41. "A Declaration of the Earl of Derby, etc." E. 566 (5). "A Message sent from the Earl of Derby, Governor of the Isle of Man, to his dread Sovereign Charles II., 1649." E. 566 (21).

Representations were made to the Council of State about the resentment with which the prospect of admitting the Earl of Derby to his composition had been received in some parts of Lancashire and Cheshire. It was urged that if he should complete his surrender and be free to enter Lancashire again the peace of the county would be in danger; and the Council of State ordered that the matter should not be proceeded with until the pleasure of Parliament was known.[1] Evidently therefore there were insuperable obstacles on both sides. The last proposals had apparently been made through General Ireton, and in reply to these the Earl of Derby wrote his famous letter of defiance. " I scorn your proffers, disdain your favour, and abhor your treason; and am so far from delivering up this Island to your advantage, that I will keep it to the utmost of my power to your destruction. Take this for your final answer, and forbear any further solicitations; for if you trouble me with any more messages on this occasion, I will burn the paper, and hang the bearer; this is the immutable resolution, and shall be the undoubted practice of him who accounts it his chiefest glory to be his Majesty's most Loyal and Obedient Servant Derby."

It has been suggested with some force that the display of anger in this letter is so unusual in the Earl of Derby, that probably the Countess was chiefly responsible for it;[2] but in any case after this all possible chance of reconciliation between him and the Parliament was at an

1. "C. S. P.," 1649–1650, p. 278. It would seem that this was the real reason for the final breaking off of the negotiations.
2. "A Declaration of the Earl of Derby, etc." E. 566 (5). The letter has been frequently reprinted. Cf. Marlet, "Charlotte de la Tremoille," p. 186 : " Signé Derby; mais faut-il dire : écrit par lord Derby ? On est en droit de croire que sa femme eut une parte prépondérante à la redaction de ses phrases hachées, vibrantes, pareilles aux coups de canon, qui, sur les vaisseaux, saluent au lever du jour, le pavillon national, montant fièrement dans les airs : car elles sont en parfaite conformité avec ses mâles repliques aux assiegeants de Lathom-house : elles n'ont, au contraire, aucun trait de resemblance avec le style flasque et ampoulé des lettres ou des discours du comte."

end. And it must be admitted that the Earl himself from his uncompromising attitude, was largely responsible for the merciless hostility with which he was pursued to the scaffold. In a further list of those to be exempted from Parliament, containing about 30 names, the name of the Earl of Derby comes third, following those of Prince Rupert and Prince Maurice.

The Isle of Man had been put into a position of defence, and plundering expeditions were organised by the few ships which the Earl had under his command. Since the royalist defeat he had been cut off from all communication with England, but maintained intercourse with the Earl of Ormonde in Ireland. Derby addressed many letters to Ormonde urging him to send some guns and ammunition to his help, but without success; eventually Ormonde did despatch some powder, but it was lost at sea.[1] There is no doubt, however, that the piracy of the royalists' vessels was a great nuisance to the shipping in the Irish Sea. In November, 1649, the Admiralty Committee were urged to send a frigate for service upon the coast of Lancashire and North Wales in order to protect the shipping in those parts; but it does not seem to have had very much effect, for the trouble continued during the following year.[2] At length the Parliament adopted a more effective but very dishonourable means of retaliation. In May, 1650, Colonel Birch was ordered to seize the daughters of the Earl of Derby, who were at Knowsley, and any other of the Earl's relatives whom they could secure; and then to send over to Derby to release by a certain date all the Parliamentarian prisoners whom he had, otherwise he must expect retaliation.[3] Lady Katherine and Lady Amelia Stanley were kept in prison for some months;

1. "Carte MSS.," Vol. 9, fol. 55, 195; Vol. 11, pp. 326, 495; Vol. 12, fol. 127; Vol. 14, fol. 12, 249, 291; Vol. 23, fol. 105. There is also a letter referring to this matter in the "Ormonde MSS.," Hist. MSS. Com., new series, Vol. 1, p. 99.
2. "C. S. P.," 1649–50, p. 381; 1650, p. 290, etc.
3. "C. S. P.," 1650, pp. 169, 282, 470.

on October 8th, 1650, they were ordered to be set free on bail, but the order was afterwards deferred pending the development of events in the Isle of Man.

There was perhaps some fear in the court of Charles II. now at the Hague, that the Earl of Derby might yield to the proposals made to him by Parliament for surrender. At any rate in January, 1650, he was made a Knight of the Garter, an honour which he had expected in the previous reign. Of the four Knights elected at this time the Duke of Hamilton, Marquis of Newcastle, the Marquis of Montrose, and the Earl of Derby, only Newcastle lived to be installed. The letter of appointment to the Earl of Derby makes special reference to his defence of the Isle of Man; and in the following June Sir Marmaduke Langdale and Sir Lewis Dives were despatched to the Island to urge the importance of preserving it. There had been plans made in the Spring of 1650 for a royalist rising in England, and the Earl of Derby had been named as General in Lancashire; and when Charles II. had a prospect of regaining power, his advisers realised that the Earl of Derby could give substantial assistance in any attempt on the North of England.[1]

It was in June, 1650, that Charles landed at Speymouth in Scotland, took the Covenant, and six months later was crowned King. To anticipate the inevitable invasion of England Cromwell crossed the border and signally defeated Leslie at Dunbar (Sept. 3rd, 1650). After his victory all the South of Scotland submitted to the English. The following summer Cromwell again took the field; Lambert turned the Scots' position by a flank march through Fife, and Leslie, realising that Scotland was lost, staked all on the desperate venture of

1. "Ashmolean MSS.," 1110, ff. 164, 165; 1112, ff. 43, 45. The particulars are from the Garter Records of Sir Edward Walker; but, curiously enough, the date in one of the volumes is given incorrectly as January, 1651. The fact that the patent was directed from Castle Elizabeth in Jersey, however, is proof of the correctness of the earlier date.

an invasion of England. Perhaps it did not seem so desperate as it was. They were convinced, as the Jacobites were convinced half a century later, that the country would rise in force out of affection for the House of Stewart; and there was certainly more reason for the expectation in 1651 than in 1715. For the majority of Englishmen after all favoured monarchy, and the prospect of a military despotism alarmed most people. The tyranny of Charles I. was being forgotten, and his tragic death had to a large extent effaced the memory of his incompetence and duplicity. But still more powerful than this feeling was the desire for peace and quietness. The country would probably have accepted Charles II. in 1651 as in 1660, if it could have done so peaceably. Perhaps a majority of the nation, certainly a majority of the inhabitants of Lancashire would have already preferred the restoration of the King to the rule of Cromwell but they were not so anxious for his restoration that they would support it by force of arms. And the old Parliamentarian leaders in Lancashire, estranged as they were from Cromwell, had no more sympathy with their old royalist enemies who now emerged from their retirement in the Isle of Man to welcome Charles' march.[1]

Early in the year the King had opened a correspondence with the Earl of Derby through the medium of Sir John Birkenhead, and had received loyal letters from the Earl in return. It was not to be expected that Charles' submission to the Scots and his taking of the Covenant would be in accord with Derby's views, but it made no difference to the latter's loyalty. When the danger from Scotland seemed imminent the Parliament had made fresh efforts to secure the Isle of Man by force. Derby defeated an attempt of five Parliamentarian ships on the Calf of Man on March 29th, 1651, and shortly afterwards repulsed a second invasion of the Island.

1. It must, however, be remembered that few of the original Parliamentarian leaders in Lancashire were now left. Assheton had died in February of this year, and Moore and Rigby in 1650.

There was some other design of the royalists in England during the Spring of this year for which several people were imprisoned; and by Cromwell's order there were seized at Greenock a party of royalists who were on their way to the Isle of Man to concert measures with the Earl of Derby.[1]

The Scots began their march into England in June, 1651, and entered Lancashire early in August. They had about 16,000 men, 'I daresay near double the number of those that the King of Sweden entered Germany with if not more," wrote one of the officers. Charles was proclaimed King at Penrith on August 7th, and afterwards at all the market towns through which he passed. On Saturday, August 9th, the army was at Kendal; two days later they entered Lancaster, and on the following day Charles was proclaimed at the Cross, and all the prisoners in the Castle were released.[2] That night the King slept at Ashton Hall, near Lancaster, and on the 13th at Myerscough Lodge, Sir Thomas Tyldesley's house. Next day they passed through Preston, and leaving there the same day, Charles stayed on August 14 at Sir William Gerrard's house at Bryn Hall, six miles from Warrington. The conduct of the royal army was very different from that of the Scotch Invasion of 1648. No plundering was allowed, and violence was strictly forbidden. No one was forced to join the army, and Charles marched swiftly, staying only a night or two at each place so as not to be too great a burden on the country. Yet in spite of this no great enthusiasm was allowed. Few recruits joined the royal standard, and there were a number of desertions. At Preston Charles rode on horseback through all the streets of the town; but even here he was disappointed by the coolness of his reception. There were already misgivings among his followers. "We have quit Scotland," wrote Hamilton

1. Gardiner, "Commonwealth and Protectorate," Vol. 2, p. 12.
2. Cary's "Memorials," Vol. 2, pp. 299, 306.

on August 8th, "being scarce able to maintain it; and yet we grasp all; nothing but all will satisfy us or to lose all. I confess I cannot tell you whether our hopes or fears are greatest; but we have one stout argument, despair; for we must now either stoutly fight it or die. All the rogues have left us; I shall not say whether for fear or disloyalty; but all now with His Majesty are such as will not dispute his commands."[1]

The Council of State had not been idle in view of the projected Scotch invasion. On April 19th they had issued instructions to Major-General Harrison to go down to Lancashire with three troops of horse, of his own regiment, and on his arrival to replace Colonel Rich, who was to return to headquarters with the three troops under his command. Harrison remained in Lancashire to keep order. When the Scots approached nearer, Colonels Duckenfield, Birch, and Mackworth were commissioned to raise ten new companies of foot of 100 men each out of the late militia forces in the counties of Lancashire, Cheshire and Salop. Liverpool was to be especially guarded, and Duckenfield, who was Governor of Chester, addressed an appeal to the Council of State for the replacement of forty barrels of powder and a quantity of arms which he had previously furnished out of the magazine under his charge for use of the troops in Ireland.[2] The Council of State were evidently quite satisfied with the preparations which were being made in these three counties for resistance. Meanwhile Cromwell had sent Major-General Lambert with a detachment of cavalry to follow the Scots, and he hung on their rear all along the line of march without being strong enough to engage them. On their way through Lancashire, however, Lambert slipped round them and effected a junction with Harrison somewhere south of the Ribble

1. Cary's "Memorials," Vol. 2, p. 305. "Discourse," p. 70. The latter has high praise for the moderate conduct of the royal troops.
2. "C. S. P.," 1651, pp. 97, 156, 302. "Rawlinson MSS.," a. 184, ff. 390, 392.

(Wed., Aug. 13th). Their combined forces, together with the newly raised local troops, amounted in all to 12,000 horse, foot and dragoons; but they were still unwilling to engage the Scots before they had been joined by Cromwell. When Lambert and Harrison met Charles was still north of Preston, and still retreating before him they passed through Bolton on Thursday, August 14th.[1] On reaching Warrington, however, Lambert decided to oppose the Scots' advance. Sending out a few troops to skirmish with their advance guard, he occupied Warrington Bridge by a detachment of foot, whose retreat was secured by cavalry. The skirmishing party encountered the royalists two miles north of Warrington, and were soon dispersed; the royalist scouts entered the town about noon, and being followed by the rest of the army, at once attacked the bridge. The Cheshire foot who were posted there, held their ground for an hour and a half; as 2,000 of the Scots pressed upon them their position was for a time somewhat perilous; but at length, breaking down as much of the bridge as they could, they regained the main body of the army in safety. The Scots following, engaged the Parliamentarian rearguard, consisting of Major-General Lambert's, General Whalley's and Colonel Twistleton's regiments, but they were beaten off; and Lambert withdrew in safety to Knutsford, a more favourable place for cavalry operations, expecting Charles to follow him; but the King continued his march through Cheshire in a more direct line.[2]

The Parliamentarians had really the better of the skirmish, but it was magnified by the royalists into a great victory for themselves. Charles issued from Higher Whitley on the same evening, a statement of his affairs in which he declared that he might have crossed the Mersey by several fords, but attacked the

1. "C. S. P.," 1651, p. 322.
2. "C. W. T.," p. 290. "Discourse," p. 71.

bridge directly in order to give his troops confidence.[1]
The fact that it was thought necessary to magnify so
greatly this small success, showed how much the royalists
lacked confidence. Even Clarendon admits that the
extent of the achievement was to force Lambert to retire
somewhat faster than he had intended; and it was
thought that the disorder of his retreat was partly feigned
in order to draw the royalists on. And even in the army
there was misgiving in spite of the apparent success.
The King perceiving David Leslie's gloomy expression,
rallied him upon it, and asked him what he thought of
the troops now. Leslie replied that however well the
army looked it would not fight.[2]

This was on August 16th. It seems to have been the
day before this that the Earl of Derby landed his men
from seven ships on Preesall Sands, on the eastern side
of the estuary of the River Wyre. He had been delayed
by contrary winds from sailing out of Douglas Harbour
for some days. After all the announcements of his
coming, which had been talked about in Lancashire for
months beforehand, the country was surprised to find
that he had with him only some 300 foot and 60 horse,
not very well armed. On account of the delay Derby
had arrived too late to meet Charles in Lancashire, but
at once hastening after the main army he had an interview with his royal master between Northwich and
Nantwich on August 17th. On the previous day a
warrant had been made out to Derby as Captain-General
of all the royal forces in Lancashire, authorising him to
raise troops by summoning all men "of what quality and
condition soever from sixteen to sixty years of age."
He was instructed not to make "any distinction of
persons with reference to former differences." On
Derby's arrival at the royal camp he was directed to

1. "A Brief Statement of His Majesty's Affairs, etc." ("Tanner
MSS.," Vol. 54, fol. 155, 156.)

2. "Clarendon" (Macray), Vol. 5, p. 180 (book 13, par. 62).

return to Lancashire in order to put the warrant into force.[1] According to Clarendon this was a mistake, for Derby's following consisted for the most part of officers and gentlemen, whose presence in the main army would have given it a strength which it very much needed. The Earl thereupon returned to Lancashire, and on August 20th met at Warrington a deputation of the Presbyterian ministers of the county, Major-General Massey also being present. Massey was regarded as a martyr for the Presbyterian cause, and had been especially commissioned by the King to remain behind; he was also personally known to many of the Lancashire Presbyterians. It would almost appear that it had been originally intended to hold this meeting in Manchester, and that the place was afterwards altered on account of the approach of some hostile troops. Massey wrote from Cadishead on August 19th that his journey to Manchester had been interrupted, and he had therefore been unable to meet the gentlemen as expected, but he had sent for them to have an interview with Ashhurst and himself the same evening; and he urged Derby to send a detachment of horse to Manchester. A large number of the local Presbyterians, however, met Derby and Massey at Warrington the following day (Aug. 20); but the conference was of no service to the royalist party. The estrangement between the local leaders and the

---

1. "C. W. T.," p. 297. The "Discourse," p. 71, says : "Besides men of quality, some 300 Manck soldiers." In the previous month Derby had declared himself ready to join the King with 500 men well armed. Cary's "Memorials," Vol. 2, p. 288. "Seacome," p. 111, says that the Earl of Derby landed with "300 gallant gentlemen." For the warrant to Derby *vide* "Tanner MSS.," Vol. 54, fol. 170. It was directed "To our Right Trusty and Right Well-beloved Cosen the Earl of Derby, our Captain Generall in our County Palatine of Lancaster," and states that owing to his rapid march the King had been unable to send particular summonses to Lancashire; he was now pursuing the enemy, who had been dislodged from Warrington Bridge. Gardiner, "Commonwealth and Protectorate," Vol. 2, p. 37, gives the date of Derby's meeting with Charles as August 17.

ruling powers was complete; "they are the men who are
grown here more bitter and envious against you than
others of the old Cavaliers stamp," wrote Robert Lilburne to the Speaker : and Manchester itself was "very
malignant." But the Presbyterians would not go so
far as to make an alliance with their old enemies. The
Earl of Derby before his coming over had been promised
substantial help by them; but when it came to the point,
the Presbyterian ministers, who really ruled the councils
of their party, would give no help except on their own
terms. There was indeed no bond between these two
ill-assorted allies but hatred of the Sects, and that was
not sufficient to bridge over the gulf which otherwise
divided them. The ministers began with a demand that
Derby should put away all the papists whom he had
brought with him from the Isle of Man, and himself take
the Covenant. The Earl replied that on those terms he
might long ago have been restored to all his estates, and
the late King to his throne; and urged that this was not
a time to argue but that everyone who was desirous for
the restoration of Charles II. should fight for him. He
added that he would refuse none who came to him with
that purpose. The Presbyterians, however, refused to
make the slightest concession, and after Derby and
Massey had both argued in vain for some time, the
meeting broke up without having arrived at any decision.
The Earl made one last appeal for support; if this was
refused "I cannot hope to effect much, I may perhaps
have men enough at my command, but all the arms are
in your possession without which I shall only lead naked
men to slaughter; however I am determined to do what
I can with the handful of Gentlemen now with me for
His Majesty's service, and if I perish I perish; but if
my master suffer, the blood of another Prince and all
the ensuing miseries of this nation will lie at your
doors." This appeal, however, was equally unavailing;
and Derby had to abandon all prospect of aid from the

Presbyterians, and depend on the royalists.   Massey
thereupon hastened after the King.[1]

On landing from the Isle of Man on August 15th, the
royalists had marched that night to Weeton, near
Kirkham, and next day over the Ribble to Lathom,
proceeding the same evening to Upholland.   It would
have been a sad sight for the Earl to have visited the
ruins of his formerly splendid home, but he was probably
not with the march that day, having hurried on after the
King.   The main body had, however, reached Warrington before he returned there, and on his arrival a Council
of War was held on the day before the abortive meeting
with the Presbyterians.   There were present the Earl of
Derby, Lord Widdrington, Sir Thomas Tyldesley, Sir
William Throgmorton, Sir Francis Gamul, Sir Theo-
philus Gilbey, Sir Edward Savage, and Colonels Vere,
Standish, James Anderton, Hugh Anderton, Robinson
and Legge.   It was resolved to raise out of Lancashire
altogether 1,300 horse and 6,000 foot.   The Hundreds
of Leyland and West Derby were to provide 500 horse
and 2,000 foot, Amounderness and Lonsdale Hundred
the same number, and the proportion of the others was
to be assessed on Derby's further advance.   Rates of
pay were fixed.   The Earl had previously issued Commissions to officers to serve under him; they were particularly directed that there was to be no plunder.   Derby
issued an appeal to the Gentlemen of Lancashire, urging
his royal warrant, and for a few days the prospect seemed

1. "Clarendon" (Macray), Vol. 5, p. 177, (book 13, par. 58).
Massey's letter of August 19 is printed in "Cary," Vol. 2, p. 324.   He
says that his advance has been checked by a regiment of Lilburne's
horse quartered near Middleton; but this cannot have been Lilburne's
own regiment, which only left Stockport on the 22nd.   Some prisoners
were made by Massey.   "Seacome," pp. 112, 113, is the authority for
the meeting at Warrington, but his statements are accepted by Mr.
Gardiner.   Seacome's account that Massey strongly seconded Derby's
appeals is, however, not compatible with a sentence of Mr. Gardiner's:
"Too late Charles discovered that a letter carried by Massey from the
Scotch ministers attending the army contained a warning against a too
close conjunction with malignants."   "Commonwealth," Vol. 2, p. 38.
It must be supposed that Seacome overrated Massey's part in the
meeting.

bright.[1] "He thought himself master of Lancashire (as indeed he was)" wrote Lilburne. There were at present no troops near to the county, and no one dared rise against the royalists in Lancashire. But Derby might well be disappointed at the response with which his appeals were met; for not one-fifth of the numbers estimated were raised, and probably never would have been raised even if there had been more time. It might reasonably have been expected that in this county where royalism was so strong, many more troops could have been raised. It was not Derby's fault; no one could have done so much as he, but partly the difficulty already referred to of Presbyterians and royalists acting together was responsible, and above all the general wearisomeness of the war.

And even in the royalist Fylde the Earl's enemies were already active. Some of the Commissioners of the Militia collected a few soldiers, and surprised the crews of Derby's ships at Preesall, took them prisoners and seized the ships. The prisoners were taken first to Preston, and then on an alarm of the royalists' march thither, to York, narrowly escaping a rescue party under Tyldesley. The chief of them, Captain Cotterell, who had done much service for the royalists at sea, was tried and executed.[2] Moreover, Colonel Robert Lilburne had been ordered to Lancashire with his regiment, and was now marching in hot haste. From Warrington the Earl of Derby moved northwards to Preston, and remained there for some days. He issued warrants for raising troops in the Fylde, and arranged for musters at Singleton and at Kirkham on August 25th; but these musters were never held. Lilburne, having made a forced march from Cheshire, reached Wigan on August 21st,

1. "Portland MSS.," Vol. 1, p. 614. Several warrants issued by Derby are given, and orders against plundering; companies on the march, however, were to have free quarter. The Earl's appeal to the Gentlemen of Lancashire is printed in " Cary," Vol. 2, p. 333.
2. "Discourse," pp. 72, 73.

thinking to have surprised the royalists; but they had retreated to Chorley. Next day (Friday, August 22nd) he advanced to Preston, and in the night sent 40 horse to make a surprise attack. Colonel Vere was wounded in the skirmish and apparently took no part in the further fighting. The royalists had now increased their numbers to about 600 horse and 900 foot, and held a rendezvous at Preston on Saturday, August 23rd.

Lilburne was not anxious to force on an engagement, as he had no infantry with him, and his men were tired with their long marches from Cheshire. Cromwell's own regiment of foot under Major-General Worsley were following him as fast as possible, and he resolved to wait for this reinforcement. On the same day the royalists delivered a surprise attack on their own account. Lilburne had now encamped at Brindle, four miles from Preston, and the royalists were informed by a secret enemy " they being all enemies hereabouts " that the horses were turned loose and the men off their guard. A party of about 20 horse, mostly gentlemen's sons from the Fylde and their servants, rode out of Preston for the adventure, and guided by byways reached the Parliamentarian camp unperceived. Lilburne's troopers were lying on the grass by their saddles, half asleep in the summer afternoon, with their horses grazing near by in the fields between Brindle and Preston. Suddenly the royalists, who had evaded the guard in the lane below burst out upon them. For a few moments all was confusion; but "the finest soldiers in Europe" were more than a match for a few hot-headed youths, even caught thus at a disadvantage. Recovering their horses they fell upon the assailants and pursued them as far as Ribble Bridge; and all the royalists were either taken or slain, excepting one who escaped like Charles II. after Worcester, by climbing into a tree and hiding there until the following day. Among those killed were the sons of Mr. Butler of Rawcliffe and Mr. Hesketh of Maines

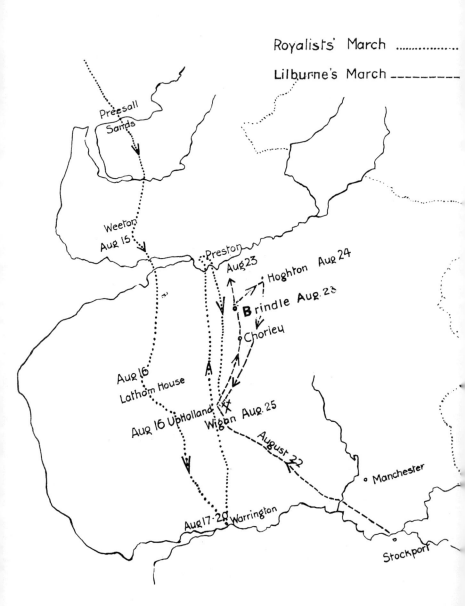

The Campaign of

Wigan Lane

Royalists' March ....

Lilburne's March _ _ _ _ _ _

Preesall
Sands

Weeton
Aug 15

Preston
Aug 23
Hoghton Aug 24
Brindle Aug 23
Chorley

Aug 16
Lathom House

Aug 16 Upholland
Wigan Aug 25
August 22

Manchester

Aug 17-20 Warrington

Stockport

Hall, near Poulton-le-Fylde. John Clifton, the second
son of Mr. Clifton of Lytham, was badly wounded and
taken prisoner.

Not knowing what other surprises might be delivered
in such a hostile country Lilburne moved his camp next
morning (Sunday, August 24th) two miles further east
to Hoghton, and that day Colonel Richard Shuttleworth
and a number of others from the neighbourhood came to
him at Hoghton Tower and remained till evening;
showing that the county was not entirely hostile to the
Cromwellians. On the previous evening Lilburne had
received two companies of foot from Chester, and there
also arrived another company of newly raised foot from
Liverpool; but he was still waiting for Cromwell's
regiment which was now reported to be at Manchester.
The royalists, however, had also heard of their advance,
and thinking to surprise Worsley before he could join
the cavalry, and having also the promise of reinforcements in Manchester themselves, they marched out of
Preston towards midnight on Sunday and proceeded
south. The movement was not one of flight as has been
suggested, and as Lilburne at first thought. He did not
hear of their march until 8 or 9 o'clock next morning
when intelligence was brought by an old woman. At
once he started off in hot pursuit, and came up with the
royalists about mid-day near Wigan. But Lilburne,
when he found that the royalists were not flying, still
held off, hoping to be able to march on their flank to
Manchester. The royalists, however, had now resolved
to give him battle, and about 3 o'clock in the afternoon
they were seen advancing along the lane which led out
of the town towards Standish.

It was a gallant company of royalists who rode out of
Wigan that August afternoon to make their last stand
for the King in Lancashire. In command was the Earl
of Derby, the uncompromising enemy of the Parliament;
and with him were Sir Thomas Tyldesley, the hero of

many fights, the perfect exponent of all the cavalier
virtues; Lord Widdrington, "one of the most goodly
persons of that age, being near the head higher than
most tall men, and a gentleman of the best and most
ancient extraction";[1] Sir William Throgmorton, who
had been Major-General in Newcastle's Yorkshire army;
Colonel Boynton, some time Governor of Scarborough
for the Parliament, and their chief instrument in the
discovery of the Hothams' plot to betray Hull; with
many others of equal bravery but of less note. Opposed
to them were the stern, well disciplined cavalry of the
Cromwellian army. The two forces were absolutely
typical of the opposing armies of the Civil War. It is
said that when Lilburne's men saw that they must fight
they turned on the country people who had come out to
see their march and dispersed them with harsh words.

The two forces were nearly equal in cavalry,[2] for the
Earl of Derby had by now 600, and Lilburne his own
regiment, which would be 600 if the ranks were full; and
Lilburne also had about 60 horse and dragoons which
Birch had mounted for him from the Liverpool garrison.
The royalists were superior in foot, having 800 to the
Cromwellians 300; but the advantage was not so great
as it appeared, for the Manxmen whom Derby had

1. "Clarendon" (Macray), Vol. 5, p. 185 (book 13, par. 69).

2. The fullest accounts of the Battle of Wigan are: "A Great
Victory, etc." ("C. W. T.," p. 296); "Two Letters from Col. Robert
Lilburne, etc." ("C. W. T.," p. 300); "Seacome," pp. 113, 114; Whitelock's "Memorials," p. 504; and "Discourse," pp. 72–76. The last gives
most details, probably from personal knowledge; Major Robinson was
one of the Lancashire officers to whom a commission was given in the
reorganisation of the Militia in 1650. His narrative and that of
Lilburne, as those written by eye-witnesses, may be taken as the most
reliable.
With regard to the numbers of the respective forces, there can be
little doubt that they were very nearly equal. Seacome's wild estimates,
which are, as usual, unhesitatingly followed by Canon Raines, may be
dismissed as impossible; he gives Lilburne 3,000 horse and foot. It has
already been mentioned that Derby landed with less than 100 horse,
and either 250 or 300 foot (p. 187). All the accounts substantially agree
in respect to these figures. In the few days after landing these numbers
were considerably increased; Seacome acknowledges that Derby had
600 horse at the battle, while Lilburne says that the royalists had

brought over with him were poor fighters; and moreover
the battle was essentially a cavalry engagement, in
which infantry played only a subordinate part. Wigan
Lane was then a broad sandy lane bordered by hedges,
and was thus as unsuitable a position for manœuvring
cavalry as could be imagined; but the time was too short
for Lilburne to choose any other ground. Placing his
musketeers behind the hedges, he awaited the royalist
onset. The place had other memories for him, and
perhaps for some of his men; for it was here that he had
driven in Hamilton's rearguard in the campaign of
1648.

Difficult as the ground was, the combat which ensued
was the fiercest of all the 10 years fighting in Lancashire.
So furious was the royalist charge that they drove back
the Cromwellians far along the lane. In the confined
space no manœuvring was possible, and for nearly an
hour the cavalry fought at close quarters. At length at
the third charge Lilburne brought up a small reserve,
and the superior steadiness of the veterans of the new
Model prevailed over the impetuous bravery of the
cavaliers. The royalists wavered and began to give
ground; Widdrington fell dead, Tyldesley was unhorsed
and shot down as he attempted to extricate himself from

---

increased to 1,400 or 1,500 men, and the "Discourse" gives them
1,000 foot and 500 horse. Lilburne's estimate of his own army, as
stated in the letter to Cromwell, may be accepted as correct. He writes :
"I had only my own regiment, and those three companies of foot, and
the 60 horse and dragoons." His own regiment of horse he had brought
with him; two of the foot companies had been sent from Chester, and
one, together with the 60 dragoons, from the garrison at Liverpool.
"Discourse," p. 75 ; "C. W. T.," p. 297. The latter of these references
is to a letter from Birch, the Governor of Liverpool, who writes : "All
that could be afforded in assistance were two foot companies from
Chester, one of my Regiment, left about Manchester, not being so ready
as the rest to march out, and what musketeers I horsed from hence
with some few countrymen." A regiment of cavalry in the New Model
Army numbered 600 men. Firth, "Cromwell's Army," p. 42. Dragoons
in the seventeenth century were not cavalry, but mounted infantry.
Mr. Gardiner's account of the Battle is not quite correct ("Commonwealth," Vol. 2, p. 39). He says : "Lilburne fell back through Wigan.
. . . . Entangled in the lanes south of the town he was compelled to
fight, etc." Wigan Lane is the road out of Wigan to the north.

the press;[1] Derby himself was wounded, and Lilburne's men chased the now broken royalist squadrons down the hill into Wigan. The pursuit and slaughter continued through the streets and town. The route was complete; Throgmorton and Boynton were also among the slain which numbered 300; 400 prisoners were taken, and the rest of the force melted away. In an hour the hopes of the royalists in Lancashire had been destroyed.

The Earl of Derby, who had fought with his accustomed bravery, was surrounded by six of his men and succeeded in reaching the town, where he slipped in through an open door of a house in the Market Place and lay concealed until nightfall. He had a number of slight wounds about the arms and shoulders, and his beaver which he wore over a steel cap was picked up afterwards in the Lane with thirteen sword cuts upon it. In the middle of the night he left his place of refuge disguised in a trooper's old coat, and accompanied only by Colonel Roscarrock and two servants, made his way out of the town and rode away to join the King.

Events had moved with too tragic suddenness for news to come to those waiting in the Isle of Man. There is in the Tanner MSS. a short letter written by Henrietta Stanley on August 11th from Castle Rushen to Tyldesley who was superintending the embarkation of the troops at Douglas. The girl writes light-heartedly, in high hopes of the success of the expedition which fair winds were just about to set free to sail, and closes with a playful message to Colonel Roscarrock about a book. Now, just fourteen days later, the royalist army had been scattered, Tyldesley was slain, and Roscarrock one of the three who rode away under cover of darkness with the wounded Earl of Derby. But no tidings of the

1. A monument to Tyldesley was erected on the spot where he fell by his cornet, Alexander Rigby, of Layton, when the latter was Sheriff of Lancashire in 1677. The monument still stands: it was restored by the Corporation of Wigan in 1886. The long inscription is printed by Canon Raines. "Stanley Papers," pt. 3, Vol. 2 (C. S. 67), p. cccxxxiii.

disaster came to Castle Rushen for many weeks. After long waiting, the Countess sent out a pinnace but it was driven by contrary winds upon the coast of Cheshire, and fell into the enemy's hands.[1]

Journeying as quickly as his wounds and weariness would permit, Derby reached the house of a Mr. Watson at Newport in Shropshire, where he met a friend, who conducted him to Boscobel House, which was then only occupied by two servants, William Penderel and his wife (Friday, August 29th). This was just a fortnight after he had landed at Preesall. Resting there until Sunday, the Earl was then guided by Penderel to Gatacre, and so reached Worcester. Pursued by ill-fortune to the last, he arrived there bringing the news of his own disaster, only two days before the Battle of Worcester; where Cromwell, with an army more than twice as numerous as the Scots, had no difficulty in gaining a complete victory. Derby fought in the battle, and after the defeat his chief care was for Charles' safety. He was one of the few noblemen who attended the King to Kinver Heath near Kidderminster; and it was by Derby's advice that Charles was conducted to White Ladies, and from there, under the care of the Penderels Richard and William, to Boscobel. "This is the King," said Derby to William Penderel, "thou must have a care of him and preserve him as thou didst me." Thus saved from the first pursuit, Charles after many narrow escapes reached Brighton and crossed to France.[2]

Derby then joined the retreat northwards with Leslie, the Earl of Lauderdale, Lord Talbot and others. They were attacked by Colonel Blundell, but managed to make their escape. Soon afterwards, however, they fell in with another skirmish and were captured. A Lancashire captain named Oliver Edge was riding by himself to see

1. This letter is printed in "Cary," Vol. 2, p. 320; Marlet, "Charlotte de la Tremoille," p. 239.

2. Hughes' "Boscobel Tracts," pp. 174, 190.

what had become of the 'forlorn,' when he noticed a party
of horse in the field behind him. Fearing they were
enemies he hastened back towards his regiment; when to
his surprise all the horsemen dismounted and surrendered themselves prisoners. The Earls of Derby and
Lauderdale were the most important of those captured.
Edge gave the prisoners quarter but his action was
over-ruled by the Parliament through no fault of his
own. Derby afterwards wrote of Edge as "one that
was so civil to me, that I and all that love me are beholden
to him." The Earl with some other prisoners was
carried to Chester Castle.[1]

After the battle of Wigan Lane, Lilburne sent up
Lieutenant Turner to London with letters to the House
of Parliament which were read on August 30th. After
hearing the letters Turner was called in to give an
account of the battle; and the House made him a present
of £100, at the same time voting to Lilburne the sum
of £500 and lands to the yearly value of £200. This
was to be raised out of some delinquent's lands, and was
in satisfaction of two former votes of £1,000 each which
remained undischarged. The Sunday after the battle
(August 31st) was named as a public thanksgiving.[2]

The Earl of Derby's papers were referred to the
Council of State to see whether they contained anything
of importance (August 30th); for so hasty had been his
flight from Wigan that all his baggage, including his
cloaks with his Orders, fell into Lilburne's hands. On
the following Monday Sir Harry Vane, the younger,
reported to the House that papers of great importance
had been found in the Earl's hampers, and as a result of

1. For the narrative of Derby's capture we are indebted to Capt.
Hodgson ("Autobiography," p. 48). Little seems to be known about
Edge; but the name of Oliver Edge occurs in a statement about the
seating of Manchester Church in 1649, which was largely signed by
the inhabitants of the town, and this signature is very probably his.
("Manchester Municipal Records.") He belonged to the family of
Edge of Birch-Hall Houses near Manchester. Halley's "Lancashire
Puritanism and Nonconformity (2nd ed. in 1 vol., 1872), p. 286.
2. "C. J.," Vol. 7, pp. 8, 9.

their examination the Council of State decided on September 10 to represent to Parliament that Derby was a fit person to be brought to trial and made an example of justice; and that he should be tried by court-martial at Chester.[1] Parliament made the required vote on the following day, September 11th.

The irreconcilable hostility of the Earl to the Parliament, his high rank, and especially his prominent part in the last campaign, rather than his personal character, probably decided the Council of State to deal hardly with him. He was not a dangerous man. But it was thought necessary that an example should be made. Much has been written by royalists of the perfidy of putting him on trial for his life after quarter had been given; but Derby must have known that Edge's promise was liable to be over-ruled by a higher authority; and in any case it could have made little difference, for if Derby and his companions had not surrendered at Newport, they must have been captured during the next few days.

The trial began at Chester on September 29th. The Earl of Lauderdale had been sent to the Tower, and Giffard, another of those who had surrendered, escaped from Bunbury in Cheshire. Two other prisoners, Sir Timothy Featherstonhaugh and Captain Benbow were tried at Chester with Derby. After the resolution of Parliament on September 11th, a commission was directed to Major-General Mitton, Colonel Duckenfield, Colonel Mackworth, Colonel Birch, Colonel Henry Brooke, Colonel Henry Bradshaw, Colonel Thomas Croxton, Colonel Gilbert Ireland, Colonel John Carter, Colonel Twistleton, Colonel Mason or any three of them. Most of the names were those of officers of the Cheshire Militia Regiments enrolled in Hamilton's invasion of 1648. Birch and Ireland were the only two Lancashire names, and neither of them attended any of the sittings of the court martial. Mackworth was chosen President.

1. "C. S. P.," 1651, pp. 422, 423. "C. J.," Vol. 7, pp. 9, 16.

He was Governor of Shrewsbury, and on Charles' march it was thought that he might be prevailed upon to surrender the town, but he returned a rude denial. Most of the other members of the commission were comparatively unknown; indeed it was not a dignified court by which to try a great nobleman.[1]

The articles against Derby were that he had in defiance of the Act of Parliament of August 12th, 1651, making it treason to hold correspondence with Charles Stewart, received a commission from him, proclaimed him King at several places in Lancashire, had raised forces to assist him, and on their defeat had himself fought in the Battle of Worcester. The Earl did not attempt to deny his acts, but he asked for more time to consider his answer, and the court was adjourned until the following day, Derby being furnished with a copy of the articles. Next morning (September 30th) at 8 o'clock in the morning the other two prisoners were tried. Derby was then brought to the bar, and pleaded that he was in the Isle of Man on August 12th and had never heard of the Act under which he was being convicted. His request for counsel was considered and allowed, and at the Earl's own suggestion Mr. Zancthy, a Chester lawyer, was named. The court then adjourned, and it was decided that the Earl should have liberty at 9 o'clock next morning to plead his own case. Later in the day a request was made on his behalf that he might have Sir Maurice Enslow or Sir Robert Brerewood as counsel instead of Zancthy, but this was refused.

Next day the Earl again pleaded that he was ignorant of the Act of Parliament of August 12th, and further that Captain Edge had given him quarter, and therefore that a court-martial had no authority over him; and he

1. The official record of the trial of the Earl of Derby, from the original in the Library of the House of Lords, is printed by Canon Raines in the appendix to his "Stanley Papers," pt. 3, Vol. 2 (C. S. 67), pp. cccxxxiv-ccclvii, as well as other valuable documents relating to the Earl's trial and death. *Vide* also "Discourse," pp. 78-85; "C. W. T.," pp. 311-323.

appealed to Cromwell to support his claim. The court, however, over-ruled the plea, and decided with two dissentients that there was cause to proceed to a conviction according to the articles proved. It was objected that quarter could not be allowed to traitors, and it cannot be supposed that Derby would have acted otherwise had he known of the Act of August 12th. The two voting in the negative were Twistleton and Delves, and the former desired his vote to be recorded. When the court met in the afternoon, however, and decided that the Earl was worthy of death and should be executed at Bolton on October 16th, Twistleton was one of those who voted. Delves was apparently not present, but of the nineteen members, none voted in the negative. Regarding the place of execution ten voted for Bolton, and eight for Manchester; against the name of Lieutenant-Colonel Finch no place is given. So that it was only by a bare majority that Bolton was fixed upon.

The trial of the Earl of Derby was really only a pretence of justice. As in the case of Charles I., two years before, the verdict had been decided upon before the court met. The result was a foregone conclusion, for Parliament had resolved to put Derby out of the way. As a matter of law his excuses were good enough; but no one could suppose that the trial would be decided by technical points. Of course the Earl had not heard of the Act of August 12th, but it would have made no difference if he had; and he knew quite well that he had been exempted from pardon by the Parliament years before, and must have been fully conscious of the risk he ran in taking part in the invasion of the Scots. The Council of State had evidently decided also that the sentence of the court-martial should be carried into effect. They had written to Colonel Duckenfield on September 30th "As to what you mention of the Earl of Derby, order has been given by Parliament concerning him, which is to be effectually pursued, without

expecting any interposition from Council."[1] Nevertheless great efforts were naturally made to secure a reprieve.
On September 29th, after the first day's sitting of the
court, Derby himself directed two petitions, one to the
Council, and the other to Parliament, promising to
surrender the Isle of Man if his life should be spared.
He also wrote to Lady Derby to surrender the Island,
but no hope was given that his petition would be granted
even on these terms.

As a matter of fact the Isle of Man was not surrendered
until November. After the Earl's death Duckenfield
and Birch led an expedition against it, and landed
troops; but the Countess asked for terms, and before any
fighting took place capitulated. Castle Rushen was
given up on November 1st, and Peel Castle on November 3rd. Duckenfield thought that the terms were
satisfactory, because "these Castles might have cost a
great expense of blood, time and charge, besides several
other difficulties which in this Island are to be undergone
in a siege, which are only obvious to such as be upon
the place.[2]

To return, however, to the trial of the Earl of Derby,
Charles, Lord Strange, now appeared upon the scene.
He was a worthless person of whom his father had
written "I have no good opinion of him; he is not
ashamed of his faults."[3] Strange was only 14 on the
breaking out of the war, and had therefore been too
young to have any considerable part in affairs. But a
few years later the exile of the Isle of Man became
irksome to him and he left his parents and went to
France, where he spent most of the next few years.
Now, however, he returned, and a reconciliation was
made; and to do him justice Strange seems to have used
great efforts on his father's behalf. He journeyed to

1. "C. S. P.," 1651, p. 457.
2. Duckenfield and Birch to Lenthall. Ramsey, Nov. 2. ("Tanner
MSS.," Vol. 55, fol. 87.
3. Marlet, "Charlotte de la Tremoille," p. 151.

London, but no one in London would intercede for the Earl, the intention of Parliament being evidently too well known. Derby then applied personally to Cromwell, emphasising the illegality of his condemnation by a court-martial after having received quarter. There seems to have been no doubt that Cromwell was anxious to secure the Earl's reprieve;[1] but Parliament would not listen to him. Other means were then used. President Bradshaw was tried through his brother, Colonel Henry Bradshaw, one of the Earl's judges, and Brideoak, one of Derby's Chaplains, applied to Speaker Lenthall. Brideoak pleaded so well for himself that he was made Lenthall's own chaplain and Preacher at the Rolls, but he failed to secure his patron's pardon.

Finding there was no hope of reprieve the Earl made an attempt to escape which was very nearly successful. One night he found some pretext for being on the lead roof above his chamber, and procuring a rope slid down and escaped from the city. The alarm, however, was raised, and he was recaptured on the roodee, having unawares discovered himself to his pursuers. Before attempting to escape, he left on his table a letter to the Countess advising her to make the best terms she could with Colonel Duckenfield "who being so much a gentleman born will doubtless for his own honour's sake deal fairly with you."[2]

After this Derby was of course more carefully watched. He made one final attempt in a petition to Lenthall on October 11th. In this he offered no vindication, but cast himself himself entirely on the Parliament's mercy, stating that he had been persuaded by Colonel Duckenfield that Parliament would spare his life. He again

---

1. Gardiner ("Commonwealth," Vol. 2, p. 62, note) quotes a Newsletter of Salvetti, which seems decisive on this point. As the Earl's death has been attributed to Cromwell's own influence the quotation may be repeated here : "Il General Cromwell fa buonissimi uffizii per salvarlo la vita, con conditione che consegni nelle mane del Parlamento la sua isoletta di Man, della quale se ne intitole Re."
2. "Seacome," p. 133.

offered to surrender the Isle of Man, to take no further
action against the Government, and to be imprisoned or
banished as the House might direct. If this was refused
he particularly asked that the place of his execution
might be altered from Bolton, because " the nation will
look upon me as a sacrifice for that blood which some
have unjustly cast upon me"; and he claimed that the
charge of cruelty at the capture of Bolton was never once
mentioned during his trial, which indeed was quite true.
This petition was not brought forward in the House till
Tuesday, October, 14th, the day before that which had
been fixed for the execution. The House voted by 22
votes to 16 that the petition should be read, Sir William
Brereton being one of the tellers for the ayes; but no
action could be taken, for if a reprieve had been intended
it would have been decided upon long before.[1]

The Earl's last hours were moving and dignified
enough; and told chiefly by Rev. Humphrey Bagguley,
who was in attendance upon him during the few days
before his death, they lose nothing in effect. Bagguley,
with the Rev. Henry Bridgeman, Vicar of Wigan and
brother of Orlando Bridgeman, together with Lord
Strange, were the three who remained to the last. The
authorities at Chester showed unnecessary cruelty in
forbidding the Earl's children intercourse with him; but
his second and third daughters, Lady Katherine and
Lady Amelia were allowed to spend most of Monday,
October 13th, with their father. Next day Derby was
informed that he must start for Bolton on the following
morning, and that evening he wrote his two last affec-

1. "Raines," *op. cit.*, p. ccxvii, ccvxiii. Canon Raines here repeats
a wild story from Seacome, to the effect that this petition would have
been allowed by the House, had not Cromwell and Bradshaw contrived
to reduce the number of Members present to less than 40, so that no
question could be put. There is no foundation for this statement. As
a matter of fact, the House voted that Derby's petition should be read,
but it could not possibly be dealt further with owing to the impossibility
of sending a messenger into Lancashire in time to stop the execution,
had that been intended. ("C. J.," Vol. 7, p. 27.) For Cromwell's real
attitude towards the reprieve, *vide* note on p. 201.

tionate letters to his wife and children in the Isle of Man. Next morning he duly set out for Bolton, after his fellow-prisoners had been permitted to say farewell to him at the Castle gate. There was one sadder farewell still to be gone through. The Earl rode on horseback and about half a mile out of the town was met by his two daughters in a coach. Alighting from his horse he kneeled down and prayed for them before taking a final farewell. "This was the deepest scene of sorrow my eyes ever beheld," says the narrator, "so much grief, and so much tender concern and tender affection on both sides, I never was witness of before. That night the cavalcade rested at Leigh, and next day with a guard of 60 foot and 50 horse the Earl reached Bolton about noon. His request to be allowed to visit Sir Thomas Tyldesley's grave had been refused. After resting two hours at an inn the Earl was conducted to the scaffold, which had been built near the Cross partly of timber brought from the ruins of Lathom House.

Not very many people were present besides the soldiers on guard; but a tumult arising from some unexplained cause interrupted Derby in his last speech. He seems to have been afraid of the hostility of the crowd, but the soldiers with more reason feared a demonstration in his favour, for most of the onlookers evidently pitied him.[1] The Earl's last words were heard by few of those present, but they were taken down in shorthand and afterwards printed. In them he again repudiated the charges of cruelty made against him. After having spent some time in private prayer, the Earl gave the signal to the executioner by lifting his hands, and his head was severed at one blow. The body was taken by Lord

1. "The Earl of Derby's Speech on the Scaffold, etc." ("C. W. T.," p. 320). The best account of the Earl's last hours is naturally given by Seacome, who quotes Bagguley's "Narrative" (pp. 120–127), "Discourse," pp. 82–85: "The Earl was no good Orator, and the tumult put him out of speaking what he intended; he was much afraid of being reviled by the people of the town, but they rather pitied his condition."

Strange to Haigh Hall, near Wigan, and the next day to Ormskirk, to be buried with the former Earls of Derby. So died, if not the wonderful possessor of all the virtues which partisan biographers afterwards pretended, a brave, upright and Christian gentleman, weak rather than offending, who deserved a better fate.[1]

And with his death the Civil War in Lancashire really ends.

1. "The Earl of Darby was a man of unquestionable loyalty to the King, and gave clear testimony of it before he received any obligations from the Court, and when he thought himself disobliged by it. . . . . He was a man of great honour and clear courage; and all his defects and misfortunes proceeded from his having lived so little time among his equals, that he knew not how to treat his inferiors : which was the source of all the ill that befell him, having thereby drawn such a prejudice from the persons of inferior quality, who yet thought themselves too good to be contemned, against him, that they pursued him to death." ("Clarendon," Macray, Vol. 5, p. 184 (bk. 13, par. 68).

Index.

INDEX.

INDEX

INDEX

225

Twistleton, Col., one of Lord Derby's judges, 197, 199.

Tyldesley, Sir Thomas, royalist Col. and Maj.-Gen., 13, 20, 74, 95, 131, 164, 191.

—— —— notice of, 28.

—— ——· at siege of Manchester, 42.

—— —— at Whalley, 81–83.

—— —— retreats before Assheton, 84, 86.

—— —— joins the Queen, 86.

—— —— at Bolton, 121.

—— —— besieges Lancaster, 170.

—— —— surrenders at Appleby, 172.

—— —— at campaign of Wigan, 188.

—— —— his death, 193.

Upholland, 188

Uttoxeter, defeat of Scots at, 170.

Vane, Sir Harry, at York, 126.

—— —— appointed to examine Earl of Derby's Papers, 196.

Venables, Capt., afterwards General, 61n.

—— —— taken prisoner, 61.

Vere, Col., at second siege of Lathom, 143, 146.

—— —— wounded a Preston, 190.

Wakefield, 89.

Walton, 132, 167.

Warrington, 81, 140, 165, 167.

—— proposal to raise royal standard at, 21.

—— Lord Strange's muster at, 41.

—— made royalist headquarters, 57.

—— unsucessful siege of, 80.

—— captured by Sir W. Brereton, 86–7.

—— Scots surrender at, 170.

·—— meeting at, 186–7.

—— royalist Council of War at, 188.

Wensleydale, 164.

Wetherby, 165.

West Derby Hundred, 54, 95, 131, 188.

Westhoughton, royalist victory at, 61.

Whalley, battle of, 82–4.

Wharton, Lord, Lord-Lieutenant of Lancashire, 11, 15, 16.

Whitchurch, 116, 142, 149.

Whitley, Higher, 184.